D1536758

Siegel's

CONTRACTS

Essay and Multiple-Choice Questions and Answers

BRIAN N. SIEGEL
J.D., Columbia Law School
and

LAZAR EMANUEL
J.D., Harvard Law School

ASPEN
PUBLISHERS

111 Eighth Avenue, New York, NY 10011
www.aspenpublishers.com

© 2005 Aspen Publishers, Inc.
a Wolters Kluwer business
www.aspenpublishers.com

All rights reserved. No part of this publication may be reproduced or transmitted in any form or by any means, electronic or mechanical, including photocopy, recording, or any information storage and retrieval system, without permission in writing from the publisher. Requests for permission to make copies of any part of this publication should be mailed to:

Aspen Publishers
Attn: Permissions Department
111 Eighth Avenue, 7th floor
New York, NY 10011

Printed in the United States of America.

1 2 3 4 5 6 7 8 9 0

ISBN 0-7355-5686-5

This book is intended as a general review of a legal subject. It is not intended as a source of advice for the solution of legal matters or problems. For advice on legal matters, the reader should consult an attorney.

Siegel's, Emanuel, the judge logo, Law in a Flash and design, CrunchTime and design, Strategies & Tactics and design, and The Professor Series are registered trademarks of Aspen Publishers.

About Aspen Publishers

Aspen Publishers, headquartered in New York City, is a leading information provider for attorneys, business professionals, and law students. Written by preeminent authorities, our products consist of analytical and practical information covering both U.S. and international topics. We publish in the full range of formats, including updated manuals, books, periodicals, CDs, and online products.

Our proprietary content is complemented by 2,500 legal databases, containing over 11 million documents, available through our Loislaw division. Aspen Publishers also offers a wide range of topical legal and business databases linked to Loislaw's primary material. Our mission is to provide accurate, timely, and authoritative content in easily accessible formats, supported by unmatched customer care.

To order any Aspen Publishers title, go to *www.aspenpublishers.com* or call 1-800-638-8437.

To reinstate your manual update service, call 1-800-638-8437.

For more information on Loislaw products, go to *www.loislaw.com* or call 1-800-364-2512.

For Customer Care issues, e-mail *CustomerCare@aspenpublishers.com;* call 1-800-234-1660; or fax 1-800-901-9075.

Aspen Publishers
a Wolters Kluwer business

Acknowledgment

The authors gratefully acknowledge the assistance of the California Committee of Bar Examiners, which provided access to questions on which many of the questions in this book are based.

Introduction

Although law school grades are a significant factor in obtaining a summer internship or entry position at a law firm, no formalized preparation for finals is offered at most law schools. For the most part, students are expected to fend for themselves in learning how to take a law school exam. Ironically, law school exams ordinarily bear little correspondence to the teaching methods used by professors during the school year. Professors require you to spend most of your time briefing cases. Although many claim this is "great preparation" for issue-spotting on exams, it really isn't. Because, in briefing cases, you are made to focus on one or two principles of law at a time, you don't get practice in relating one issue to another or in developing a picture of an entire problem or the entire course. When exams finally come, you're forced to make an abrupt 180-degree turn. Suddenly, you are asked to recognize, define, and discuss a variety of issues buried within a single multi-issue fact pattern. In most schools, you are then asked to select among a number of possible answers, all of which look inviting but only one of which is right.

The comprehensive course outline you've created so diligently, and with such pain, means little if you're unable to apply its contents on your final exams. There is a vast difference between reading opinions in which the legal principles are clearly stated, and applying those same principles to hypothetical essay exams and multiple-choice questions.

The purpose of this book is to help you bridge the gap between memorizing a rule of law and **understanding how to use it** in an exam. After an initial overview describing the exam writing process, you see a large number of hypotheticals which test your ability to write analytical essays and to pick the right answers to multiple-choice questions. **Read them — all of them!** Then review the suggested answers which follow. You'll find that the key to superior grades lies in applying your knowledge through questions and answers, not through rote memory.

Note: References in the questions and answers to the Uniform Commercial Code are to the Code prior to the revisions in 2001 to Article 1 and to the revisions in 2003 to Article 3. Where appropriate, answers according to the pre-revision and revised Code have been provided. The Table of References to the Uniform Commercial Code on page 221 provides references to the pre-revision Code, with revised Code numbers in brackets.

GOOD LUCK!

Table of Contents

Essay Exam Answers

Multiple-Choice Questions

Multiple-Choice Answers

Tables and Index

Preparing Effectively for Essay Examinations[1]

To achieve superior scores on essay exams, a law student must (1) learn and understand "blackletter" principles and rules of law for each subject; (2) analyze how those principles of law arise within a test fact pattern; and (3) write clearly and succinctly a short discussion of each principle and how it relates to the facts. One of the most common misconceptions about law school is that you must memorize each word on every page of your casebooks or outlines to do well on exams. The reality is that you can commit an entire casebook to memory and still do poorly on an exam. Our review of hundreds of student answers has shown us that most students can recite the rules. The students who do **best** on exams are able to analyze how the rules they have memorized relate to the facts in the questions, and how to communicate their analysis to the grader. The following pages cover what you need to know to achieve superior scores on your law school essay exams.

The "ERC" Process

To study effectively for law school exams you must be able to "*ERC*" (*E*lementize, *R*ecognize, and *C*onceptualize) each legal principle covered in your casebooks and course outlines. *Elementizing* means reducing each legal theory and rule you learn to a concise, straightforward statement of its essential elements. Without knowledge of these elements, it's difficult to see all the issues as they arise.

For example, if you are asked, "What is self-defense?", it is **not** enough to say, "self-defense is permitted when, if someone is about to hit you, you can prevent him from doing it." This layperson description would leave a grader wondering if you had actually attended law school. An accurate statement of the self-defense principle would go something like this: "When one reasonably believes she is in imminent danger of an offensive touching, she may assert whatever force she reasonably believes necessary under the circumstances to prevent the offensive touching from occurring." This formulation correctly shows that there are four separate, distinct elements which must be satisfied before the defense of self-defense can be successfully asserted: (1) the actor must have a **reasonable belief** that (2) the touching which she seeks to prevent is **offensive**, and that (3) the offensive touching is **imminent**, and

---

1 To illustrate the principles of effective exam preparation, we have used examples from Torts and Constitutional Law. However, these principles apply to all subjects. One of the most difficult tasks faced by law students is learning how to apply principles from one area of the law to another. We leave it to you, the reader, to think of comparable examples for the subject-matter of this book.

(4) she must use no greater force than she **reasonably believes necessary under the circumstances** to prevent the offensive touching from occurring.

Recognizing means perceiving or anticipating which words or ideas within a legal principle are likely to be the source of issues, and how those issues are likely to arise within a given hypothetical fact pattern. With respect to the self-defense concept, there are four *potential* issues. Did the actor reasonably believe the other person was about to make an offensive contact with her? Was the contact imminent? Would the contact have been offensive? Did she use only such force as she reasonably believed necessary to prevent the imminent, offensive touching?

Conceptualizing means imagining situations in which each of the elements of a rule of law can give rise to factual issues. **Unless you can imagine or construct an application of each element of a rule, you don't truly understand the legal principles behind the rule!** In our opinion, the inability to conjure up hypothetical fact patterns or stories involving particular rules of law foretells a likelihood that you will miss issues involving those rules on an exam. It's **crucial** (1) to **recognize** that issues result from the interaction of facts with the words defining a rule of law; and (2) to develop the ability to **conceptualize** or **imagine** fact patterns using the words or concepts within the rule.

For example, a set of facts illustrating the "reasonable belief" element of the self-defense rule might be the following:

> One evening, A and B had an argument at a bar. A screamed at B, "I'm going to get a knife and stab you!" A then ran out of the bar. B, who was armed with a concealed pistol, left the bar about 15 minutes later. As B was walking home, he heard someone running toward him from behind. B drew his pistol, turned, and shot the person advancing toward him (who was only about ten feet away when the shooting occurred). When B walked over to his victim, he realized that the person he had shot was dead and was not A, but another individual who had simply decided to take an evening jog. There would certainly be an issue whether B had a reasonable belief that the person who was running behind him was A. In the subsequent wrongful-death action, the victim's estate would contend that the earlier threat by A was not enough to give B a reasonable belief that the person running behind him was A. B could contend in rebuttal that given the prior altercation at the bar, A's threat, the darkness, and the fact that the incident occurred soon after A's threat, his belief that A was about to attack him was "reasonable."

An illustration of how the word "imminent" might generate an issue is the following:

> X and Y had been feuding for some time. One afternoon, X suddenly attacked Y with a hunting knife. However, Y was able to wrest the knife

away from X. At that point, X retreated about four feet away from Y and screamed: "You were lucky this time, but next time I'll have a gun and you'll be finished." Y, having good reason to believe that X would subsequently carry out his threats (after all, X had just attempted to kill Y), immediately thrust the knife into X's chest, killing him. While Y certainly had a reasonable belief that X would attempt to kill him the ***next time*** the two met, Y would probably ***not*** be able to assert the self-defense privilege because the element of "imminency" was absent.

A fact pattern illustrating the actor's right to use only that force which is reasonably necessary under the circumstances might be the following:

D rolled up a newspaper and was about to strike E on the shoulder with it. As D pulled back his arm for the purpose of delivering the blow, E drew a knife and plunged it into D's chest. While E had every reason to believe that D was about to deliver an offensive impact on him, E probably could not successfully assert the self-defense privilege because the force he utilized in response was greater than reasonably necessary under the circumstances to prevent the impact. E could simply have deflected D's blow or punched D away. The use of a knife constituted a degree of force by E which was ***not*** reasonable, given the minor injury which he would have suffered from the newspaper's impact.

"Mental games" such as these must be played with every element of every rule you learn.

Issue-Spotting

One of the keys to doing well on an essay examination is issue-spotting. In fact, issue-spotting is ***the*** most important skill you will learn in law school. If you recognize a legal issue, you can always find the applicable rule of law (if there is any) by researching the issue. But if you fail to see the issues, you won't learn the steps that lead to success or failure on exams or, for that matter, in the practice of law. It is important to remember that (1) an issue is a question to be decided by the judge or jury; and (2) a question is "in issue" when it can be disputed or argued about at trial. The bottom line is that ***if you don't spot an issue, you can't raise it or discuss it***.

The key to issue-spotting is to learn to approach a problem in the same way as an attorney does. Let's assume you've been admitted to practice and a client enters your office with a legal problem. He will recite his facts to you and give you any documents that may be pertinent. He will then want to know if he can sue (or be sued, if your client seeks to avoid liability). To answer your client's questions intelligently, you will have to decide the following: (1) what principles or rules can possibly be asserted by your client; (2) what defense or defenses can possibly be raised to these principles; (3) what issues may arise if these defenses are asserted; (4) what arguments can each side make to persuade the fact-finder to resolve the issue in his favor; and (5) finally, what will the *likely* outcome of each issue be. *All the issues which can possibly arise at trial will be relevant to your answers.*

How to Discuss an Issue

Keep in mind that *rules of law are the guides to issues* (i.e., an issue arises where there is a question whether the facts do, or do not, satisfy an element of a rule); a rule of law *cannot dispose of an issue* unless the rule can reasonably be *applied to the facts.*

A good way to learn how to discuss an issue is to study the following mini-hypothetical and the two student responses which follow it.

Mini-Hypothetical

A and B were involved in making a movie which was being filmed at a local bar. The script called for A to appear to throw a bottle (which was actually a rubber prop) at B. The fluorescent lighting at the bar had been altered for the movie—the usual subdued blue lights had been replaced with rather bright white lights. The cameraperson had stationed herself just to the left of the swinging doors which served as the main entrance to the bar. As the scene was unfolding, C, a regular patron of the bar, unwittingly walked into it. The guard who was usually stationed immediately outside the bar had momentarily left his post to visit the restroom. As C pushed the barroom doors inward, the left door panel knocked the camera to the ground with a resounding crash. The first (and only) thing C saw was A (about 5 feet from C), who was getting ready to throw the bottle at B, who was at the other end of the bar (about 15 feet from A). Without hesitation, C pushed A to the ground and punched him in the face. Plastic surgery was required to restore A's profile to its Hollywood-handsome pre-altercation look.

Discuss A's right against C.

Pertinent Principles of Law:

1. Under the rule defining the prevention-of-crime privilege, if one sees that someone is about to commit what she reasonably believes to be a felony or misdemeanor involving a breach of the peace, she may exercise whatever degree of force is reasonably necessary under the circumstances to prevent that person from committing the crime.

2. Under the defense-of-others privilege, where one reasonably believes that someone is about to cause an offensive contact upon a third party, she may use whatever force is reasonably necessary under the circumstances to prevent the contact. Some jurisdictions, however, limit this privilege to situations in which the actor and the third party are related.

First Student Answer

Did C commit an assault and battery upon A?

An assault occurs when the defendant intentionally causes the plaintiff to be reasonably in apprehension of an imminent, offensive touching. The facts state that C punched A to the ground. Thus, a battery would have occurred at this point. We are also told that C punched A in the face. It is reasonable to assume that A saw the punch being thrown at him, and therefore A felt in imminent danger of an offensive touching. Based upon the facts, C has committed an assault and battery upon A.

Were C's actions justifiable under the defense-of-others privilege?

C could successfully assert the defense-of-others and prevention-of-crime privileges. When C opened the bar doors, A appeared to be throwing the bottle at B. Although the "bottle" was actually a prop, C had no way of knowing this fact. Also, it was necessary for C to punch A in the face to assure that A could not get back up, retrieve the bottle, and again throw it at B. While the plastic surgery required by A is unfortunate, C could not be successfully charged with assault and battery.

Second Student Answer

Assault and Battery:

C committed an assault (causing A to be reasonably in apprehension of an imminent, offensive contact) when A saw that C's punch was about to hit him, and battery (causing an offensive contact upon A) when (1) C knocked A to the ground, and (2) C punched A.

Defense-of-Others/Prevention-of-Crime Defenses:

C would undoubtedly assert the privileges of defense-of-others (when defendant reasonably believed the plaintiff was about to make an offensive contact upon a third party, he was entitled to use whatever force was reasonably necessary to prevent the contact); and prevention-of-crime defense (when one reasonably believes another is about to commit a felony or misdemeanor involving a breach of the peace, he may exercise whatever force is reasonably necessary to prevent that person from committing a crime).

A could contend that C was not reasonable in believing that A was about to cause harm to B because the enhanced lighting at the bar and camera crash should have indicated to C, a regular customer, that a movie was being filmed. However, C could probably successfully contend in rebuttal that his belief was reasonable in light of the facts that (1) he had not seen the camera when he attacked A, and (2) instantaneous action was required (he did not have time to notice the enhanced lighting around the bar).

A might also contend that the justification was forfeited because the degree of force used by C was not reasonable, since C did not have to punch A in the face after A had already been pushed to the ground (i.e., the danger to B was no longer present). However, C could argue in rebuttal that it was necessary to knock out A (an individual with apparently violent propensities) while the opportunity existed, rather than risk a drawn-out scuffle in which A might prevail. The facts do not indicate how big A and C were; but assuming C was not significantly larger than A, C's contention will probably be successful. If, however, C was significantly larger than A, the punch may have been excessive (since C could presumably have simply held A down).

Critique

Let's examine the First Student Answer first. It mistakenly treats as an "issue" the assault and battery committed by C upon A. While the actions creating these torts must be mentioned in the facts to provide a foundation for a discussion of the applicable privileges, there was no need to discuss them further because they were not the issue the examiners were testing for.

The structure of the initial paragraph of First Student Answer is also incorrect. After an assault is defined in the first sentence, the second sentence abruptly describes the facts necessary to constitute the commission of a battery. The third sentence then sets forth the elements of a battery. The fourth sentence completes the discussion of assault by describing the facts pertaining to that tort. The two-sentence break between the original mention of assault and the facts which constitute assault is confusing; the facts which call for the application of a rule should be mentioned *immediately* after the rule is stated.

A more serious error, however, occurs in the second paragraph of the First Student Answer. While there is an allusion to the correct principle of law (prevention of crime), the *rule is not stated*. As a consequence, the grader can only guess why the student thinks the facts set forth in the subsequent sentences are significant. A grader reading this answer could not be certain whether the student recognized that the issues revolved around the *reasonable belief* and *necessary force* elements of the prevention-of-crime privilege. Superior exam-writing requires that the pertinent facts be *tied* directly and clearly to the operative rule.

The Second Student Answer is very much better than the First Answer. It disposes of C's assault and battery upon A in a few words (yet tells the grader that the writer knows these torts are present). More importantly, the grader can easily see the issues which would arise if the prevention-of-crime privilege were asserted (i.e., "whether C's belief that A was about to commit a crime against B was reasonable" and "whether C used unnecessary force in punching A after A had been knocked to the ground"). Finally, it also utilizes all the facts by indicating how an attorney would assert those facts which are most advantageous to her client.

Structuring Your Answer

Graders will give high marks to a clearly written, well-structured answer. Each issue you discuss should follow a specific and consistent structure which a grader can easily follow.

The Second Student Answer basically utilizes the *I-R-A-A-O format* with respect to each issue. In this format, the *I* stands for the word *Issue*; the *R* for *Rule of law*; the initial *A* for the words *one side's Argument*; the second *A* for *the other party's rebuttal Argument*; and the *O* for your *Opinion as to how the issue would be resolved*. The *I-R-A-A-O* format emphasizes the importance of (1) discussing *both* sides of an issue, and (2) communicating to the grader that where an issue arises, an attorney can only advise her client as to the *probable* decision on that issue.

A somewhat different format for analyzing each issue is the *I-R-A-C format*. Here, the *I* stands for *Issue;* the *R* for *Rule of law;* the *A* for *Application of the facts to the rule of law;* and the *C* for *Conclusion. I-R-A-C* is a legitimate approach to the discussion of a particular issue, within the time constraints imposed by the question. The *I-R-A-C format* must be applied to each issue in the question; it is not the solution to the entire answer. If there are six issues in a question, for example, you should offer six separate, independent *I-R-A-C* analyses.

We believe that the *I-R-A-C* approach is preferable to the *I-R-A-A-O* formula. However, either can be used to analyze and organize essay exam answers. Whatever format you choose, however, you should be consistent throughout the exam and remember the following rules:

First, *analyze all of the relevant facts.* Facts have significance in a particular case *only as they come under the applicable rules of law.* The facts presented must be analyzed and examined to see if they do or do not satisfy one element or another of the applicable rules, and the essential facts and rules must be stated and argued in your analysis.

Second, you must communicate to the grader the *precise rule of law* controlling the facts. In their eagerness to commence their arguments, students sometimes fail to state the applicable rule of law first. Remember, the *R* in either format stands for *Rule of Law.* Defining the rule of law *before* an analysis of the facts is essential in order to allow the grader to follow your reasoning.

Third, it is important to treat *each side of an issue with equal detail.* If a hypothetical describes how an elderly man was killed when he ventured upon the land of a huge power company to obtain a better view of a nuclear reactor, your sympathies might understandably fall on the side of the old man. The grader will nevertheless expect you to see and make every possible argument for the other side. Don't permit your personal viewpoint to affect your answer! A good lawyer never does! When discussing an issue, always state the arguments for each side.

Finally, don't forget to *state your opinion or conclusion* on each issue. Keep in mind, however, that your opinion or conclusion is probably the *least* important part of an exam answer. Why? Because your professor knows that no attorney can tell her client exactly how a judge or jury will decide a particular issue. By definition, an issue is a legal dispute which can go either way. An attorney, therefore, can offer her client only her best opinion about the likelihood of victory or defeat on an issue. Since the decision on any issue lies with the judge or jury, no attorney can ever be absolutely certain of the resolution.

Discuss All Possible Issues

As we've noted, a student should draw *some* type of conclusion or opinion for each issue raised. Whatever your conclusion on a particular issue, it is essential to anticipate and discuss *all of the issues* which would arise if the question were actually tried in court.

Let's assume that a negligence hypothetical involves issues pertaining to duty, breach of duty, proximate causation, and contributory negligence. If the defendant prevails on any one of these issues, he will avoid liability. Nevertheless, even if you feel strongly that the defendant owed no duty to the plaintiff, you *must* go on to discuss all of the other potential issues as well (breach of duty, proximate causation, and contributory negligence). If you were to terminate your answer after a discussion of the duty element only, you'd receive an inferior grade.

Why should you have to discuss every possible issue if you are relatively certain that the outcome of a particular issue would be dispositive of the entire case? Because at the commencement of litigation, neither party can be *absolutely positive* about which issues he will prevail upon at trial. We can state with confidence that every attorney with some degree of experience has won issues he thought he would lose, and has lost issues on which victory was assured. Since one can never be absolutely certain how a factual issue will be resolved by the fact-finder, a good attorney (and exam-writer) will consider *all* possible issues.

To understand the importance of discussing all of the potential issues, you should reflect on what you will do in the actual practice of law. If you represent the defendant, for example, it is your job to raise every possible defense. If there are five potential defenses, and your pleadings only rely on three of them (because you're sure you will win on all three), and the plaintiff is somehow successful on all three issues, your client may well sue you for malpractice. Your client's contention would be that you should be liable because if you had only raised the two additional issues, you might have prevailed on at least one of them, and therefore liability would have been avoided. It is an attorney's duty to raise *all* legitimate issues. A similar philosophy should be followed when taking essay exams.

What exactly do you say when you've resolved the initial issue in favor of the defendant, and discussion of any additional issues would seem to be moot? The answer is simple. You begin the discussion of the next issue with something like, "Assuming, however, the plaintiff prevailed on the foregoing issue, the next issue would be . . ." The grader will understand and appreciate what you have done.

The corollary to the importance of raising all potential issues is that you should avoid discussion of obvious non-issues. Raising non-issues is detrimental in three ways: first, you waste a lot of precious time; second, you usually receive absolutely no points for discussing a point which the grader deems extraneous; and third, it suggests to the grader that you lack the ability to distinguish the significant from the irrelevant. The best guideline for avoiding the discussion of a non-issue is to ask yourself, "Would I, as an attorney, feel comfortable about raising that particular issue or objection in front of a judge"?

Delineate the Transition from One Issue to the Next

It's a good idea to make it easy for the grader to see the issues you've found. One way to accomplish this is to cover no more than one issue per paragraph. Another way is to underline each issue statement. Provided time permits, we recommend that you use both techniques. The essay answers in this book contain numerous illustrations of these suggestions.

One frequent student error is to write two separate paragraphs in which all of the arguments for one side are made in the initial paragraph, and all of the rebuttal arguments by the other side are made in the next paragraph. This is *a bad idea*. It obliges the grader to reconstruct the exam answer in his mind several times to determine whether all possible issues have been discussed by both sides. It will also cause you to state the same rule of law more than once. A better-organized answer presents a given argument by one side and follows that immediately in the same paragraph with the other side's rebuttal to that argument.

Understanding the "Call" of a Question

The statement *at the end of* an essay question or of the fact pattern in a multiple-choice question is sometimes referred to as the "call" of the question. It usually asks you to do something specific like "discuss," "discuss the rights of the parties," "what are X's rights?" "advise X," "the best grounds on which to find the statute unconstitutional are:," "D can be convicted of:," "how should the estate be distributed?," etc. The call of the question should be read carefully because it tells you exactly what you're expected to do. If a question asks, "what are X's rights against Y?" or "X is liable to Y for: . . ." you don't have to spend a lot of time on Y's rights against Z. You will usually receive absolutely no credit for discussing issues or facts that are not required by the call. On the other hand, if the call of an essay question is simply "discuss" or "discuss the rights of the parties," then *all* foreseeable issues must be covered by your answer.

Students are often led astray by an essay question's call. For example, if you are asked for "X's rights against Y" or to "advise X," you may think you may limit yourself to X's viewpoint with respect to the issues. This is *not correct*! You cannot resolve one party's rights against another party without considering the issues which would arise (and the arguments which the other side would assert) if litigation occurred. In short, although the call of the question may appear to focus on the rights of one of the parties to the litigation, a superior answer will cover all the issues and arguments which that person might *encounter* (not just the arguments she would *make*) in attempting to pursue her rights against the other side.

The Importance of Analyzing the Question Carefully Before Writing

The overriding *time pressure* of an essay exam is probably a major reason why many students fail to analyze a question carefully before writing. Five minutes into the allocated time for a particular question, you may notice that the person next to you is writing furiously. This thought then flashes through your mind, "Oh, my goodness, he's putting down more words on the paper than I am, and therefore he's bound to get a better grade." It can be stated *unequivocally* that there is no necessary correlation between the number of words on your exam paper and the grade you'll receive. Students who begin their answer after only five minutes of analysis have probably seen only the most obvious issues, and missed many, if not most, of the subtle ones. They are also likely to be less well-organized.

Opinions differ as to how much time you should spend analyzing and outlining a question before you actually write the answer. We believe that you should spend at least 12 to 18 minutes analyzing, organizing, and outlining a one-hour question before writing your answer. This will usually provide sufficient time to analyze and organize the question thoroughly *and* enough time to write a relatively complete answer. Remember that each word of the question must be scrutinized to determine if it (1) suggests an issue under the operative rules of law, or (2) can be used in making an argument for the resolution of an issue. Since you can't receive points for an issue you don't spot, it is usually wise to read a question *twice* before starting your outline.

When to Make an Assumption

The instructions for a question may tell you to *assume* facts which are necessary to the answer. Even when these instructions are *not* given, you may be obliged to make certain assumptions about missing facts in order to write a thorough answer. Assumptions should be made only when you are told or when you, as the attorney for one of the parties described in the question, would be obliged to solicit additional information from your client. On the other hand, assumptions should *never be used to change or alter the question*. Don't ever write something like "if the facts in the question were . . . , instead of . . . , then . . . would result." If you do this, you are wasting time on facts which are extraneous to the problem before you. Professors want you to deal with *their* fact patterns, not your own.

Students sometimes try to "write around" information they think is missing. They assume that their professor has failed to include every piece of data necessary for a thorough answer. This is generally *wrong*. The professor may have omitted some facts deliberately to see if the student *can figure out what to do* under the circumstances. In some instances, the professor may have omitted them inadvertently (even law professors are sometimes human).

The way to deal with the omission of essential information is to describe (1) what fact (or facts) appear to be missing, and (2) why that information is important. As an example, go back to the "movie shoot" hypothetical we discussed above. In that fact pattern, there was no mention of the relative strength of A and C. This fact could be extremely important. If C weighed 240 pounds and was built like a professional football linebacker, while A tipped the scales at a mere 160 pounds, punching A in the face after he had been pushed to the ground would probably constitute unnecessary force (thereby causing C to forfeit the prevention-of-crime privilege). If the physiques of the parties were reversed, however, C's punch to A's face would probably constitute reasonable behavior. Under the facts, C had to deal the "knockout" blow while the opportunity presented itself. The last sentences of the Second Student Answer above show that the student understood these subtleties and correctly supplied the essential missing facts and assumptions.

Assumptions should be made in a manner which keeps the other issues open (i.e., they lead to a discussion of all other possible issues). Don't assume facts which would virtually dispose of the entire hypothetical in a few sentences. For example, suppose that A called B a "convicted felon" (a statement which is inherently defamatory, i.e., a defamatory statement is one which tends to subject the plaintiff to hatred, contempt, or ridicule). If A's statement is true, he has a complete defense to B's action for defamation. If the facts don't tell whether A's statement was true or not, it would *not* be wise to write something like, "We'll assume that A's statement about B is accurate, and therefore B cannot successfully sue A for defamation." So facile an approach would rarely be appreciated by the grader. The proper way to handle this situation would be to state, "If we assume that A's statement about B is not correct, A cannot raise the defense of truth." You've communicated to the grader that you recognize the need to assume an essential fact and that you've assumed it in a way that enables you to proceed to discuss all other issues.

Case Names

A law student is ordinarily *not* expected to recall case names on an exam. The professor knows that you have read several hundred cases for each course, and that you would have to be a memory expert to have all of the names at your fingertips. If you confront a fact pattern which seems similar to a case which you have reviewed (but you cannot recall its name), just write something like, "One case we've read held that . . ." or "It has been held that. . . . " In this manner, you have informed the grader that you are relying on a case which contained a fact pattern similar to the question at issue.

The only exception to this rule is in the case of a landmark decision (e.g., *Roe v. Wade*). Landmark opinions are usually those which change or alter established law.[2] These cases are usually easy to identify, because you will probably have spent an entire class period discussing each of them. *Palsgraf v. Long Island Rail Road* is a prime example of a landmark case in Torts. In these special cases, you may be expected to remember the case by name, as well as the proposition of law which it stands for. However, this represents a very limited exception to the general rule which counsels against wasting precious time trying to memorize and reproduce case names.

How to Handle Time Pressures

What do you do when there are five minutes left in the exam and you have only written down two-thirds of your answer? One thing ***not*** to do is write something like, "No time left!" or "Not enough time!" This gets you nothing but the satisfaction of knowing you have communicated your personal frustrations to the grader. Another thing ***not*** to do is insert in the exam booklet the outline you may have made on a piece of scrap paper. Professors will rarely look at these.

First of all, it is not necessarily a bad thing to be pressed for time. The person who finishes five minutes early has very possibly missed some important issues. The more proficient you become in knowing what is expected of you on an exam, the greater the difficulty you may experience in staying within the time limits. Second, remember that (at least to some extent) you're graded against your classmates' answers and they're under exactly the same time pressure as you. In short, don't panic if you can't write the "perfect" answer in the allotted time. Nobody does!

The best hedge against misuse of time is to ***review as many old exams as possible***. These exercises will give you a familiarity with the process of organizing and writing an exam answer, which, in turn, should result in an enhanced ability to stay within the time boundaries. If you nevertheless find that you have about 15 minutes of writing to do and five minutes to do

2 In Constitutional Law and Criminal Procedure, many cases will qualify as "landmark" cases. Students studying these subjects should try to associate case names with the corresponding holdings and reproduce both in their exam answers.

it in, write a paragraph which summarizes the remaining issues or arguments you would discuss if time permitted. As long as you've indicated that you're aware of the remaining legal issues, you'll probably receive some credit for them. Your analytical and argumentative skills will already be apparent to the grader by virtue of the issues that you have previously discussed.

Write Legibly

Make sure your answer is legible. Students should **not** assume that their professors will be willing to take their papers to the local pharmacist to have them deciphered. Remember, your professor may have 75 to 150 separate exams to grade. If your answer is difficult to read, you will rarely be given the benefit of the doubt. On the other hand, a legible, well-organized paper creates a very positive mental impact upon the grader.

Many schools allow students to type their exams. If you type your exam, you'll probably be in a room with a lot of other people who are typing theirs. Some schools may have programs that allow you to type on your laptop or on a school laptop. If it's your own laptop, the school will provide software that blocks you from accessing any other programs or information on your hard drive while you type the exam. Computer-typing is not widely available, however, so if you type you will more than likely be typing on a typewriter. If the constant clack-clack-clack of typewriters keeps you from concentrating, you shouldn't type. If you do write your exam on a typewriter, be sure to leave at least one blank line between typewritten lines, so that handwritten changes and insertions in your answers can be made easily.

If you decide against typing, your answer will probably be written in a "bluebook." It is usually a good idea to write only on the odd numbered pages (i.e., 1, 3, 5, etc.). You may also want to leave a blank line between each written line. These things will usually make the answer easier to read. If you discover that you have left out a word or phrase, you can insert it into the proper place by means of a caret sign (∧). If you feel that you've omitted an entire issue, you can write it on the facing blank page. A symbol can be used to indicate where the additional portion of the answer should be inserted. While it's not ideal to have your answer take on the appearance of a road map, reference to an adjoining page by means of a symbol is much better than trying to squeeze six lines into one, and the symbol will help to indicate to the grader where the same symbol appears in another part of your answer.

The Importance of Reviewing Prior Exams

As we've mentioned, it is *extremely important to review old exams*. The transition from blackletter law to essay exam can be a difficult experience if the process has not been practiced. Although this book provides a large number of essay and multiple-choice questions, *don't stop here*! Most law schools have recent tests on file in the library, by course. We strongly suggest that you make a copy of every old exam you can obtain (especially those given by your professors) at the beginning of each semester. The demand for these documents usually increases dramatically as "finals time" draws closer.

The exams for each course should be scrutinized *throughout the semester*. They should be reviewed as you complete each chapter in your casebook. Generally, the order of exam questions follows the sequence of the materials in your casebook. Thus, the first question on a law school test may involve the initial three chapters of the casebook; the second question may pertain to the fourth and fifth chapters; etc. In any event, *don't wait* until the semester is nearly over to begin reviewing old exams.

Keep in mind that no one is born with the ability to analyze questions and write superior answers to law school exams. Like any other skill, it is developed and perfected only through application. If you don't take the time to analyze numerous examinations from prior years, this evolutionary process just won't occur. Don't just *think about* the answers to past exam questions; take the time to *write the answers down*. It's also wise to look back at an answer a day or two after you've written it. You will invariably see (1) ways in which the organization could have been improved, and (2) arguments you missed.

As you practice spotting issues on past exams, you will see how rules of law become the sources of issues on finals. As we've already noted, if you don't *understand* how rules of law translate into issues, you won't be able to achieve superior grades on your exams. Reviewing exams from prior years should also reveal that certain issues tend to be lumped together in the same question. For instance, where a fact pattern involves a false statement made by one person about another, three potential theories of liability are often present—defamation, invasion of privacy (false, public light), and intentional infliction of severe emotional distress. You will need to see if any or all of these legal remedies apply to the facts.

Finally, one of the best means of evaluating if you understand a subject (or a particular area within a subject) is to attempt to create a hypothetical exam for that subject. Your exam should contain as many issues as possible.

If you can write an issue-packed exam, you probably know that subject well. If you can't, then you probably haven't yet acquired an adequate understanding of how the principles of law in that subject can spawn issues.

As Always, a Caveat

The suggestions and advice offered in this book represent the product of many years of experience in the field of legal education. We are confident that the techniques and concepts described in these pages will help you prepare for, and succeed, at your exams. Nevertheless, particular professors sometimes have a preference for exam-writing techniques which are not stressed in this book. Some instructors expect at least a nominal reference to the *prima facie* elements of all pertinent legal theories (even though one or more of those principles is *not* placed into issue). Other professors want their students to emphasize public policy considerations in the arguments they make on a particular issue. Because this book is intended for nationwide consumption, these individualized preferences have *not* been stressed. The best way to find out whether your professor has a penchant for a particular writing approach is to ask her to provide you with a model answer to a previous exam. If a model answer is not available, speak to upper-class students who received a superior grade in that professor's class.

One final point. While the principles cited in the answers to the questions in this book have been drawn from commonly used sources (i.e., casebooks, hornbooks, etc.), it is conceivable that they may be inconsistent with those taught by your professor. In instances where a conflict exists between our formulation of a legal principle and the one which is taught by your professor, *follow the latter!* Since your grades are determined by your professors, their views should always supplant the views expressed in this book.

Essay Exam Questions

Question 1

Sam had developed a secret-formula sauce that makes hamburgers taste better.

Frank asked Sam about the rights to the commercial use of the sauce. Sam replied that he was willing to sell these rights, but that he wanted $40,000. Frank said he would think it over.

The next day Sam tried to call Frank to tell him that he had changed his mind and wanted $50,000 instead of $40,000, but he could not reach Frank.

When they met for lunch two days later, Frank told Sam that $40,000 was all right. Sam replied that it was too late; that the price would be $50,000. Frank then said: "I don't know about all this and want to see my lawyer about the $40,000 deal that I have accepted. But just in case, let's keep the $50,000 deal open for a week." Sam replied: "If you want me to keep the deal open, you ought to pay for lunch today."

Frank agreed to pay for the lunch, and he and Sam drafted a memorandum saying that Sam offered to sell to Frank the right to use his hamburger sauce if Frank would agree to pay Sam $50,000 within thirty days after accepting the offer. The memorandum also stated that in return for Frank's paying for lunch on that day Sam agreed to keep the offer open for one week. They both signed the memorandum. Then Sam said: "Look. If you can't pay the $50,000 right away, I would be willing to take $40,000 plus 20% of your net profits for a year instead." Frank replied: "I'll think about it," but they did not alter the memorandum.

When the lunch bill was presented, Frank discovered that he had forgotten his wallet, so Sam paid for both of them.

Five days later Sam told Frank the deal was off. Frank replied: "No it isn't. I hereby accept your offer to let me use the sauce for $40,000 plus 20% of my net profits for one year." Sam said: "Since you didn't pay for lunch and since the $40,000 plus 20% offer wasn't contained in our written agreement, there isn't even an offer you can prove in court!"

Does Frank have any rights against Sam? Discuss.

Question 2

At the wedding of Tom and Mary, Tom's father, Frank, told them that he wanted them to live with him and to care for him for the rest of his life. He said, "If you agree to do this, I will deliver to you, within a year, a deed to my home." Tom and Mary told Frank they accepted his offer and promised to look after Frank with loving care in Frank's home. They immediately moved in with him.

Soon after moving into Frank's home, Tom and Mary used their own money to add a new wing to the house, pay the outstanding property taxes, and pay off an existing mortgage of $25,000.

One year after Tom and Mary moved into the home, Tom reminded Frank of his promise to convey the property to them. Frank became angry, refused to execute the deed, and ordered Tom and Mary to leave the premises.

Tom and Mary consult you concerning the rights and the remedies that may be available to them.

How would you advise them? Discuss.

Question 3

For several weeks, Seller and Buyer had been dickering about the possible sale of a farm owned by Seller. Seller professed only a mild interest in selling, and Buyer, who had brought up the subject in the first place, thought the price mentioned was too high. On Thursday, September 1, Buyer signed and sent the following letter to Seller:

> During our last talk you insisted you could not possibly sell your farm, Blackacre, for less than $50,000. I need more time to decide whether to pay that much, but I would like to receive your offer to sell the farm for that amount. I need 30 days to decide. Enclosed is my check for $50. If you are interested, answer this letter within 10 days.

Seller received this letter on Tuesday, September 6. On Thursday, September 15, Seller replied by mail, his signed letter reading in part as follows:

> Receipt is acknowledged of your check. I could not possibly sell Blackacre for less than $50,000.

Seller's letter, which contained an adequate legal description of the property, was received by Buyer on Monday, September 19. Thirty days later, on October 19, Buyer decided to purchase. He called Seller at both his residence and office but received no answer. He searched around town without avail (Seller was in another town playing golf with other doctors on their usual day off), and he then, still acting on the 19th, dropped in the mailbox a properly addressed and stamped letter that stated, "I hereby accept your offer to sell Blackacre." Seller received that letter on October 21.

Seller refused to convey the farm. Assuming Buyer could obtain specific performance, is he entitled to such relief?

Question 4

In response to Buyer's request for a firm annual price on fuel oil, Seller wrote Buyer on December 20, "I offer to supply you with any no. 2 fuel oil ordered by you during the next year beginning January 1: 14 cents a gallon, to be ordered only in 3,000 gallon tank cars. Because of your past favors, this offer will not be withdrawn during the year." On December 22, Buyer wrote: "I accept your offer." Seller received Buyer's communication on December 24.

During January and February of the next year, Buyer ordered 400 tank cars of fuel oil; the oil was delivered and paid for at the rate of 14 cents a gallon. Early in March the price of no. 2 fuel oil rose to 17 cents a gallon generally throughout the trade. On March 9, Seller mailed a letter to Buyer reading: "I revoke my December offer." Seller's letter was misdirected by the post office and did not arrive until March 16. Buyer placed the following March orders, all by mail: on March 10, for 50 tank cars; on March 17, for 50 tank cars; on March 30, for 100 tank cars. Seller received all orders two days after mailing, but has refused to fill any March order.

On April 5, Buyer purchased 200 tank cars of no. 2 fuel oil from Petro (a competitor of Seller) at Petro's regular price of 18 cents a gallon, although Buyer admits that by shopping around he might have been able to buy at 17 cents a gallon.

What rights, if any, does Buyer have against Seller? Discuss.

Question 5

Cliff Johnson owned Farmland, a large parcel of undeveloped land. On August 9, he offered it to Bill for $8 an acre. Both men signed the following paper:

> Cliff Johnson hereby offers to sell Farmland to Bill Benson for $8 an acre, cash. Dated: August 9.

Bill considered the deal for two days. On August 11, he again met with Cliff. Bill wanted assurance Cliff would not sell to someone else if Bill went out to look at Farmland. After a long discussion, Cliff gave Bill a memorandum signed by him stating:

> If Bill will look at Farmland, I'll keep the offer open until he's had awhile to think about it.

Bill replied:

> Okay. I will examine Farmland.

On August 11, Bill took the 100-mile round trip to Farmland and inspected it. On August 12, he made arrangements to borrow the money to buy Farmland.

On August 14, Bill was on his way to Cliff's home to tell him that he accepted the offer when he met Cliff's brother. The brother told Bill that on August 13, Cliff had discovered oil on Farmland, so Cliff probably wouldn't be interested in selling it now. Bill went to the post office the next day and sent Cliff a letter (received by Cliff on August 17), stating:

> I accept your offer to sell Farmland for $8 an acre.

Cliff called Bill when he received the letter and told Bill that he wasn't going to let him "snap up" the deal now.

Discuss Bill's rights against Cliff.

Question 6

Bird Aircraft Company manufactured four different models of airplanes called Gull, Tern, Lark, and Eagle. Mills, a retail dealer of planes, wished to buy a number of Bird planes. After extended oral negotiations between Mills and Crow, the secretary of Bird Aircraft Company, Crow wrote out and handed Mills the following:

Purchase Agreement

Bird Aircraft Company agrees to sell and Mills agrees to buy 50 planes to be delivered as ordered within the next year at these prices: Gulls — $24,000 ea.; Terns — $32,000 ea.; Larks — $48,000 ea.; Eagles — $60,000 ea.

To be shipped f.o.b. factory, Mills to specify shipping dates. Number of each type wanted on each shipment to be specified by Mills at least 30 days before each shipping date. Usual form of sales contract to be executed later.

July 15, 1977

Bird Aircraft Company, by Crow, Secty.

Mills did not sign this instrument but looked it over, expressed himself as satisfied, and retained it. Two days later, Mills telegraphed Bird, "Ship me 4 Eagles and 6 Larks by September 1." On the same day he dictated the following letter, which he later signed and mailed to York, an automobile dealer friend of his.

Do you want to try selling planes as a sideline until business picks up? I am selling the Bird line now. I have 10 planes — Eagles and Larks — ordered and hold a purchase agreement under which I will receive 40 more planes during the year.

To this letter, York replied that he was not interested. Through oversight, Bird Aircraft Company never sent Mills a formal sales contract for execution. Finding little demand for Bird planes, Mills telegraphed Bird Aircraft Company on August 1: "Disregard July 17 telegram. Am dropping all plans to handle your line." Mills has since refused to accept delivery of any airplanes from Bird.

Advise Bird, which now has possession of the letter written by Mills to York, of its rights against Mills.

Question 7

Acme Hospital planned to construct an addition to its present facilities. It placed the following advertisement in the local newspapers:

> Sealed bids will be received until 3 p.m., November 1, from all contractors interested in participating in the construction of the addition to Acme Hospital. All bids must be delivered to the Business Office of Acme Hospital no later than 3 p.m., November 1.

Buildem Construction Company sent the following letter to various subcontractors:

> We intend to bid for the general contract on the addition to Acme Hospital. If you wish to subcontract for any portion of the job, your bid must be received in our office no later than 2 p.m., November 1.

On November 1, Buildem was receiving the bids of the subcontractors at its office and using the lowest bids for the computation of its final overall bid to Acme. Buildem had its representative located in the Acme Business Office for the purpose of receiving the final overall bid and submitting it to Acme before 3 p.m.

Coast Company delivered a bid to Buildem for the foundation work in the amount of $140,000. The bid was delivered to Buildem at 1:30 p.m. on November 1 and was the lowest. At 1:45 on the same day, Coast realized it had made a mistake in the computation of its bid and immediately advised Buildem by telephone of the mistake and revised its bid to $170,000. At that time, the final bid had already been submitted to Acme by Buildem's representative at the Acme office. Buildem advised Coast that its bid could not be canceled.

Buildem was awarded the general contract two days later, but Coast refused to perform the foundation work for $140,000. The second lowest bid for the foundation work received by Buildem was $150,000, and Buildem unsuccessfully attempted to have the second lowest bidder perform the work. Buildem was subsequently obliged to have the foundation work done for $200,000.

What are Buildem's rights, if any, against Coast? Discuss.

Question 8

On October 15, Coll, a collector of art, telephoned Art, a well-known painter, and said, "In February I saw your painting of sunflowers. Is it still available, and, if so, how much do you want for it?" Art responded, "You can have it for $25,000. I can deliver it on November 1, but I want a valid liquidated damage clause stating that if either of us decides not to go through with the deal, the other party is entitled to $5,000." Coll replied, "You've got a deal. Draw up the papers and mail them to me."

The painting that Coll had in mind was entitled "Sunflowers." In July, unknown to Coll, Art had painted another picture of sunflowers, which he entitled "Sunflowers II."

Art prepared, signed, and mailed to Coll a typewritten document stating: "October 16. I hereby sell to Coll my sunflower painting for $35,000, the price to be paid and the painting to be picked up by Coll on November 1. In the event either party fails to perform, it is agreed that, because of the difficulty of proving the damages that have been sustained by the non-breaching party, the nonbreaching party shall be entitled to damages in the sum of $5,000." There was a handwritten note attached to the document that stated: "Please sign and return to me. I'll then send you a copy."

Coll received the document on October 17. He telephoned Art that day and said, "I accept your offer and will pick up the painting on November 1." Coll did not sign the typewritten document or return it to Art. The $35,000 figure in the writing was a typographical error made by Art's secretary. Neither Art nor Coll noticed that the figure was $35,000, rather than the $25,000 they had specified in their October 15 telephone conversation.

On November 1, when Coll tendered $25,000, Art tendered to Coll the painting entitled "Sunflowers II." Coll refused to accept "Sunflowers II." Art advised Coll that their transaction was terminated.

What are Coll's rights and remedies against Art, if any?

Question 9

During each month of the preceding calendar year, Buyer, a retail florist, had placed telephone orders with Seller, a flower wholesaler, for cut long stem roses. In each instance, the telephone order was followed by a signed printed "acknowledgment" form from Seller to Buyer. In each instance, the roses were shipped by Seller and accepted and paid for by Buyer.

On May 1 (for the first time in the new calendar year), Buyer telephoned Seller and placed an order for 1,000 long stem roses at 60 cents each. Seller orally accepted the order and sent her signed "acknowledgment" form, which arrived on May 2. The printed form included a statement, not included in the prior acknowledgment forms, that "all disputes are to be settled by arbitration."

On May 2, Seller shipped the roses and they arrived a day later. When Buyer inspected the shipment, she discovered that all the roses were red, rather than of assorted colors as had been the roses received in all prior shipments.

Buyer immediately consults you, tells you she wants to reject this shipment, and asks for your analysis of the following:

1. Must the dispute be settled by arbitration rather than litigation?
2. If she (Buyer) rejects the shipment, will Seller have a cause of action against Buyer for breach of contract, and, if so, what would be Seller's recovery?
3. If she (Buyer) rejects the shipment, will she have a cause of action against Seller, and, if so, what would be Buyer's recovery?

What advice would you give Buyer as to each inquiry? Discuss.

Question 10

In December, during his last year of high school, Paul applied for post-graduation employment with Dryden, an accountant. On January 15, Dryden wrote to Paul: "I offer you employment with my firm, beginning August 1, at $15,000 a year." A few hours after mailing the letter, Dryden telephoned Paul. Dryden stated that a letter offering employment was in the mail and that he wanted to make it clear that "I expect you to stay for at least a year to see how things work out if you accept the job." Paul stated that he would reply promptly.

After a few days, Paul responded by letter, "I accept your employment offer of January 15."

On March 3, Paul received a letter from Dryden stating: "It was my intention in hiring you to have you work with my International Union account. However, the Union no longer retains my firm. Therefore, I lack the funds and will not hire you. Good luck in securing other employment."

Thereafter, several weeks of communication ensued in which Paul demanded at least $5,000 in compensation and Dryden refused to pay more than $200. At last Dryden wrote: "I am tired of hassling. I enclose a check for $500 to settle this mess." The check was conspicuously marked: "In full satisfaction of all claims of Paul against Dryden." On April 15, Paul cashed the check, but printed above the endorsement: "Under protest, reserving all rights."

On May 1, Paul consults you regarding his rights, if any, against Dryden. Advise him.

Question 11

Buyer ("B") telephonically agreed to buy, and Seller ("S") telephonically agreed to sell, 1,000 widgets at $2.00 per widget. S sent B an acknowledgment form (which was not manually signed by S) after their conversation. S also ordered 1,000 clips at $.04 each from a manufacturer. These clips would be integrated into the widgets. S subsequently sent an initial installment of 200 widgets to B. B accepted the 200 widgets, but called S two days later and claimed that he never had a "firm" contract with S. B also said he was going to ship the 200 widgets back to S.

Does S have any rights against B? Discuss.

Question 12

On January 15, Jones agreed with Buyer in a writing signed by both to supply Buyer with 10,000 pounds of specifically described bolts each month, for a period of ten months, beginning March 1. The stated price was $.85 a pound. On February 1, Jones, in good faith, notified Buyer that he could not afford to sell the bolts at the agreed price. He said he would charge $.90 a pound. Buyer orally agreed to the increase in price.

In a written confirmation, signed by Jones, Jones's secretary mistakenly typed the new price as "$.91 a pound" rather than "$.90 a pound." Buyer received the confirmation but did not read or reply to it.

Prior to March 1, Jones notified Buyer that he would deliver no bolts because he had just contracted to sell his entire output to Ted at $1.10 a pound.

Despite diligent efforts, Buyer was unable to buy bolts from a new supplier until May 1, and then at $1.00 a pound.

Because of the 61-day delay in obtaining a new source of supply, Buyer was delayed in delivering motors to Electric, a company with which Buyer had a contract that contained a valid liquidated damages clause providing for damages of $10,000 a day for delays in delivery of motors.

Although Jones knew that Buyer sold motors, he did not know specifically, nor did he have reason to know, that Buyer had a contract with Electric or that the contract contained a liquidated damages clause.

In a suit by Buyer against Jones commenced on October 1, Buyer prays for the following damages.

Count 1: $15,000 in damages for the difference between the price paid by Buyer ($1.00) and the original contract price ($.85) for 100,000 pounds;

Count 2: $610,000 in damages for the amount Buyer had to pay Electric in liquidated damages;

Count 3: $1,000,000 in punitive damages, alleging that Jones's breach was malicious.

In his answer, Jones denies liability and contends that should he be found liable under Count 1, his liability would be limited to $9,000, the difference between the price paid by Buyer ($1.00) and the modified price in the written confirmation ($.91). What result on each count? Discuss.

Question 13

American's relationship with Citadel, a company facing financial difficulty, had been a profitable one for American. Therefore, American undertook to make various commitments to or on behalf of Citadel.

Citadel was in debt to General. American orally advised Citadel, "Don't worry about what you owe General. We will pay it if you can't, and you can repay us later."

Citadel was also in arrears on its rent on its business premises, and the lease there had two years to run. With Citadel's approval, American called Citadel's landlord, Lanco, and told him orally, "Don't worry about Citadel's past due rents. If necessary, we will lend Citadel the money to pay the rent it owes you."

Citadel was indebted to National on a promissory note given to National by Citadel for a loan by National to Citadel. The note was past due. With Citadel's approval, American wrote National as follows: "If you agree to give Citadel additional time to pay its note, we guarantee its payment." National replied by signed note as follows: "In consideration of your guarantee, we promise to hold Citadel's note until such time as we need payment."

To provide Citadel with operating funds, American purchased from Citadel various accounts receivable held by Citadel. American immediately gave each of the account debtors written notice of its purchase. One of the accounts purchased was for certain goods sold by Citadel to Debco, which goods proved to be totally defective. At the time of the purchase of the accounts, American was not aware of the defective nature of the goods.

Despite American's efforts, Citadel failed financially two months after the foregoing events took place.

What liability has American incurred to (1) General, (2) Lanco, (3) National? Discuss.

What are American's rights to recover from Debco on the assigned accounts receivable? Discuss.

Question 14

At the request of B, A, an attorney, represented B in protracted business negotiations. About a month after termination of these negotiations, B wrote a letter to A in which B stated: "Your services were most helpful. You have not sent me a bill as yet, but I appreciate what you have done and am going to pay you $10,000."

At the time A received the letter, she was feeling very affluent and was trying to think of something to do for her favorite nephew, N. A telephoned B and said: "The $10,000 fee you are giving me is very generous; it's more than I was going to charge you. However, I really don't need it now. Why don't you pay me off by going down to the Cadilline Car Agency and buying my nephew, N, one of their Goldray Specials?" B responded: "If that's what you want, I'll be glad to do it. I'll arrange it as soon as I can." Goldray Specials are worth $7,000.

One week later, A, who had suffered reverses in the stock market and felt impoverished, again telephoned B as follows: "If you haven't done anything about that Goldray, forget it; I need the money myself." B replied: "I'm a little short at present. How much do you want?" A said: "If you can pay me $5,000, I'll take that as my fee." B paid A the $5,000.

A later told the story to N, who was not amused. A Cadilline stockholder heard the story from N. After thinking matters over, A decided that B still owed her about $2,000 more, bringing her total fee to $7,000. Cadilline and N also decided to sue B to enforce whatever rights they had against him.

What are the rights of A, N, and Cadilline against B? Discuss.

Question 15

M, when solicited for a gift to his alma mater, Mayberry University, wrote a letter stating: "I am giving you $50,000 because of the outstanding contributions Mayberry has made to education and research over the past years. M." Mayberry replied, "Thank you. We shall use your gift to solicit matching funds from other alumni." Mayberry did, in fact, send out postcards to its alumni describing M's gift and requesting similar donations.

M had patented a new gadget that was potentially very valuable but that he had not been able to sell because the process for putting it into mass production had never been perfected. The patent had ten years to run. D, a manufacturer who had a use for the gadget, offered to buy the patent from M. D showed M some diagrams that, D claimed, described a process that would allow M to mass-produce the gadget. M was skeptical of the efficacy of D's plans, but nevertheless offered to transfer to D the exclusive right to make and market the gadget if D would pay Mayberry the $50,000 that M owed to it. D agreed.

After two months, M wrote a letter to D that said: "I've changed my mind. Send the payments to me." D wrote back: "Re your letter. I'll send the money to you. D." Thereafter, D determined that his process was defective and that it was not economically feasible to manufacture the gadget. He advised M that he was surrendering his rights to the gadget and considered himself relieved of any obligation to M. M then advised Mayberry that he would not honor his pledge.

Does Mayberry have any rights against M or D? Does M have any rights against D? Discuss.

Question 16

Xact and Young contracted in writing. Xact was to clear and level a designated tract of land owned by Young. Young was to pay $12,000 when the work was half done and a final $12,000 when the work was completed. The contract recited: "Each of the said payments shall be made only on the presentation by Xact of receipts showing he has paid all his workmen and suppliers who, by statute, might have lienable claims against Young's land."

Xact showed Will a copy of the Xact-Young contract and said: "If you will finance my labor costs on this job by loaning me each week a sum sufficient to cover my payroll for that week, I will repay you with interest at the highest lawful rate, when Young pays me; this contract will be your security."

Will replied: "I will make the loans you request."

At the end of each week for the next four weeks Will loaned Xact a sum sufficient to cover Xact's payroll. When the work was half done, Xact took receipts to Young showing that the workers had been fully paid. Young said he must also have receipts showing payment for the petroleum products used on the job by Xact's automotive and machine equipment. Xact insisted that suppliers of such products did not have lienable claims under any statute. Young insisted to the contrary. The dispute continued. Meanwhile, Xact went ahead with the work.

The fifth weekly payroll is about due. Young has paid Xact nothing. Will has received nothing from Young or Xact.

You are counsel to Will. What advice do you have for him? Your advice should specifically address these two questions:

1. What will be the legal position of Will as to Xact when the fifth weekly payroll comes due if Will's four loans have not then been repaid?

2. What are Will's rights against Young?

Question 17

Ace Construction and Beta Milling signed a contract whereby Ace was to construct the concrete base and the covering for a new 50-ton flour mill that Beta was purchasing. Ace's engineers analyzed the soil beneath where the base was to be built and found that it was generally firm and underlaid with a solid rock layer about 15 feet down. They planned to construct concrete pillars on the rock and put the concrete base on them, which, they calculated, would give ample support for holding the mill. All this was explained to Beta as the basis for Ace's estimate of what the cost of the project would be.

The contract provided for a "firm" price of $100,000 — $20,000 to be paid on signing and the remaining $80,000 to be paid on completion. The contract also contained the following statements:

> This contract constitutes the parties' entire agreement. Nothing has been agreed to or is otherwise a part of this contract that is not expressly included in it. This contract cannot be amended, varied, modified, or added to in any respect except by a writing signed by both parties.

Beta paid Ace the $20,000 and Ace started construction. After Ace had laid four of the ten pillars, an earthquake cracked all four pillars and caused the holes to be filled back in by dirt falling from the sides. Ace's supervising engineer told Beta's plant manager that it would cost $10,000 to remove the dirt that had fallen in and to remove and replace the four pillars. He also said the rock layer would have to be restored to its former strength. This, he estimated, would cost $50,000. He told Beta's president that he had been authorized to proceed with construction only if Beta promised to pay an additional $45,000. This was $15,000 less than the additional cost caused by the earthquake, but Ace was willing to waive its $15,000 profit in order to be of help to Beta in this emergency. Beta's president agreed and the construction was then resumed.

When construction was completed, Ace asked to be paid the sum of $125,000 ($145,000, less the $20,000 paid before construction started). Beta refused but tendered $80,000, saying that it would not honor the modified agreement.

Ace has now sued Beta. Discuss.

Question 18

Bert owned a chemicals manufacturing plant. Walt contacted Bert about the production of a new cleaning solvent that Walt had developed. Bert analyzed the cost of producing Walt's solvent and quoted a price of $7 a gallon for 5,000 gallons a month to be delivered in 1-gallon containers, effective for a period of one year. Walt advised Bert that his offer would be acceptable, provided Bert agreed to pay for the containers. Bert made no further reply to Walt. Bert ordered the necessary materials, including the containers, and began production and delivery. Walt paid Bert at the rate of $7 for each gallon of solvent delivered.

After two weeks of production, Bert discovered that the solvent required special zinc-lined containers, which raised the cost to $8 a gallon to make the same amount of profit. At the same time, the local water pollution district found that chemical wastes from Bert's manufacturing process were polluting a nearby river and ordered Bert to install a water purification system at a cost of $50,000. Walt refused to adjust the price to reflect these factors. Bert had neither the $50,000 nor sufficient credit to enable him to finance installation of the purification system.

Bert then advised Walt that he could not continue with the project and proposed that Gray, a larger manufacturer, be substituted in Bert's place. Gray consented and quoted a price of $9.00 a gallon. Walt advised Bert he would accept Gray's offer and release Bert from further liability, if Bert would agree to pay Walt the $2 difference between Bert's and Gray's prices for each gallon manufactured by Gray during the remainder of the one-year period. Bert agreed, and Gray began to manufacture the solvent.

Two weeks later, Gray's plant was totally destroyed by fire.

Walt demanded that Bert immediately resume production and deliver solvent at the rate of $7 a gallon. Bert refused to do so. Walt obtained solvent from Mafco at the rate of $10 a gallon for the remainder of the year.

Walt consults you at the end of the year about what rights, if any, he has against Bert. What would you advise Walt? Discuss.

Question 19

Manor, the owner of Blackacre, engaged Broker to sell the property under the terms of a signed, written agreement that provided, in part:

> I, Manor, agree to pay Broker a commission of 5% of the gross sale price of any sale of said property which is arranged by Broker for a consideration of not less than $15,000, such commission to be payable on consummation of the sale.

Shortly thereafter, Broker procured a buyer, Valley, who agreed to purchase the property for $16,000. On March 1, Valley paid Manor $1,000 down and signed a contract of sale that stated, *inter alia*:

> Valley agrees to pay an additional $2,000 in cash with a five-year note for the balance of $13,000 at 6% interest, on delivery by Manor of a deed conveying good and clear title to Blackacre.

On March 15, Valley learned that Manor had that week obtained a bank loan in the amount of $12,000 payable in five years and that he had given the bank as security for the loan a mortgage on Blackacre. On April 15, Valley entered into a contract to buy the house of another, Smith, and demanded that Manor return his $1,000 deposit. A few days later, Manor paid off the mortgage loan and on May 1, tendered a sufficient deed to Valley, which Valley refused.

What are the rights of Valley and Manor against one another, and of Broker against Manor? Discuss.

Question 20

In January, Owner contracted in a signed writing to sell Greenacre, a 50-acre square parcel of unimproved realty, to Byer for $50,000. Byer was to pay $5,000 on March 1. The remainder of the purchase price and the deed were to be exchanged on April 1.

On February 1, in a signed writing, Byer assigned to Ellis all his rights under the contract, and Ellis, also in a signed writing, agreed with Byer to pay the contract price to Owner. Byer then notified Owner that he had assigned the contract to Ellis, that Ellis had agreed to pay the contract price, and that, therefore, Byer considered himself "free and clear of any further obligations under the contract." Owner received, but did not reply to, this communication.

On March 1, Owner accepted the $5,000 installment paid to him by Ellis. On March 15, Owner notified Byer and Ellis that he had just discovered that he did not own a strip 3 feet wide along the western edge of Greenacre.

On April 1, Owner tendered to Byer and Ellis a deed to Greenacre, excluding from the description of the property the 3-feet strip. Both Byer and Ellis refused to accept the deed or to pay the remaining $45,000. Owner thereon commenced a suit for specific performance against both Byer and Ellis. Ellis cross-complained against Owner for restitution of the $5,000 installment he had paid to Owner.

1. What result in Owner's suit against Byer? Discuss.

2. What result in Owner's suit against Ellis and Ellis's cross-complaint against Owner? Discuss.

Question 21

O owned land adjacent to City Airport that he wished to develop. A was an architect whose designs had won national acclaim. On January 2, A and O entered into a valid written contract whereby A agreed to produce and deliver a design, on or before May 1, of a 10-story hotel that O wished to build on the land. O agreed to pay $300,000 for that design. The contract provided that "This contract may not be assigned."

On January 15, A was advised by his personal physician that he was on the verge of a nervous breakdown and should take a six-month rest from his work. On January 20, A and B entered into a written agreement that stated that "A hereby assigns B all A's rights under his January 2 contract with O." B was also a well-known architect and occasional collaborator with A on construction design projects. On January 22, B visited O for preliminary discussions on the hotel design. Thereafter, B started work and needed to communicate with O only by telephone on various aspects of the emerging design.

On March 31, it was announced that City Airport flight operations would cease at the end of the calendar year. This decision of the City Airport Authority was reached after a year of mounting public protest over noise and safety problems associated with the airport operations. The protests had figured prominently in the local news media since their inception.

On May 1, B tried to deliver the completed hotel design to O, who refused to accept it. O has refused to pay B anything.

Discuss the contractual rights and measure of damages, if any, of B against O.

Question 22

Art and Betty own adjoining farms in County, an area where all agriculture requires irrigation. Art bought a well-drilling rig and drilled a 400-foot well from which he drew drinking water. Betty needed no additional irrigation water, but in January 1985, she asked Art on what terms he would drill a well near her house to supply better tasting drinking water than the County water she had been using for years. Art said that because he had never before drilled a well for hire, he would charge Betty only $10 a foot, about $1 more than his expected cost. Art said that he would drill to a maximum depth of 600 feet, which was the deepest his rig could reach. Betty said, "Okay, if you guarantee June 1 completion." Art agreed and asked for $3,500 in advance, with any refund or additional payment to be made on completion. Betty said, "Okay," and paid Art $3,500.

Art started to drill on May 1. He had reached a depth of 200 feet on May 10 when his drill struck rock and broke, plugging the hole. The accident was unavoidable. It had cost Art $12 a foot to drill this 200 feet. Art said he would not charge Betty for drilling the useless hole, but he would have to start a new well close by and could not promise its completion before July 1.

Betty, annoyed by Art's failure, refused to let Art start another well, and on June 1, she contracted with Carlos to drill a well. Carlos agreed to drill to a maximum depth of 350 feet for $4,500. Betty paid Carlos the $4,500 in advance, but Carlos could not start drilling until October 1. He completed drilling and struck water at 300 feet on October 30.

In July, Betty sued Art seeking to recover her $3,500, plus the $4,500 paid to Carlos.

On August 1, County's dam failed, reducing the amount of water available for irrigation. Betty lost her apple crop worth $15,000. The loss could have been avoided by pumping from Betty's well if it had been operational by August 1. Betty amended her complaint to add the $15,000 loss.

In her suit against Art, what are Betty's rights and what damages, if any, will she recover? Discuss.

Question 23

D is a chair manufacturer. P is a chair distributor. Three and one-half years ago, D entered into a five-year, written agreement with P, which provided that: (1) D would furnish one of its models of chairs (the Luxuriator) exclusively to P (or the business entity designated by P) for 25% below the prevailing retail price; and (2) P would pay for the chairs within 60 days after their delivery to the location specified.

During the initial three years of the agreement, D supplied P with 330, 100, and 250 chairs, respectively. Halfway into the fourth year, P had already ordered 475 chairs. However, P was 12 days behind in his payments to D for 30 previously ordered and delivered chairs. When reminded of this fact by D, P replied that a few of his customers had been tardy in paying him, but that all overdue payments would be made within two weeks. To this explanation, D simply replied, "that better be the case." P's next order (made the next day) from D was for 150 chairs, to be delivered to A. Before sending the chairs, D called A and advised the latter that, due to P's outstanding delinquencies, D would not provide the chairs unless A guaranteed P's payment to D for them. A promised to pay D if P didn't, and the chairs were shipped to A the next day.

Five days later, D advised P in writing that "he had exceeded his quota for the year" and that no more orders would be filled this year. Although A paid P for the 150 chairs that were delivered to A, P has refused to pay D for them, claiming he is entitled to offset that amount against D's damages to him. P has also refused to pay D for the 30 chairs represented by his late payment (even though P has been paid by his customers), based on the same rationale. D has now advised P that their agreement is terminated. P desires to sue D, and D desires to sue A.

Discuss.

Essay Exam Answers

Answer to Question 1

There are three possible bases on which a contract may have been formed. Whether Frank ("F") has any rights against Sam ("S") will turn on the resolution of the following issues.

Was an enforceable contract formed based on the first ($40,000) "offer"?

Whether a statement constitutes *a negotiation* (which is not capable of acceptance) or *an offer* depends on how a reasonable offeree would construe the offeror's statement. F will argue that S's initial statement constituted an offer because (1) it was in response to F's request to enter into a contract, and (2) the contract price was stated. Although S will contend that his comment that "he was willing" *to sell the use of the sauce for $40,000* was merely an inquiry to determine if there was any basis on which to discuss a contract, F should prevail on the question whether S's statement was an offer.

Assuming S's statement was intended as an offer, S will also argue that it was not sufficiently definite (an offer must be definite as to all material terms) because essential details such as the method of payment (cash or credit terms?), exclusivity (was F's use to be exclusive?), the timing of payment (when was S to be paid?), as well as the length of F's use of the formula (indefinitely?) were not mentioned. F will contend it would probably be implied into the agreement that (1) payment would be made in cash concurrently with tender of the formula, and (2) he would have the exclusive use of the formula during his life. Because of the ambiguities as to these details, S should prevail on this issue.

S would next argue that his telephone call to F revoked any offer to sell the formula for $40,000. However, F would contend in rebuttal that a revocation is not effective until actually communicated to the offeree. The facts do not show whether S left a message at the place where he attempted to call F (which probably would have constituted a revoking communication), and so it doesn't appear that a revocation occurred.

Before the 2001 revisions, §1-206 of the UCC required a writing signed by the party against whom enforcement is sought for sales of personal property (other than of goods) in excess of $5,000. (That provision was eliminated in the 2001 revisions but remains the law in most states at the time of this writing. If your class worked with revised article 1, you should not raise this issue.) S would argue that the transaction *constituted a "sale" of his formula* (which is personal property), and since the contract was entirely verbal, it is not enforceable beyond $5,000. F would argue in rebuttal that the contract involved a licensing agreement (the $40,000 was only for the "use" of the formula during F's life), and thus no writing was necessary. F would probably prevail on this issue.

Was a contract formed based on the second possible offer (use of the sauce for $50,000)?

The requirement of definiteness of material terms would also be applicable here. S might also contend that F *was not reasonable in believing an offer was being made because the reference to "buying lunch" showed that S was merely joking.* F would argue in rebuttal, however, that the drafting of a memo reasonably led him to believe that an offer was being made. F should prevail.

An *option contract* is formed where the offeror receives consideration in exchange for his promise not to revoke the offer for a specified period of time. F will argue that S offered him an *option contract* for seven days, which was *accepted* when F promised to pay for the lunch. S can contend that acceptance of the option required performance by payment of the lunch, and F failed to pay for the lunch. F, however, could argue in rebuttal that S's payment of the lunch was actually a loan that F was obliged to repay. In addition, an option may be valid if it "recites a purported consideration," even if not actually paid. Rest. 2d §87(1) & cmt. c.

S will argue that even if an option contract was formed, F never made the final acceptance of it (i.e., paid the $50,000 to S within 30 days); also that F failed to accept the second alleged offer within one week (F stated that he accepted only the third alleged offer). While F might argue that S's anticipatory repudiation of the alleged option contract excused F's obligation to tender $50,000, F will be obliged to prove that he was capable of tendering the $50,000 payment to S. However, F seems to have *no* adequate rebuttal to S's contention that the alleged *second offer was never explicitly accepted by F.*

Was a contract formed based on the third ($40,000 plus 20% of net profits) possible offer?

Our discussion of the requirement of definiteness of material terms would be equally applicable, with the additional problem of defining *what was intended by "net profits"*—i.e., what expenses incurred by F could be offset against gross profits derived from the sauce formula? Our discussion pertaining to UCC §1-206 (i.e., that contracts for the sale of personal property, other than goods, are not enforceable if in excess of $5,000 unless there is an adequate writing) would again be applicable.

Additionally, S could probably successfully contend that the "$40,000 plus 20%" offer was revoked prior to acceptance since the facts indicate that S told F the "deal was off" prior to F's attempted acceptance.

Summary:

Based on all of the foregoing, it appears that no contract existed between F and S, so F probably has no rights against S.

Assuming, however, a contract was formed, can F get specific performance?

Specific performance is appropriate where there is no adequate remedy at law. If F sued S for damages, S would probably successfully argue that F's losses are too speculative to be awarded any damages (would F have made a profit or suffered a loss from use of the sauce?). Since the formula is new, it has no track record. Thus, specific performance would be appropriate in this instance if a contract existed.

Answer to Question 2

Advise Tom and Mary (jointly, "T/M") that they should anticipate that the following issues will arise if they attempt to enforce the promise made by Frank ("F").

Did F make an offer to T/M?

Whether a statement constitutes an offer depends on whether a reasonable offeree would construe it as such. While F might contend that in an **intrafamilial situation** there is a presumption that legal relationships are not intended, T/M could probably successfully argue in rebuttal that F's statement appeared to be serious and in the form of a commitment, and their subsequent conduct showed that they believed an offer had been made; so ***F's statement was an offer.***

Was F's offer sufficiently definite as to material terms?

An offer must be sufficiently definite as to material terms to be enforceable. F will contend that his words were not sufficiently definite: (1) **the words "care for" are too vague,** and (2) **the type of deed to be delivered was not specified** (i.e., was it a quitclaim or warranty deed?). T/M could successfully rebut these arguments by pointing out that (1) the words "care for" are susceptible of a factual determination, and (2) an ordinary grant deed would be implied into the contract. They would also argue that F has apparently never contended that T/M did *not* take care of him.

Is the contract unenforceable by reason of the Statute of Frauds ("SOF")?

A transfer of an interest in land is within the SOF (i.e., there must be a writing, signed by the party against whom enforcement is sought, which describes the material terms of the agreement). Since F never signed such a writing, he will contend that the alleged agreement is unenforceable. T/M could assert two theories in rebuttal to this argument. First, in many states, where the grantee has completed acts that are unequivocally referable to the existence of a contract for the transfer of land, such part performance is sufficient evidence of an oral contract as to remove the agreement from the SOF. If done by strangers, acts such as adding a new wing, paying off the mortgage and satisfying the property taxes probably would be adequate to show the existence of a contract. F may argue that these acts were generous gifts from one family member to another, not unequivocally related to a contract. T/M may be able to assert that their action in reliance satisfies an exception to the Statute of Frauds. Rest. 2d §139. Paying for taxes and an addition in reliance on F's promise would produce substantial detriment if F is allowed to avoid the promise entirely. T/M should prevail on the reliance argument. The exception for reliance, however, specifies that the remedy should be limited as justice requires. Typically this permits recovery of the reliance interest (expenses incurred), but not the expectation interest (the deed or its value).

Can T/M obtain specific performance ("SP")?

Assuming T/M prevailed on the foregoing issues, the next question would be whether they can obtain SP. While land is generally considered "unique" (meaning that no amount of money can make up for the loss of a particular parcel of land), F could argue that to grant SP in this instance would not be appropriate since it would force two antagonistic parties to share a single roof (obviously, F would still have the right to live in the house until his death). Moreover, given the strong public policy against enforcing SP of personal services contracts (enforcement could amount to involuntary servitude), F would emphasize that T/M were required to care for him as well as to live with him. F could also argue that if he gave a deed to T/M, and then they sold the property prior to fulfilling their obligations (i.e., taking care of F for his entire life), the buyers might be *bona fide* purchasers and have a right to the land deemed superior to F's.

However, T/M could argue in rebuttal that (1) it was F (not T/M) who caused the situation in which the parties resided together, and so he should not be heard to complain about this problem; and (2) the court order transferring the property into T/M's names could specifically be subject to fulfillment of a condition subsequent (i.e., T/M's taking care of F for the remainder of his life). Ultimately, however, even though the public policy concerns will probably defeat them, courts are just as unlikely to award SP against an employer as they are to award it against an employee. F should therefore prevail.

Assuming that SP is not granted, what damages could T/M claim under the agreement with F?

An aggrieved party is entitled to be placed in the position he would have been in had the other side performed the contract. Thus, if the court elects to enforce the contract, T/M would be able to recover the value of the land on the date of the breach, plus interest on that amount, plus the cost of moving out, less, however, the value of benefits T/M will receive from not having to complete their own performance (i.e., expenses saved by not having to care for F, and perhaps money they will earn working for someone else, if they could not have taken those jobs while caring for F). They cannot recover the cost of the improvements they made; those will be reflected in the value of the house. Awarding the value of the house allows T/M to purchase (or rent, if they prefer) suitable substitute housing. The cost of reasonable interim housing (while seeking a permanent substitute) should be recoverable. However, T/M may need to find substitute housing immediately. Recovery for interim housing will cover a reasonable time, not necessarily the entire time between the breach and payment of the judgment.

As noted earlier, however, the Statute of Frauds might constrain the court to award only the reliance interest. If so, T/M can recover the cost of moving into and out of the house, the investments they made in the house, the cost (including their time) caring for F, and perhaps any loss suffered by postponing their search for housing for a year because they believed F's house would become theirs. Offset against this would be the fair rental value they received by living in the house for a year.

Assuming T/M are not successful with respect to their breach of contract action against F, can they recover in quasi-contract?

If T/M are not successful under breach of contract, they probably can recover for unjust enrichment. Their expenses for taxes and improvements benefited F. Because T/M incurred these expenses under the belief that F would convey the house to them, T/M were not volunteers or donors, making it unjust for F to retain the benefit. The benefit to F might be measured either by the increase in the value of the house (over what it would have been without the addition and with unpaid taxes) or by the amount F would have needed to spend to get the same benefit (probably the amount T/M spent, unless F could have hired a cheaper contractor for the addition). In addition, T/M should recover the reasonable value of their services under a *quantum meruit* theory (i.e., they rendered services in anticipation of compensation, and the defendant was aware of such expectation). Any other result would permit F to be unjustly enriched.

Answer to Question 3

Buyer ("B") can contend that a contract arose from either (1) his acceptance of the option contract, which was formed by reason of Seller's ("S") acceptance of the option offer contained in B's September 1 letter to S; or (2) his acceptance of S's September 15 offer.

If B were to assert that a contract arose based on his acceptance of the option contract, the following issues would be raised.

Was B's September 1 letter an offer or merely an invitation?

Whether a statement constitutes an offer (which is capable of acceptance) or an invitation (which is not) depends on how a reasonable offeree would construe it. S could contend that since B's September 1 letter stated that "I would like to receive your **offer**," it was merely an invitation inquiry. B, however, could argue in rebuttal that while his layperson language was somewhat awkward, the fact that he included a $50 check with the letter would lead a reasonable person in S's position to recognize that B was offering an option contract to S (whereby S, in exchange for the $50, would offer to sell Blackacre to B for $50,000 for a 30-day period). B should prevail on this issue.

Was B's September 1 offer sufficiently definite as to material terms?

A contract must be sufficiently definite as to material terms to be capable of acceptance. S could contend that the alleged offer was not sufficiently definite since there was no indication of (1) the type of deed that he was to deliver, (2) when the transaction was to be completed, and (3) what title would be acceptable (would it have to be completely "clean," or would certain liens or easements be acceptable?). However, B could contend in rebuttal that (1) the type of deed would be that which is normally required for such transactions in the area, (2) the deal would be completed within a reasonable period of time, and (3) title would have to be clean (as is ordinarily the case). Again, B should prevail.

Was B's offer for an option contract accepted by S in a timely manner?

Where an offer is not accepted within the time specified by the offeror, it **lapses automatically**. S could contend that since B's September 1 letter stated that if S were interested he was to answer it within 10 days, and S did not reply until September 15, B's offer lapsed when S did not reply to it by September 11. However, B could contend in rebuttal that where a dated communication states that the offer must be accepted within a specified period of time, the time limitation is ordinarily deemed to run from the date on which it is received by the offeree, rather that the date of the communication. In the alternative, if S's acceptance is deemed late, the acceptance would operate as an offer in and of itself, and B's silence as to S's late acceptance would operate as a manifestation of assent. Acceptance by silence is limited to a few specific situations: where the offeree accepts a benefit without objection; where an offeror invites acceptance by silence and the offeree intends silence to accept the offer; or where prior dealings make silence a reasonable means of acceptance. Rest. 2d §69. No facts support any of these theories. Thus, B probably should rely on this interpretation that S's response was timely.

Did S accept B's offer for an option contract?

An acceptance must ordinarily be unequivocal. S could contend that since his September 15 letter merely acknowledged receipt of B's check and stated that he "could not possibly sell Blackacre for less than $50,000," no acceptance of B's offer occurred. If S cashed B's check, it would be difficult for S to deny that he accepted B's offer (since the act of cashing the check would be inconsistent with a contention that he had not accepted). Even if S did not cash B's check, retaining it and reaffirming the purchase price would probably constitute an acceptance. Thus, B again should prevail.

Assuming an option contract arose, was it accepted by B in a timely manner?

S would argue that even if an option contract did arise, it **lapsed** on October 1 (30 days after B's September 1 letter to S). Additionally, S would contend, even if the 30-day option period commenced from S's September 15 reply to B, the 30-day period still expired before B's attempted acceptance on October 19. Although B would contend in rebuttal that the 30-day period should commence to run from September 19 (the date on which he received S's reply), and therefore his October 19 acceptance was timely, a reasonable offeree would probably interpret the option contract to have lapsed on October 15 (30 days after the date of S's letter to B). In either case (whether the 30-day period lapsed on October 15 or October 19), acceptance of an option contract is effective on receipt by the offeror and not on dispatch. Rest. 2d §63(2). Thus, B's acceptance was not timely since it wasn't **received** by S until October 21. S should prevail on this issue.

If, however, an option contract was formed, was it accepted by B in the proper manner?

S can contend that even if an option contract had arisen, it had to be accepted by payment of $50,000 to S. Since this did not occur on or before October 19, acceptance was not made in the proper manner. B, however, could argue in rebuttal that where the mode of acceptance is somewhat ambiguous (i.e., performance or promise), acceptance can ordinarily be made in either manner. Additionally, B could contend that S made it impossible for him to accept by making payment since S was unavailable on October 19. However, since the facts do not indicate that B intended to pay $50,000, this argument will probably be unavailing. S should therefore prevail on this issue.

Summary (1):

Since B probably did not accept the option contract in a timely manner (i.e., by S's arranging receipt of B's acceptance on or before October 15, or even October 19), B probably ***cannot*** enforce it against S.

Alternative argument by B:

B could alternatively contend that S's letter of September 15 constituted an offer that B accepted on October 19. Whether this contention would be successful depends on a resolution of the following issues.

Was S's September 15 letter a valid offer?

S could contend that his September 15 letter was **merely an invitation** because words such as "I could not possibly sell Blackacre for less than $50,000" suggest a willingness to consider offers for that amount (rather than constituting an offer itself). However, B could probably successfully argue in rebuttal that taking into consideration (1) their earlier negotiations, (2) B's September 1 letter to S, and (3) S's retention of the $50 check, B reasonably understood S's September 15 communication to be an offer.

Our discussion with respect to the requirement of definiteness as to material terms would be equally applicable here.

Was S's offer accepted in a valid manner?

Where no time is specified by the offeror, ***an offer must be accepted within a reasonable period of time***. S could contend that a one-month period is too long a span of time within which to accept his offer (if, in fact, one was made). Although B would contend in rebuttal that 30 days is not too lengthy a period of time to accept an offer to purchase a $50,000 parcel of land (i.e., it would take the average person some time to raise that amount of money and establish an escrow arrangement), S should prevail on this issue.

Our discussion with respect to whether acceptance was made in the proper manner would be equally applicable here.

Summary (2):

Based on our conclusion that B did not accept S's offer within a reasonable period of time, S is again probably *not* obligated to sell Blackacre to B.

Answer to Question 4

If Buyer ("B") were to sue Seller ("S"), the following issues would probably arise.

Was S's offer sufficiently definite as to material terms? (If it wasn't, S would not be required to fill any orders that had not already been completed.)

An offer must be sufficiently definite as to its material terms to be capable of acceptance. S could contend that his offer was not sufficiently definite as to material terms because (1) nothing was said as to place of delivery or the terms of sale (cash or credit), and (2) the amount of oil is not ascertainable since it could not be known what B's prospective purchases would be. However, B could contend in rebuttal that under the UCC: (1) where nothing is said as to form of payment, it must be made in cash; (2) the place of delivery would be the seller's business premises; and (3) the quantity of oil used by B could be ascertained by proof of the purchases B had made from other entities during prior years. Also, the fact that B and S did business in January and February (apparently without any dispute) also suggests that both parties understood the essential terms. Thus, B should prevail on this issue.

Was the offer by S an offer for a one-year requirements contract or merely an offer to make a series of unilateral contracts (an offer that, if not explicitly revoked earlier, would terminate automatically after one year)?

B would probably contend that he reasonably understood S's letter as offering a requirements contract to him, whereby S promised to supply B with all of the latter's requirements of no. 2 fuel oil throughout the next calendar year, and that this offer was accepted by B's December 22 letter to S. However, S could argue in rebuttal that since there was no "requirements" language (i.e., discussion of quantity by reference to buyer's requirements or reference to exclusivity of source) in either his letter or B's response, B should have realized that S was proposing only a *series of unilateral contracts*, which B could accept by the act of ordering no. 2 fuel oil each time. S's contention that he had made only a continuing offer (which could be revoked at any time prior to an order's actually being made by B) should prevail since there was a complete absence of "requirements" language. Thus, B's December 22 response to S probably did *not* bind S to fill all of B's requirements for the succeeding calendar year.

Was an option contract created? (If so, S would be unable to revoke his offer to make a series of unilateral contracts throughout the next calendar year.)

An option contract is created when, for consideration, the offeror relinquishes her right to revoke the offer. Although B might contend that consideration was supplied by B's past favors to S, it is well established that ***prior performance*** rendered to a promisor by the promisee cannot serve as consideration.

Despite the Rest. 2d's language requiring "purported" consideration for creation of an option contract (§87(1)(a)), it is not apparent that "true" consideration is actually required for this purpose. In fact, courts concern themselves most with the ***fairness of the exchange*** in determining whether an option contract arose. Though the December market price is not stated, it would appear to be in the vicinity of 14 cents a gallon. If S was not selling at a premium above market price before the price rose, it would seem unfair to hold S to the 14-cent price for a full year. Thus, a court would probably find that no option contract arose.

Did S make a firm offer to B?

Under UCC §2-205, an offer by a merchant (defined in §2-104 to mean a person dealing in the kind of goods in question) to buy or sell goods is irrevocable if: (a) it is in a signed writing, and (b) it gives explicit assurance that the offer will be held open. Such an offer is irrevocable even though there is neither consideration nor a recital that consideration has been paid. Since S would seem to qualify as a merchant, his December 20 offer would appear to be firm (since he states that it will not be withdrawn during the next year), provided that he has ***signed*** the offer. The fact that S mistakenly believed that past favors constituted consideration would not detract from the fact that a firm commitment had been made. However, firm offers under §2-205 (firm offers for which no consideration is given) cannot be made irrevocable for a longer period than three months. Thus, even under the firm-offer doctrine, S could revoke his offer after three months had elapsed.

Assuming B reasonably understood S's offer as being one for a requirements contract extending for one year, was the agreement illusory? (If so, S would not be required to fill any orders that had not already been completed.)

An ***illusory agreement*** is one in which one of the parties can unilaterally avoid his obligations because that party has made an "illusory" promise — i.e., has not committed himself to anything at all. S would contend that since he was required to supply B with all no. 2 fuel oil "ordered by" B, B could avoid his obligations by simply failing to place any orders with S. However, B would contend in rebuttal that it was the implicit understanding of both parties that B, in fact, would purchase no. 2 fuel oil only from S, and that the words "ordered by you" were simply the awkward language of a layperson. B would also contend that S's contention is somewhat spurious because B has purchased all of his no. 2 fuel oil from S (at least until March, when S refused to fill any more of B's orders). B should prevail on this issue.

Assuming S made a firm offer to B or offered B only a series of unilateral contracts (which B could accept by ordering no. 2 fuel from S), is S liable for the March 10, March 17, and March 30 orders made by B?

B will contend that under the firm-offer theory above, S's offer extended through March 31 (the three-month period between January 1 and March 31), and therefore S is liable for all orders placed by B up to that time. S could conceivably argue in rebuttal that B's March 30 order was not "made" until actually received by S (on April 1, two days after it was mailed). However, B could contend in rebuttal that S's offer did not state when an order had to be received by him. An acceptance normally is effective when mailed, not when received. Thus, S should be liable for all of B's orders. Alternatively, S may argue that the irrevocability extends 30 days from the time the offer was made — December 24, not January 1. If so, the offer expired on March 24, making the March 30 order too late. B may respond that the three-month period of irrevocability should begin with the first day the offer could be accepted (January 1). The UCC and comments are unclear, but seem aimed at preventing long-term options without consideration. Thus, S might prevail on the March 30 order.

In the event that S's letter to B is **not** deemed to be a firm offer, but rather a series of unilateral contracts, then S would be liable for only the March 10 order since B learned of S's revocation before B placed the March 17 order. Because the revocation became effective on receipt by B, the March 10 order accepted the offer before the revocation.

Was B's "cover" proper — i.e., is B entitled to recover the difference between the contract price and the 18 cents he paid, or the difference between the contract price and the 17 cents a gallon at which no. 2 fuel oil could have been bought?

Under UCC §2-712(1), an aggrieved buyer may, in good faith and without unreasonable delay, make any reasonable purchase of goods in substitution for those that were to be supplied by the seller. Assuming B made at least a few inquiries of other potential suppliers of no. 2 fuel oil, he probably would be deemed to have acted in good faith and therefore be able to recover the 4 cents a gallon difference between the cover price and the contract price. However, if B had made absolutely no effort (or an inadequate one) to ascertain the "going" price for no. 2 fuel, then B would probably be able to recover only 3 cents a gallon.

Summary:

If the court found that a one-year requirements contract had been entered into between B and S, then B could cover (as he apparently has been able to do) and sue S for the ***difference between the cover and contract price.***

If S merely offered B a series of unilateral contracts, then S probably would be liable for the difference between the cover price and the contract price with respect only to the order placed by B on March 10.

If the court found that S made a firm offer to B, then S probably would be liable for the difference between the cover price and contract price for the March 10 and March 17 orders, but probably will not recover for the March 30 order.

Answer to Question 5

If Bill ("B") were to sue Cliff ("C") to compel specific performance or for damages, the court would look at the following issues.

Did Cliff make a valid offer to Bill?

An offer must be sufficiently definite as to its material terms (i.e., parties, subject matter, time for performance, and price) to be capable of acceptance. C could argue that the offer was indefinite since it was silent as to the aggregate acres involved (and thereby the total price); the time for performance (when title would transfer and C would be paid); what type of deed B would receive; and the condition of title that would be acceptable at the time of transfer. However, since modern courts are generally willing to supply reasonable terms, B could contend in rebuttal that the (1) aggregate acres could be ascertained by a survey (after which the price could easily be determined by multiplying $8 times the number of acres); and (2) other aspects of the contract could be implied from what is customary in such transactions in this locale (i.e., title would be transferred at the time of payment, which would be made within a reasonable time after the offer was accepted; a standard warranty deed would be delivered; title would be clean, etc.). B should prevail on this issue.

Can the contract be avoided under the mutual mistake doctrine?

Where there is a **mutual mistake** going to the essence of the contract, either party can usually avoid the agreement. The Rest. 2d requires that the mistake concern a basic assumption of the contract with material effect and that the adversely affected party must not bear the risk of the mistake. C could argue that he should be able to avoid the contract because neither party knew of the oil lying beneath the land's surface and the oil concerned a basic assumption of the contract with material effect. However, C will almost certainly not be able to contend that he **did not** bear the risk of the mistake. Generally, the courts will follow the Restatement scheme and will allocate the risk of minerals in land to the seller. Rest. 2d §154, cmts. a and d. This allocation is almost universally adopted because a contrary rule would disturb the essential finality of real estate transactions. B should prevail on this issue also.

Was the original offer turned into an option contract under which B had a reasonable time to accept C's offer after B visited Farmland? (If so, the alleged revocation would not have been effective.)

B would contend that C's statement that he would not revoke the offer until B had "awhile" to think about it if B visited Farmland was an offer for an option contract. Thus, C *ceased to have the right to revoke his offer to sell Farmland* for a reasonable period of time after B inspected the parcel. Although C might contend that the vagueness of the terminology used in his August 11 memo indicates that it was merely a gratuitous assurance that the offer would not be revoked, B could probably successfully contend in rebuttal that a reasonable offeree in B's position would have construed C's statement (formalized in C's written memorandum) as offering B a reasonable period of time to accept if B incurred the inconvenience of a 100-mile round trip to Farmland. (B's visit probably was consideration for the promise to keep the offer open. In any event, C reasonably should have expected B to rely on the promise and incur some costs — time and perhaps expense — to visit Farmland. This reliance would make the option enforceable even without consideration.) Thus, an *option contract* was probably created.

Assuming an option contract was created, has B validly accepted C's offer?

An offer for a *unilateral contract can ordinarily be accepted* only by completed performance by the offeree. C might contend that since the August 9 writing stated "$8 an acre, cash," B could accept it only by delivering the appropriate sum to C (not by mailing a letter as B attempted to do). However, B could argue that it was not clear whether the offer was to be accepted by performance or promise (i.e., whether the offer sought a unilateral or bilateral contract); thus, either action by B would be valid. B would contend that the reference to "cash" meant only that the sale would be for cash (i.e., C was unwilling to accept credit terms). B's interpretation is strengthened by the fact that the normal means of accomplishing the sale and purchase of land is through an escrow arrangement whereby concurrent performance (i.e., the deed is transferred at the same time the seller's money is received) is assured. Thus, B should prevail on this issue.

Acceptance of an option contract occurs when the acceptance is received, not when it is posted. Thus, acceptance occurred on August 17. The August 11 promise to keep the offer open for "awhile" probably had not expired on August 13; Bill could not reasonably be expected to visit the property and make a decision in less than two days. C may argue that "awhile" expired before August 17. Because "awhile" is vague, courts may interpret it to mean a reasonable time. Having made all necessary arrangements (visit, loan, etc.) by August 14, perhaps the additional three-day delay was unreasonable. B may reply that August 17 still was less than a week after the option was created. B probably should prevail on this issue.

Assuming that no option contract was formed, was the offer revoked by C's brother?

An offer can ordinarily be revoked by an offeror or a reliable source at any time prior to acceptance. C could contend that his brother accomplished a revocation when the latter advised B that C "probably wouldn't be interested" in selling Farmland now that oil had been discovered. B could argue in rebuttal, however, that no revocation occurred because (1) C's brother was merely speculating as to what C's response to the oil discovery would be (rather than stating, "C told me that he was no longer willing to sell Farmland to you"); and (2) the words spoken by C's brother did not constitute a clear revocation (he stated only that C "probably" would no longer be interested in selling Farmland). B should prevail on this issue too.

Assuming no option contract was created and no revocation occurred, did B accept in a timely manner?

Where no time for acceptance is specified by the offeree, the offer will lapse automatically after a reasonable period of time. Although C might argue that B's mailing of a letter to C on the 15th (six days after the offer had been made) constituted an unreasonably lengthy period of time, B could probably successfully contend in rebuttal that since (1) any prudent buyer would want to view the land and obtain financing before communicating an acceptance to the offeree, and (2) the amount of money involved is probably substantial (Farmland is a ***large parcel of real estate***), six days would probably be a reasonable period of time within which to accept. B should prevail on this issue.

Can B obtain specific performance?

Since land is unique, specific performance is ordinarily available with respect to transactions for the sale of land. Additionally, since it will probably be impossible to determine the precise worth of Farmland in light of this discovery of an oil deposit beneath the surface, monetary damages are not capable of reasonable determination. Thus, specific performance should be granted. C could argue that specific performance, an ***equitable*** doctrine, would be unfair to seller since circumstances (the discovery of oil) changed substantially after his offer and before B's acceptance.

If specific performance is not granted, C will argue that the measure of damages would be the difference between the market value (without the oil, since such damages would be too speculative and unfair to the seller) and the contract price.

Answer to Question 6

Whether you will advise Bird ("B") to sue Mills ("M") will depend on a resolution of the following issues.

Was B's July 15 Purchase Agreement an offer or an invitation?

Whether a statement is an invitation (which is not capable of acceptance) **or an offer** depends on how a reasonable offeree would have construed the offeror's statement. M would contend that since B's Purchase Agreement stated, "Usual form of sales contract to be executed later," B's form was merely an invitation. However, B could probably successfully contend in rebuttal that considering that the written Purchase Agreement (1) was the culmination of extended oral negotiations, and (2) included language indicating a commitment to sell to M, the agreement could reasonably be construed as an offer. In further support of B's argument is the fact that by advising York ("Y") that he was "selling the Bird line," M obviously construed the Purchase Agreement as an offer. B should prevail on this issue.

Was B's July 15 Purchase Agreement sufficiently definite to be an offer?

An offer must be sufficiently definite as to all material terms as to be capable of enforcement. M could contend that since the quantity of each type of airplane has never been specified, the contract is not sufficiently definite to be enforceable (would M have ordered 50 Larks, 50 Eagles, or 50 Gulls, etc.?). However, B could contend in rebuttal that, under UCC §2-204(3), indefiniteness as to one or more terms will not prevent enforcement of a contract if there is a reasonably certain basis for awarding damages. Here, at least 10 of the airplanes were specified in M's order to B on July 17 (when M ordered 4 Eagles and 6 Larks). As to the remaining 40 planes to be ordered under the contract, B could contend that, at a minimum, a court could assume that M would have ordered 40 Gulls (the least expensive aircraft under the Purchase Agreement). B should prevail on these arguments, so M would probably be deemed to have ordered 40 Gulls, 4 Eagles, and 6 Larks.

Was M's alleged acceptance unequivocal?

An **acceptance must ordinarily be unequivocal**, but it may be shown by implication from words or conduct. M might contend that since he never signed the Purchase Agreement or expressly agreed to it (M simply "expressed himself as satisfied and retained" the Purchase Agreement), no unequivocal acceptance was ever made. However, B could contend in rebuttal that an acceptance by implication can be found since (1) M made an order on July 17 under the Purchase Agreement (when he requested shipment of 4 Eagles and 6 Larks); and (2) M obviously believed that he had accepted the Purchase Agreement since he advised Y that he would receive 40 more planes in the "Bird line" and solicited orders from the latter. B should prevail on this issue.

Assuming a contract was formed, can M successfully assert the Statute of Frauds as a defense?

A transaction for the sale of goods with an aggregate price of $500 or more must be evidenced by a writing that (1) indicates that a contract was made, (2) describes the quantity involved, and (3) is signed by the party against whom enforcement is sought. (In states that have adopted revised article 2, the writing required applies for goods valued at $5,000 or more. This transaction qualifies under either test.) M will contend that since he never signed the Purchase Agreement, he can successfully assert the Statute of Frauds ("SOF") as a defense against B's breach of contract action.

However, B will assert the *"aggregated documents"* rule in rebuttal. Under this theory, the "writing" necessary to satisfy the SOF may be a group of writings, provided their interrelationship is apparent. B could contend that M's July 17 telegram to B, M's letter to Y (in which M indicates that he holds a Purchase Agreement to receive 40 planes in addition to the 10 that he presently has in his possession), and M's August 1 telegram to B (advising B of his intent to drop the aircraft line) have a sufficiently apparent relationship with the Purchase Agreement. When these writings are aggregated with the Purchase Agreement, the missing signature of M is deemed supplied. Although none of these additional writings *expressly* refers to the July 15 Purchase Agreement (M wrote to Y that he held "*a* purchase agreement"), a court would probably find that the relationship of the other documents to the July 15 Purchase Agreement is apparent.

In the event that the court was willing to aggregate M's July 17 telegram to B or M's August 1 telegram to B (but not the letter to Y) with the Purchase Agreement, M might contend that the appearance of its name on a telegram does not constitute a "signature" for purposes of the SOF. However, under UCC §1-201(39) (UCC §1-201(37) in states that have adopted the 2001 revisions), any symbol executed or adopted by a party with the present intent to authenticate a writing constitutes a sufficient signature. Since M's name was presumably inserted at the conclusion of these telegrams with the intention of identifying their source, M's *failure to manually sign the wires would probably not prevent the signature requirement of the SOF from being satisfied.*

Assuming B is successful against M, what damages may be recovered?

Under UCC §1-106 (UCC §1-305 in states that have adopted the 2001 revisions), an aggrieved party is to be put in the position he would have been in had the other party fully performed. B would probably be entitled to recover the difference between the contract price for 4 Eagles, 6 Larks, and 40 Gulls and either the resale price (if B makes a good faith and commercially reasonable sale of the planes) or the market price at the time and place for tender (for any planes B does not resell). The court may need to supply the time for tender of the 40 Gulls, which the contract left to M's discretion. At a minimum, M owes the difference between the contract price and the highest market value of the 40 Gulls during the year covered by the agreement. While M might have ordered the planes at a time when they were worth less (and thus damages would be greater), using the highest market price during the period fixes the smallest damage award M could possibly have owed had M performed. If B did not resell the planes, B's recovery would be reduced by whatever benefits, if any, B would receive from not having to complete its performance (e.g., any construction costs not incurred or any warranty service not performed on these 50 planes).

This measure may be inadequate, especially if B resold all the planes at the contract price, but could have produced enough planes to meet all of its other orders in addition to the planes M agreed to buy. If so, B is a lost volume seller, one who could have earned a profit on 50 more planes if M had performed. In these circumstances, B would be entitled to its lost profit on the planes. UCC §2-708(2). B's recovery would be reduced by whatever benefits, if any, B would receive from not having to complete its performance (e.g., not having to perform warranty service on these 50 planes).

Assuming M prevailed on any of the foregoing issues, could B at least enforce M's July 17 telegram to it for 4 Eagles and 6 Larks?

Although B might contend that M's July 17 wire was an offer for 4 Eagles and 6 Larks, M could contend in rebuttal that it revoked this offer on August 1 by reason of its telegram to B on that date. This contention may prevail since B had not accepted or confirmed the order prior to the latter date.

Answer to Question 7

The following issues would arise in assessing Buildem's ("B") rights against Coast ("C").

Was C's bid to B an offer or an invitation?

Whether a communication is an offer or an invitation depends on how a reasonable offeree would construe it. C might contend that **bids are ordinarily deemed to be invitations, rather than offers.** However, B could probably successfully argue in rebuttal that bid solicitation constitutes an invitation to submit offers and that a "bid" submitted in response is ordinarily deemed to be an offer. Since the facts do not state that C indicated to B that its communication was other than an offer, B would probably prevail on this issue.

We will assume that C's offer was sufficiently definite as to its material terms to be enforceable since the facts are silent on this issue.

Was C's mistaken calculation so obvious as to negate B's acceptance?

Offers that contain a mistake can be accepted, unless the mistake should have been obvious to the offeree. C might contend that the error in its offer to do the work for $140,000 (which subsequently cost $200,000) was so obvious that B should have realized that the **offer was based on a mistaken calculation.** However, since the second-lowest bid was only $10,000 more than C's bid, it would appear that C's mistaken computation was **not** so obvious that B should have realized it. Thus, B will probably prevail on this issue also, unless C is able to prove that enforcement of the contract against it would be unconscionable.

Did C revoke its offer prior to acceptance by B?

An offer may ordinarily be revoked at any time prior to acceptance. C will contend that since it notified B at 1:45 p.m. that its offer was in error, such action constituted a revocation. Since B had not previously advised C that C's bid was accepted, the revocation was effective. B could argue in rebuttal, however, C's bid became irrevocable when B relied on it in making its overall bid to Acme. It was **reasonably foreseeable** that B would rely on bids by subcontractors, and allowing C to revoke the bid would cause B considerable harm (at least $10,000). Thus, **promissory estoppel should prevent C from revoking or withdrawing its offer** until after the contract has been awarded and B has a reasonable time to accept bids by subcontractors.

Rest. 2d §87(2). C may reply that injustice does not require an irrevocable offer if B could have advised Acme that it desired to revise its overall bid prior to 3:00 p.m. B was aware of the error at 1:45 p.m., so B might have been able to adjust its overall bid to Acme prior to the 3:00 p.m. deadline. If such a revision was possible, B could have avoided any detriment from relying on C's bid, and C would probably prevail on this issue (and, as a consequence, have no liability to B). Otherwise, B would probably be successful with respect to this issue.

Was the telephone an effective means of communicating the revocation?

A revocation may ordinarily be made by the same or a similar mode of communication as the offer. While B might contend that revocation by telephone is not effective to revoke a prior **written** offer, since the telephonic communication was actually received by B and constituted a reasonable (certainly quicker) means of communication, this contention by B should fail.

Assuming B would prevail on the foregoing issues, to what recovery is B entitled?

If the offer was irrevocable, then B's acceptance (within a reasonable time after being awarded the general contract) would be effective, and C would be bound to perform the work for $140,000. B actually spent $200,000 for this work, suffering a loss of $60,000. A party may not recover for any loss it could have avoided by reasonable conduct. C may argue that B could have avoided all but $10,000 of the loss by timely accepting the second-lowest bid ($150,000). Alternatively, B could have limited the loss to $30,000 by accepting C's revised bid of $170,000. Often it is reasonable to reject an offer by a party that proves its unreliability by refusing to perform a contract unless the price is adjusted in their favor. While this justifies rejecting C's demand, it may have been unreasonable not to accept the second-lowest bidder in a timely manner, limiting the loss to $10,000. C may prevail on this argument and owe B only $10,000 in damages.

Answer to Question 8

Coll ("C") could contend there are two independent grounds on which a contract arose: (1) when Art ("A") proposed a contract to C during their initial telephone conversation, and C accepted by his words, "You've got a deal"; or (2) when C accepted A's typewritten document offer by his telephone response. In assessing C's contention, we must consider the following issues.

Can A avoid the transaction under the misunderstanding doctrine?

If A was actually aware of the meaning that C attached to the term "Sunflowers," then there is little question that C would prevail since there would have been a meeting of the minds with respect to "Sunflowers I." We will assume, however, that A erroneously thought that C was referring to "Sunflowers II."

If a term in the offer or acceptance is ambiguous, and one party *has reason* to know of the ambiguity, but the other party has no reason to know of the ambiguity, a contract will be formed on the term *as understood by the other party (who had no reason to know).*

A would contend that since he had in mind the "Sunflowers" painting that had been created in July, and C was referring to the initial one, there was no meeting of the minds (and therefore the contract is avoidable by A). However, C could contend in rebuttal that where one party has reason to know that the other had attached a particular meaning to a term of their agreement, the other's understanding will control. Rest. 2d §201(2). Since C mentioned that he had seen the painting in question "in February," A should have recognized that C could *not* have been referring to "Sunflowers II" (which wasn't completed until July). C should prevail on this issue.

Was A's statement to C on the telephone an offer or merely an invitation?

If A's telephonic offer was valid, then the question whether C had accepted by the proper means (discussed below) would not be pertinent.

Whether a statement is an offer (which is capable of acceptance) *or merely an invitation* (which is not) depends on how a reasonable offeree would construe the offeror's statement. A could contend that C realized that A's telephonic statement was merely an invitation since C advised A to "draw up the papers" (recognizing that the offer would come in a more formal manner). However, C could contend in rebuttal that his reference to "drawing up the papers" pertained only to memorializing their agreement, especially since those words were preceded by the statement, "You've got a deal" (which suggests that C believed the verbal statement by A was sufficient to constitute an offer). C's belief is supported by the language of A's verbal statement, which indicates a serious commitment to sell. C could further contend that A's suggestion of a liquidated damages clause made it clear that the parties intended to be bound even before the legal document was drawn up. That each party tendered on the basis of their oral communications and that both ignored the typographical error in price in the written contract further strengthens C's position. C should prevail on this issue.

Was the alleged offer sufficiently definite as to material terms?

An offer must be sufficiently definite as to material terms to be capable of acceptance. A could contend that the alleged telephonic offer was not sufficiently definite as to material terms since (1) there was no agreement as to what would constitute acceptable liquidated damage language, and (2) it was not clear whether A would give C *any guarantees that the painting in question was genuine.* However, C could probably successfully contend in rebuttal that (1) the liquidated damage language would be the standard terminology (similar to that included in A's October 16 document), and, in any event, A's contention is spurious since C expressed a willingness to accept the language proposed by A; and (2) since C expressed a desire to purchase the "Sunflower" painting created by A, implicit in A's delivery would be the fact that the painting was genuine. Again, C should prevail.

Can A assert the Statute of Frauds?

Where a transaction involves the *sale of goods with an aggregate price of $500* (or $5,000 in a state that adopts the 2003 revisions to article 2 of the UCC) *or more, it must be embodied in a writing that is signed by the party against whom enforcement is sought.* Although A might argue that the telephonic conversation does not satisfy this requirement, C could successfully contend in rebuttal that the subsequent typewritten and *signed document* that A sent to C *satisfies the requisites of the Statute of Frauds.*

Assuming A did not make a valid offer on October 15, was A's October 16 typewritten offer accepted by C?

Under UCC §2-206(1), an offer can be accepted by any reasonable means, unless the means are otherwise unambiguously indicated. A might contend that since his typewritten note stated that C was to sign and return a copy of the October 16 document to him, C's telephonic response was a non-conforming acceptance and is therefore an invalid acceptance. However, C could probably successfully contend in rebuttal that A's words merely expressed a desire that C return an executed copy of the document (i.e., they didn't "unambiguously indicate" that acceptance could be made **solely** by that means). Since A used the term "please" with reference to the language in question (rather than stating "acceptance can be made only by your returning the signed original of the document"), C should prevail on this issue. C's telephone acceptance was probably valid.

Can the typewritten contract be reformed to state a purchase price of $25,000?

A might contend that, pursuant to the **parol evidence rule**, once the parties have reduced their understandings to a writing, evidence of a prior understanding that varies that writing is not admissible. However, where there has been a mutual mistake in reducing an agreement to writing, evidence of the actual agreement is ordinarily admissible. Since there was a mistake in expression, we have a very different sort of mistake in that the error was in the writing (a later "expression" of the parties' intentions) and not in the original agreement itself. In such an instance, amending the writing does not vary the parties' agreement, but merely reflects their true understanding. A might contend that reformation is an equitable doctrine and that, since C did not read the document that had been sent to him with reasonable care, reformation should be barred. However, most courts would probably permit reformation (provided it can be established by clear and convincing evidence) in this instance since the difference between a typed "2" and "3" is small and hard for the eye to discern.

Can C obtain specific performance?

The majority rule is that a **liquidated damage clause** ("LDC") does **not** ordinarily preclude the aggrieved party from seeking specific performance. Such clauses are usually interpreted as applying only where the aggrieved party is seeking monetary damages.

Assuming, however, that this jurisdiction adheres to the minority view that an LDC constitutes the exclusive remedy of the nonbreaching party, C could contend that the LDC is not binding. (Where a **liquidated damage clause** is invalid, it is simply stricken from the agreement.) An LDC is ordinarily enforceable only if (1) the damage would otherwise be difficult to calculate; (2) the parties made a reasonable effort to calculate the likely damages; and (3) the damages specified bear a reasonable relationship to the actual damages that the aggrieved party would be likely to sustain. C could contend that the LDC is unenforceable since the $5,000 figure was arbitrarily selected by A with no effort by the parties to calculate the damages that would be incurred in the event of a breach. A could argue in rebuttal, however, that the damages would be uncertain because art items (such as paintings) are almost always subject to dispute as to their fair market value (i.e., expert testimony could be widely divergent). In light of this fact, the $5,000 figure represented a reasonable estimate as to the actual damages that the innocent party would suffer as a consequence of a breach by the other side. A should prevail on this issue.

Assuming, however, C were allowed to seek specific performance despite the LDC, whether such remedy would be granted depends on whether the goods involved are unique. UCC §2-716. Since art items ordinarily fit into this category (i.e., there is only a single "Sunflowers I," and no one can really estimate how much it will appreciate in the future), specific performance would probably be granted. If specific performance is impossible (e.g., if another person bought "Sunflowers I" before the contract between Art and Coll), the court probably would award damages instead.

Summary:

C should be able to obtain specific performance with respect to the "Sunflowers I" painting for a price of $25,000.

Answer to Question 9

In analyzing Buyer's questions, you will consider the following.

I. Must the dispute be settled by arbitration rather than litigation?

Section 2-207 of the Uniform Commercial Code ("UCC") would be controlling since the transaction involves a sale of goods. The analysis will depend on whether the state has adopted the 2003 revisions to article 2 of the UCC.

Under the revised UCC: A contract appears to have been formed during the telephone conversation. Buyer ("B") offered to buy 1,000 roses and Seller ("S") "accepted the order." Alternatively, shipping the goods might constitute an acceptance. In either case, the contract was formed on the terms of B's offer once S accepted it. The acknowledgment seeks to confirm the contract but contains terms that are different from or additional to those in the contract formed on the phone. Under these circumstances, the contract consists of (a) terms that appear in the records of both parties, (b) terms to which both parties agree, and (c) terms supplied under the UCC. UCC §2-207. The arbitration clause is not provided by the UCC and was not in any record (or writing) sent by B. Thus, unless B agrees to the term, it will not become part of the contract. Because silent acquiescence (e.g., paying for the flowers without objection) might be interpreted as agreement, B should promptly object to the term—unless arbitration would be in B's best interests. (While oral objection is sufficient, a written objection is easier to prove later.)

If S did not orally accept B's offer, the acknowledgment itself may be an acceptance if it contains "a definite and seasonable expression of acceptance." UCC §2-206(3). The existence of different or additional terms in the acknowledgment will not prevent it from operating as an acceptance. If so, the analysis above applies equally here. However, if the acknowledgment contains language that negates assent—such as a clear statement that S is unwilling to do business unless B accepts the additional or different terms—then it is a counteroffer and not an acceptance. If the acknowledgment is a counteroffer, B may reject it by promptly notifying S that the terms are unacceptable. Keeping the roses without objection, however, may be interpreted as assent to the counteroffer. If B notifies S of any objections to the terms, B may then negotiate more appropriate terms or reject the goods and seek another supplier.

Under the UCC before revision: If S actually accepted B's offer on the telephone (i.e., after B placed the order, S stated that the flowers would be delivered), then S's acknowledgment form would merely be a post-agreement confirmation. Between merchants (which both B and S appear to be since B is a retail florist and S is a wholesaler), additional terms contained in a confirmation or acknowledgment become part of the contract unless (1) they materially alter the contract, *or* (2) notice of objection to the additional terms is given within a reasonable time after notice is received. B should therefore be advised to send notice immediately of objection to S's acknowledgment form. Even if B does not make a timely objection to the additional terms, B could contend that an arbitration clause is a "material" alteration of the contract entered on the phone since, by agreeing to arbitrate, a party waives certain rights (such as a jury trial). Of course, S will probably contend that it is not material since the clause only affects the type of proceeding in which the claim would be pursued and disputes between parties should not be reasonably anticipated. Though courts have been split on the materiality of arbitration clauses, the facts of each case will determine materiality. Given the informal course of prior dealing between B and S and the sudden interjection of binding arbitration by S, the clause is probably a material alteration of the contract. (Of course, this analysis assumes that you as B's attorney would conclude that litigation was preferable to arbitration in this instance.)

If S did not accept B's offer on the telephone, then S's acknowledgment would constitute a counteroffer if it was expressly conditional on B's assent to the additional terms. Taking physical possession of the flowers with knowledge of the arbitration provision might be construed as B's assent to the terms of the counteroffer, including the arbitration clause. However, if S's counteroffer was *not* expressly conditional on B's assent to the additional terms in the acknowledgment, the acknowledgment would be an acceptance and the additional terms would merely constitute proposals to modify the agreement. The analysis described above (with respect to what would occur if B's offer had been accepted on the telephone by S) would be equally applicable; and the arbitration clause would probably *not* be a part of the agreement between B & S. (Again, our discussion assumes that B may be construed as accepting the counteroffer by returning the flowers. Since the facts indicate that she consulted you immediately, she can still return the flowers within a reasonable time.)

II. *Will B be in breach if she rejects the shipment?*

If S were to sue for breach of contract, B could assert two defenses.

A. Is the Statute of Frauds applicable?

In contracts for the sale of goods with an aggregate price of $500 or more ($5,000 or more under revised article 2), there must be a writing that (1) indicates that a contract has been made, and (2) is signed by the party against whom enforcement is sought. An exception to this rule, however, occurs where the **party attempting to assert this defense has failed to object within 10 days** after receiving a writing from the other party that would satisfy the Statute of Frauds ("SOF"). UCC §2-201(2). Since the 10-day period has **not** expired, B should be able to avoid the application of UCC §2-201(2) by notifying S of her objection.

If B does not return the flowers, S will be able to assert that under UCC §2-201(3)(c), to the extent that goods have been accepted by the buyer, they are taken out of the SOF. If B delays, it will be deemed that she had a reasonable opportunity to inspect the flowers (and that therefore there was an acceptance under UCC §2-606), and that UCC §2-201(3)(c) controls.

B. Was it implied in the contract between B and S that the roses would be assorted?

Under UCC §1-205(1), a **course of dealing** (previous conduct between the parties that establishes a common basis of understanding for interpreting their expressions) should be given meaning to qualify the terms of an agreement. S will argue that since the previous transactions between the parties occurred at least four months before, their previous conduct of sending assorted flowers should **not** be considered a basis of understanding for the May transaction. B will contend in rebuttal, however, that since she had received and accepted assorted roses on 12 prior occasions, she had a right to assume that S would ship assorted roses. B should prevail on this issue.

C. If S prevailed on the previous issues, what would S's recovery be?

S would probably be entitled to the purchase price of the roses ($600), unless he could sell the roses and recover some or all of his loss.

III. Does B have a cause of action against S, and if so, what will be B's recovery?

If B prevails, she should be able to reject and return the flowers. B should be advised to "cover" (i.e., purchase the flowers from another vendor), and then sue S for the difference between the cover price and the contract price.

Answer to Question 10

In advising Paul, you will consider the following issues.

If Paul ("P") were to sue Dryden ("D"), the latter would probably raise the following defenses.

Was D's alleged obligation to P discharged when P cashed D's $500 check?

Where there is a good faith dispute as to the existence or extent of an obligation, and the obligor tenders to the obligee a sum in full satisfaction thereof, and the latter accepts such sum, the obligee's debt is deemed to be discharged. D will argue that since P *cashed the check with knowledge that it was tendered in full satisfaction of their dispute*, any possible liability to P has been extinguished. At one time, Uniform Commercial Code ("UCC") §1-207(1) (§1-308(a) after the 2001 revisions) offered the possibility that "A party that with explicit reservation of rights . . . assents to performance in a manner offered by the other party does not prejudice the rights reserved." P could thus contend that his right to the balance of the obligation has not been discharged since he specifically wrote the words "under protest, reserving all rights" on the check before cashing it. That provision has been amended to clarify that it does not apply to accord and satisfaction. UCC §1-207(2) (§1-308(b) after the 2001 revisions). In effect, D offered P a new contract (an accord), in which D would pay $500 for a release of P's claim. By signing the check, P appears to accept the offer. Amending the check to reflect a reservation of rights could be construed as making a counteroffer instead of accepting. But D has not accepted the counteroffer, giving P no right to keep the benefit of D's offered accord (the money). Under Rest. 2d §69(2), this wrongful retention of D's property may be considered an acceptance of D's offer or, at best, a tort (conversion of D's property).

Can D successfully assert the impracticability of performance doctrine?

When one of the parties to a contract cannot reasonably perform his obligations (through no fault of his own) as a consequence of an unforeseeable, post-agreement event, that party is relieved of his prospective obligations. D might contend that he could not foresee the loss of the Union account, and that it is a consequence of this occurrence that he can no longer afford to retain P. However, the facts do not indicate that honoring the contract with P will force D into insolvency or prevent him from satisfying P's damages. Thus, P can probably successfully contend in rebuttal that it is *not impracticable* (as opposed to merely unprofitable) to pay P $15,000 over a one-year period.

Can D successfully assert the frustration of purpose doctrine?

Where one of the parties has a special purpose for entering into a contract (of which the other side is aware), and that **purpose is frustrated** by an unforeseeable, post-agreement event, each side is relieved of his prospective obligations. While D might contend that he is relieved of his obligations to P as a result of the supervening loss of the Union contract, P could successfully contend in rebuttal that while D may have had a special reason for hiring P, this purpose was not communicated to him. Thus, the frustration of purpose doctrine cannot be successfully asserted by D.

Can D avoid his obligations if P is a minor?

Since P was in his last year of high school, it may well be that he has **not obtained the age of majority** within the applicable jurisdiction (ordinarily between the ages of 18 and 21 years). If this is the case, D will contend that P was **not capable of entering into a valid contract.** However, P can probably successfully contend in rebuttal that agreements with a minor are avoidable only by the minor. (This is the majority view.)

Assuming P prevailed on all the foregoing issues, was D's offer of employment sufficiently definite?

An offer must be sufficiently definite as to material terms to be capable of acceptance by a reasonable offeree. D will argue that his offer of January 15 was not sufficiently definite in that it failed to indicate at what intervals P would be paid, how much vacation time P would receive, the hours per week P would be required to work, etc. However, P could probably successfully contend that all of those terms could be implied into the agreement based on D's ordinary employment practices (i.e., if D ordinarily pays his employees biweekly, that's when P will be paid).

Can P introduce evidence of D's telephone call? (If he cannot, there would be little point in suing D because employment contracts are ordinarily terminable at will, and the original note from D to P did not specify a term of employment.)

Under the **parol evidence rule,** where a writing (or related group of writings) constitutes a total integration (i.e., the writing represents the entire and complete understanding of the parties), evidence of any prior or contemporaneous agreement is **not** admissible. Where a writing (or a related group of writings) represents only the entire **written** contract of the parties, but not their complete agreement, it is merely a partial integration and evidence of *consistent* verbal understandings are ordinarily admissible. A court will ordinarily consider all relevant evidence in reaching its determination as to whether the parties intended the written contract to be a total or partial integration (the traditional view was that this determination had to be made exclusively from the writing itself).

D might initially contend that his January 15 letter to P, and P's written response (which referred to D's January 15 letter, but *not* the telephone call) constituted a total integration; and therefore testimony as to the telephone conversation is not admissible. Without evidence of D's verbal statement to P, P would have little likelihood of successfully contending that D offered him a one-year (in contrast to an at-will) employment agreement. However, P could probably successfully contend that given the relative informality and brevity of D's letter to him, the writings do not indicate a total integration.

Assuming the P-D letters constituted merely a partial integration, D would next contend that the alleged telephone conversation contradicted the writings (i.e., the letters make no reference to a one-year term of employment, while the telephone conversation arguably does), and therefore was *not* admissible. While P could contend that the telephone conversation did not contradict D's writing (it merely explained what D intended by "employment with my firm ... at $15,000 a year"), this contention would probably not refute the at-will relationship suggested by D's January 15 letter. D's verbal statements probably would *not* be admissible.

The parol evidence rule (in most states) does not bar consideration of *subsequent* oral agreements. P could argue that D's verbal statements were admissible because they were made after the written offer was mailed. D could probably successfully argue that the verbal statements were made before the contract came into existence; i.e., that P accepted in writing after (and without mentioning) the telephone conversation.

Even if D's verbal statement to P is admissible, did D offer P a one-year employment agreement?

Whether D's statement to P that he expected the latter to "stay for at least a year" constituted an offer for a *one-year term of employment* would depend on how a reasonable offeree would interpret that statement. D would contend that his words merely expressed a hope that P remain with him for one year (if D had desired to offer a one-year contract he could have easily said something like: "I am offering a one-year employment agreement").

While P would contend in rebuttal that he reasonably believed that he was contractually bound to stay as employee for a one-year period as a consequence of D's explicit "expectation," D's language would probably be interpreted as merely a wish (rather than an offer for a binding one-year agreement). Thus, P's employment arrangement with D was probably terminable at will by either party.

Summary:

Based on the issues described above, P would appear to have a questionable lawsuit against D.

Assuming, however, P prevails with respect to all of the foregoing issues, what are his remedies?

While P might desire an order requiring D to specifically perform the agreement (and thereby gain a year of valuable experience), courts will rarely grant specific performance with respect to a **personal service contract** since they do not want to mandate an obviously antagonistic relationship. Therefore, P would be expected to obtain substantially similar employment and thereby mitigate his damages. He could then sue D for the difference.

Note: We have not discussed what rights the parties have to the proceeds of the $500 check mailed by D and cashed by P. If our conclusion is correct that P has no cause of action against D, what happens to the $500? Does P have an obligation to return it? May he keep it? What is your advice?

Answer to Question 11

S will obviously want to sue B for breach of their contract. B will probably set up the Statute of Frauds ("SOF") as a defense to S's action. Since the transaction involves a sale of goods with a value of $500 or more, §2-201 of the Uniform Commercial Code ("UCC") is applicable. S will argue that one or more of the exceptions (discussed below) to the SOF is present.

Note: The 2003 revisions to article 2 of the UCC applies the SOF to sales of goods valued at **$5,000** or more. Because the contract in this case involves only $2,000 in goods, the SOF would not apply. Because no jurisdictions have adopted the 2003 revisions at the time of this writing, the analysis below applies today. Because professors can alter their questions easily— say, by changing the price to $5 per widget—the analysis below is worth studying even under revised article 2.

Is the nonobjecting merchant exception applicable?

Under UCC §2-201(2), if (i) both of the parties are merchants; (ii) within a reasonable time after a contract has been made a confirmation is sent from one party to the other; **and** (iii) the **recipient fails to object** to the writing within 10 days, the SOF is deemed to be satisfied against the recipient, provided the writing involved would be sufficient (i.e., enforceable) against the shipper. Assuming that B and S are both merchants, S would argue that the acknowledgment he sent was a writing that sufficiently indicated that a contract had been made. Since B did not respond, the SOF defense asserted by B is lost.

B could contend, however, that since S's acknowledgment was not signed by S, it would not be valid against S, so the nonobjecting merchant exception is not applicable. Assuming, however, that the acknowledgment at least had S's name printed on it, S could contend that the term "signature" encompasses "any symbol . . . adopted by a party . . . to authenticate a writing." UCC §1-201(39) (UCC §1-201(37) after the 2001 revisions). At least one case has held that the preprinted name of an entity on a form may constitute a signature. B will argue in rebuttal, of course, that S's name was not preprinted on the acknowledgment form for the purpose of "authenticating" the transaction with S, but rather, for the convenience of not having to insert such information each time the form was utilized. B should prevail on this issue, and therefore the §2-201(2) exception will **not** be available.

Is B estopped from asserting the SOF?

Estoppel principles are still applicable to the UCC in most instances. UCC §1-103. Since S ordered 1,000 clips from another manufacturer in reliance on the contract, S might contend that B should be estopped (i.e., S foreseeably relied to his substantial detriment on B's promise) from asserting the SOF in this instance. However, S probably has **not** been substantially prejudiced (the total cost of the clips was $40), and therefore it is doubtful that S will be able to sustain the entire contract on this theory. In addition, B may argue that UCC §2-201(3) supplants common law estoppel by providing specific situations in which reliance provides an exception to the SOF (such as specially manufactured goods). Unless S satisfies one of these statutory reliance provisions, S seems unlikely to prevail on estoppel.

Can S at least recover the contract price for the 200 widgets that B accepted?

Section 2-201(3)(c) of the UCC states that a **contract is enforceable with respect to goods that have been "received and accepted."** The facts indicate that B accepted 200 of the widgets before advising S that he would be sending them back. Assuming B had a reasonable opportunity over two days to inspect the widgets, acceptance within UCC §2-606 would probably have occurred. Thus, B would be liable to S for $400 ($2 times 200 widgets).

We assume that the widgets involved in this instance are suitable for sale to others in the ordinary course of S's business. Therefore, the "specially manufactured" goods exception to the SOF rule is not applicable. UCC §2-201(3)(a).

We also assume that B's rejection is not based on any defect or nonconformity in the goods. If B has a right to reject the goods under UCC §2-601, S may not be able to collect the price even of the delivered widgets. B did not mention any concern with their quality, only a denial of a binding contract, suggesting that no concerns for the quality of the goods arose.

Summary:

Based on the foregoing conclusions, B's only liability to S would be the purchase price for the 200 widgets that B accepted (i.e., $400). If either of S's **nonobjecting merchant** or **estoppel** arguments was successful, however, B would be liable to S for the entire contract ($2,000, less whatever expenses could be saved by S in not producing the remaining 800 widgets).

Answer to Question 12

In his defense against the lawsuit by Buyer ("B"), Jones ("S"), will probably raise the following issues:

The original contract was not sufficient as to material terms.

A contract must be sufficiently definite as to its material terms to be capable of enforcement. Focusing on the original writing, S will contend that **numerous material terms have been omitted**: the alleged contract fails to state where the **bolts are to be delivered** (at B's or S's place of business); whether cash or credit terms are intended; whether there was any warranty, etc. However, B can probably successfully contend in rebuttal that the contract is sufficiently definite because the missing terms can be supplied from usage of trade or by reference to the Uniform Commercial Code ("UCC"). **When not specified**: (1) delivery is at the seller's place of business, (2) payment must be at the time of delivery, and (3) the normal implied warranties will accompany the sale. Additionally, since S repudiated the agreement prior to any attempt at its performance, **there was no dispute arising from any supposedly missing terms.**

The contractual modification was valid.

B will contend that the contractual modification is not valid because (1) there was no consideration for the increased purchase price (S was already under a **preexisting contractual duty to supply the bolts at $.85**), and (2) the modification did not satisfy the Statute of Frauds ("SOF"). Under UCC §2-201(1), contractual modifications pertaining to the sale of goods with an aggregate value of $500 or more ($5,000 or more if the 2003 revisions to article have been enacted) are not enforceable unless embodied in a writing that is signed by the party against whom enforcement is sought.

S can reply that (1) under the UCC, good faith modifications need no consideration to be enforceable (UCC §2-209(1)); and (2) under the UCC's nonobjecting merchant rule (§2-201(2)), where confirmation of an agreement within the UCC's SOF is sent by one party within a reasonable time after the contract is made, and the recipient fails to object to it within 10 days after receipt, the SOF is satisfied if the writing would be enforceable against the sender. Since the confirmation was signed by S (and presumably is enforceable against him), it is enforceable against B. Thus, the UCC's SOF is satisfied, and the modification is valid.

The controlling price is $.91.

S will argue for but will not be able to insist on the price of $.91 inserted by his secretary in error. Where a written agreement fails to reflect the parties' understanding as a consequence of some *clerical mistake*, the aggrieved party can ordinarily have the contract reformed to coincide with such actual understanding. There is therefore little question that B can have the contract reformed to conform to their actual agreement of $.90 a pound.

Count 1.

Based on the discussion above, it appears that B is entitled to damages in the amount of $10,000 (the difference between B's cover price of $1.00 a pound and the modified contractual price of $.90). The fact that all of B's damages might not have accrued on October 1 when B began his lawsuit would probably be of no consequence since UCC §2-610 permits an aggrieved party to seek any remedy for breach where the defendant has made an anticipatory repudiation (defined in the 2003 revisions to article 2 as "language that a reasonable person would interpret to mean that the other party will not or cannot make a performance still due under the contract" (UCC §2-610(2)); the older version of the UCC contains no definition, leaving courts to apply the common law definition of an unequivocal statement that performance will not be forthcoming). This occurred when S informed B that he would deliver no bolts.

Count 2.

Under the UCC, an aggrieved buyer can recover *consequential damages that were reasonably foreseeable* and that could not be prevented by the buyer's cover. Since the facts indicate that B made "diligent efforts" to cover, the only question is whether S could have reasonably foreseen damages of this magnitude to B. S will certainly contend that it could not be expected to foresee damage to B in the amount of $610,000 resulting from the nondelivery of bolts costing $.90 a pound and $9,000 in all. The facts are silent as to whether S should have recognized the possibility of such damages to B (i.e., whether S should have realized that B would enter into agreements with other parties based on its ability to obtain the bolts from S; whether liquidation clauses requiring payments of $10,000 a day were common in that industry, etc.). Without more facts, it would *not* appear that B can recover its obligation to Electric from S.

Count 3.

Punitive damages are ordinarily not recoverable in breach of contract actions. While the failure to perform a contractual obligation that has been undertaken is, in some states, a basis for a tort action, S never commenced performance of its agreement with B. It therefore appears unlikely that B will be able to recover punitive damages (even though S's breach appears to have been deliberate).

Answer to Question 13

General v. American:

Since American's promise to pay Citadel's debt to General was made to Citadel (the obligor), rather than to General (the obligee), it was a third party *promise (rather than a guarantee)*. Thus, General would have to seek recovery from American as a third party beneficiary (3PB) of American's promise to Citadel.

Did a 3PB relationship arise by reason of American's promise to Citadel?

A 3PB relationship arises where (1) the promisee's primary intention is to bestow a benefit on the third party, and (2) the promisor's performance is to be rendered directly to such person. General could probably successfully contend that both of these requisites were present because (1) Citadel intended that General receive the benefit of the contract (payment of a debt owed by Citadel to General), and (2) American's performance was to be rendered directly to General. American might reply that the parties did not intend to provide General with a right to enforce American's promise, but intended that right to remain at Citadel's discretion.

Was there consideration for American's promise?

Assuming a 3PB relationship existed, a promisor can assert against the 3PB any defenses that are available under the contract to the promisee. American can therefore contend that since it received nothing in exchange for its promise to Citadel, that promise is unenforceable for lack of consideration. While General might contend in rebuttal that *American should be estopped* (because of foreseeable, detrimental reliance by the promisee of a substantial nature) from asserting the lack of consideration since Citadel remained in business for two more months, there is nothing to indicate that Citadel (1) did, in fact, rely on American's promise in continuing its operations, or (2) was, in fact, substantially damaged by maintaining its operations for that two-month period. Thus, American should prevail on the issue of consideration.

Summary:

General cannot successfully bring suit against American.

Lanco v. American

Did American guarantee Citadel's obligation to Lanco?

Lanco will contend that American's statement to Lanco (i.e., American will lend Citadel the money necessary to pay the present rent owed by Citadel to Lanco) was a guarantee promise, and therefore American was liable for such rent. However, American can argue in rebuttal that it did not promise to pay Lanco directly, but only to lend the money to Citadel. While Lanco may attempt to counter this argument by asserting that in the context of Citadel's financial problems, Lanco reasonably understood American's statement as a promise to it, American should prevail on this issue because guarantees must ordinarily promise payment to the obligee in an unequivocal manner to be enforceable.

If American's statement to Lanco was a guarantee promise, was there consideration for, and acceptance of, the guarantee?

American can also contend that Lanco never accepted its offer to guarantee Citadel's delinquent rent obligations (i.e., the facts do not indicate that Lanco made any response to American's statement). Additionally, it is unclear what consideration American may have received for its guarantee promise. Although Lanco may contend that (1) the implicit consideration was permitting Citadel to remain at the premises without immediately attempting to evict the latter; and (2) Lanco's conduct in refraining from seeking to evict Citadel constituted an acceptance of American's promise, American should prevail on these issues.

If American's statement to Lanco was a valid guarantee, is it unenforceable by reason of the Statute of Frauds ("SOF")?

American could additionally contend that **guarantee promises** must ordinarily be embodied in a writing that has been signed by the guarantor to be enforceable. Since the alleged promise was made on the telephone, it cannot be enforced by Lanco. However, where the **primary purpose of the guarantor** was to benefit itself (rather than the debtor), the guarantee is enforceable despite the absence of an adequate writing. Lanco will therefore argue that American was primarily concerned with preserving a profitable business relationship for itself, rather than assisting Citadel. Lanco may also contend that American should be estopped from asserting the SOF, but there is nothing in the facts to indicate that Lanco actually relied on American's statement or that such reliance constituted a substantial detriment to Lanco (at most, it would appear only that Lanco may have permitted Citadel to remain at the premises for two months). Thus, Lanco's estoppel argument would probably **not** be successful.

Summary:

Lanco can probably not successfully sue American (although it may succeed on the SOF issue).

National v. American

Did American receive consideration for its guarantee?

A promise must ordinarily induce a detriment for consideration to be present. American (the promisor) can contend that since National **promised only to forbear** from attempting to collect on the note "until such time as we need payment," National has incurred no detriment in exchange for American's promise to pay Citadel's obligation. The weight of modern decisions, however, suggests that National should prevail regardless of consideration: a writing signed by the promisor is the only requirement for such a guaranty under UCC §3-408, while Rest. 2d §88(a) requires a "purported" consideration. Though action under a promissory estoppel theory is also possible, on that theory National would need to show that it in fact relied on the guaranty in not immediately pursuing action against Citadel and also on the consequent detrimental effect of refraining from collecting Citadel's debt for the two months before Citadel failed financially. National need not rely on promissory estoppel, however, since it should be able to prevail in an action based on the contractual guarantee, as we have noted.

Summary:

National can probably successfully bring suit against American.

American v. Debco:

An **assignee** normally takes subject to any **defenses under the contract** that the **obligor could have asserted** against the obligee-assignor (assuming there is no explicit agreement between the assignor and obligor to the contrary). Thus, assuming Debco validly rejected the goods or revoked its acceptance, it should be able to assert the failure of consideration (i.e., the defective goods) against American. American's lack of knowledge of the defect at the time of the assignment to it is irrelevant.

Summary:

Debco can probably successfully defend against a suit by American on the account receivable.

Answer to Question 14

A v. B:

A could conceivably sue B for $5,000 or $2,000, contending that she is entitled to the difference between the $5,000 she already received and either (1) B's initial promise (of $10,000) or (2) their later agreement to pay $7,000 for a Goldray as compensation for her services.

As to the first, there appears to be no consideration to support B's promise to pay a sum in excess of the amount A had actually earned. Since A and B apparently did not agree on A's compensation, an *implied-in-fact contract* only for A's normal hourly rate would probably be found. While this amount has not been stated by A in an invoice as yet, it can be liquidated (the figure that results from multiplying A's normal hourly rate by the number of hours expended on B's negotiations). We'll assume for our analysis that this amount would be approximately $6,000.

As to A's possible contention that B had agreed to pay her the value of a Goldray ($7,000), B would assert the consideration argument above and also contend that A's offer to accept the purchase of a Goldray for N as compensation was an offer for a unilateral contract, which he never accepted as required, i.e., by purchasing the car. A, however, could probably successfully argue in rebuttal that there is at least some ambiguity as to whether A's offer to B was unilateral or bilateral (i.e., it is capable of being accepted by a promise, which B gave). In such instances, the courts will usually construe the contract as being bilateral in nature.

B will next contend, however, that even if a bilateral contract was formed, it was *modified* when A offered to accept a lesser sum if such amount were paid immediately. While A might attempt to argue in rebuttal that she received no consideration for agreeing to accept the lesser sum (i.e., B was already under a *preexisting duty* to pay $7,000 for the Goldray), B could probably successfully argue in rebuttal that there was consideration since he had promised to purchase the Goldray "as soon as I can" (which would be taken to be within a reasonably prompt period of time); and so by paying A $5,000, he did something (paid a sum of money more quickly than he otherwise might have) he was not previously obligated to do. This latter argument would probably be successful, and therefore B would owe A nothing more.

N v. B:

N might contend that he was a third party beneficiary ("3PB") of the A-B contract, and that his rights vested when the A-B contract for the Goldray was formed. One is a 3PB where the promisee (in this case A), primarily for the purpose of benefiting the 3PB, bargains for performance by the promisor (in this case B) directly to the 3PB (here, N). Since it appears (especially in light of the familial relationship between A and N) that A primarily sought to benefit N and performance was to be rendered to N, N's contention seems correct.

B will also assert the "consideration," "bilateral contract," and "modification" arguments discussed above against N (the promisor is entitled to assert against the 3PB any defenses that he could have asserted under the contract against the promisee).

B would alternatively contend that the majority rule is that a *3PB's rights do not vest until he has relied to his detriment on the contract or expressly assented to it* (neither of which events appear to have occurred). In a *minority of jurisdictions, however, since N was a donee beneficiary, his rights vested automatically on formation of the underlying agreement.* If this state follows the latter view, N would prevail on this issue and (assuming he prevailed on the issues discussed above) would be able to enforce the 3PB contract against B. (In such event, B would be able to recover the $5,000 previously paid to A since B's payment to N would constitute payment to A.)

Under Rest. 2d §311(3), the beneficiary's rights vest when he sues, detrimentally relies, or manifests assent to the contract *before notice of modification.* Since N brought suit only after A modified the contract, this provision cannot operate to support N's claim.

Cadilline ("C") v. B:

Although **C may contend that it was a 3PB of the A-B contract,** C probably has no rights against B because there is no indication that A actually intended to benefit C. Presumably A mentioned C by name because she was aware that it had Goldrays in stock, without intending to specifically confer a benefit on C. Thus, C is not a 3PB (C is merely an "incidental" beneficiary, which means C has no rights under the original contract).

Answer to Question 15

Mayberry University ("MU") v. D:

MU is a donee third-party beneficiary ("3PB") of the initial contract between M and D since (1) M intended to benefit MU, and (2) D promised to render performance directly to MU.

Did MU's rights vest prior to the modification?

Since M and D agreed to modify the rights of MU (the 3PB) in a manner that resulted in MU's receiving nothing from D, MU would contend that its rights as a 3PB vested prior to the modification.

The Rest. 2d §311(3) (which probably represents the majority view) states that the **rights of a 3PB vest** when the latter detrimentally relies on the contract between the promisor and the promisee, commences a lawsuit against the promisor, or expressly indicates its assent to the contract. While MU made reference to M's donation in the mailing that it sent to its alumni, the facts do not indicate that MU's reliance on M's pledge was detrimental (unless, possibly, it can be shown that MU was subsequently obliged to return whatever donations it received based on the campaign built around M's pledge). Thus, there appears to be no detrimental reliance by MU on M's promise, and therefore MU would probably lose on this issue in most states.

A minority view holds that the rights of a "donee" beneficiary (one, like MU, to whom the promisee is not indebted) vest when the contract is made, while the rights of a creditor beneficiary (one to whom the promisee is indebted) vest only when it detrimentally relies on the contract. If this minority view were followed, MU would argue that it was a donee beneficiary (in which instance, M and D could not subsequently modify MU's 3PB rights). (We'll assume that in our jurisdiction a pledge to a nonprofit entity is **not** enforceable. If it were deemed enforceable, MU would be a creditor beneficiary.)

In a minority-view state, MU will argue that M probably did **not** believe that he was legally obligated to MU, as evidenced by the fact that M later repudiated his pledge (and that therefore MU was a donee beneficiary). D, however, will contend that M probably thought his pledge to MU was legally enforceable (despite the fact that he reneged on it) since he actually promised to make the $50,000 payment to MU (and that therefore MU was a creditor beneficiary). MU will probably prevail on this issue because most persons realize that a gratuitous promise is **not** legally enforceable.

Does D have any defenses against MU?

A promisor under a 3PB arrangement can ordinarily assert against the 3PB any defenses that could have been raised against the promisee.

Was there a lack of consideration for M's initial pledge to MU?

A promisee must ordinarily incur some detriment for a promise to be binding. (We've assumed that this is not a state in which the consideration requisite is suspended for nonprofit organizations.) Although MU will argue that M should be estopped from repudiating his *pledge* since it relied on M's promise in doing another mailing to its alumni, the facts do not show any significant detriment to MU as a consequence of M's promise. MU will reply that D's right to assert any defense it has against M does not extend to defenses M has against MU. Rest. 2d §309(3). Donee beneficiaries would rarely receive rights as 3PBs if lack of consideration for the promisee's gift was a defense the promisor could assert. MU will probably prevail on this issue.

Is the frustration of purpose doctrine applicable?

A party is discharged from his prospective obligations where the **basic purpose** of the contract, recognized as such by both parties, is **frustrated** by an unforeseeable post-agreement event. D will contend that M was aware of the purpose for which the patent was to be used, and that this purpose was frustrated by the subsequent discovery that D's process was not economically viable. However, MU will argue that D's frustration arises from a judgmental error, not an "event." Also, the inability to perfect the process was not unforeseeable to both parties since M was skeptical of the feasibility of D's plans. Thus, MU should prevail on this issue.

Is the mutual mistake doctrine applicable?

Where both parties are mistaken with respect to an essential fact going to the essence of the contract, the adversely affected party can avoid the contract (assuming the risk of such mistake was not borne by that party). D will argue that M knew that the ability to market the gadget successfully as a consequence of D's new process was an essential fact on which the contract was premised. Since the process could not be used in a financially successful manner, there was a **mutual mistake** that discharges D from liability to M and to MU. MU will contend in rebuttal, however, that simply because one party explains its rationale for entering into a contract with the other side, he is not relieved of liability if his thought process proves to be faulty. Since M never indicated agreement with D's claim that the process would make production of the gadget economically feasible, MU should prevail on this issue also.

Was there an implied condition subsequent in the M-D agreement that D's obligations would be discharged if D's new process proved unsuccessful?

A condition subsequent may be implied in a contract where, had the parties contemplated the condition sought to be implied, they would almost certainly have agreed to it. Where such a condition occurs, each side is relieved of his prospective obligations. D could conceivably contend that since he had explained his basis for entering into the agreement with M, M should have realized that D would not expect to be contractually bound if the process did not permit the new gadget to be marketed successfully. However, MU would contend in rebuttal that there is no indication that M, had he and D considered this aspect, would have agreed to allow D to rescind the agreement if the process proved to be unsuccessful. In fact, since M apparently was skeptical about the efficacy of D's plans, it is unlikely that M would have agreed that D should be discharged if mass production of the gadget proved economically unfeasible.

Thus, MU would probably prevail on this issue also.

Summary:

However, because MU's rights probably did not vest prior to the modification and, in the majority view, there was a lack of consideration for M's promise to MU, MU probably has no rights against D.

MU v. M:

The discussion above with respect to the "consideration" issue would be applicable here. Even though D cannot assert lack of consideration, M can assert that defense and seems likely to prevail.

M v. D:

The discussions above with respect to frustration of purpose, mutual mistake, and implied condition subsequent would be equally applicable here. Since it was concluded above that MU would be successful against D with respect to these issues, M should be able to obtain a judgment against D for $50,000. Note that the result if M sues is different from the result if MU sues.

Answer to Question 16

Counsel to Will should consider the following issues.

Will ("W") v. Xact ("X"):

There is no indication that a novation occurred (i.e., that W ever agreed to look solely to Young ("Y") for repayment of the loan made to X). Additionally, we'll assume that the term "highest lawful rate" is sufficiently definite (i.e., there is in this jurisdiction a law or rule that states the highest interest rate that may be charged by a lender to a borrower).

Was payment to X by Y a condition precedent to X's obligation to repay W?

If a **condition precedent** to a promise fails to occur, neither party to the contract has any prospective obligations to the other. X might contend that since he told W that he would repay the latter when Y paid him, he was not bound to repay W at all until such event occurred. However, W will argue in rebuttal that Y's payment to X described only the approximate time when X's loan to W would become due. Any other interpretation of the W-X agreement would be illogical since W could not have reasonably intended that X be able to avoid repayment of the loan if Y defaulted in his obligations to X. W should prevail on this issue.

Has X materially breached his contract with W? (If so, W has no obligation to make any further loans to X and may commence an action for damages against X.)

If Y is correct in his assertion that X was obliged to deliver receipts showing payment for the petroleum products used on Y's jobs (i.e., that such claims are lienable under law), then X would probably be deemed to have breached the implied covenant that neither side will do anything to prevent the other from obtaining the full benefits of the agreement. By failing to provide proof that the petroleum product suppliers had been paid when he was obligated to pay them, X has caused the nonpayment by Y. This would constitute a **material breach** of the W-X agreement (since because of the breach, the payment by Y will not be made when originally anticipated), entitling W to (1) suspend further payments to X, and (2) commence an action for the loans (and accrued interest) previously made to X.

Even if X is not in default under the Y-X agreement, W could still contend that the words "when Y pays me" should be taken to mean "when Y would have been obliged to pay X, assuming each side performed its obligations in a timely manner." This construction would prevent X from arguing that his obligation to pay W was uncertain because Y might never pay him. Despite the apparently clear meaning of the words "when Y pays me," X probably intended that W be repaid in accordance with the Y-X contractual schedule, so X's failure to pay W when one-half of the X-Y job was finished probably constituted a material (albeit unintentional) breach of their agreement. Thus, W is not obligated to make additional advances to X and may sue X for the prior loans and accrued interest.

Can W successfully sue Y?

Whether W can also successfully sue Y depends on resolution of the following issues.

Did an assignment of X's rights against Y occur?

W is not in privity with Y and therefore would have no rights against Y unless an **assignment** of X's rights had actually occurred. Y would initially contend that X merely indicated a **source of funds** for repayment of X's obligation to W. (X's words, "this contract will be your security" are different from stating, "I hereby assign you my rights under my contract with Y"). W, of course, would contend that X's words, coming in the context of X's showing him a copy of the agreement, were reasonably understood by W as an outright assignment of X's rights. However, Y would probably prevail on this issue, and therefore W cannot successfully maintain an action against Y.

Assuming, however, an assignment did occur, can W enforce the X-Y contract against Y?

An assignee ordinarily stands in the shoes of the assignor. The **obligor**, however, **may assert against the assignee any defenses** under the contract that he had against the assignor. Thus, if Y's assertion that X was obliged to provide him with receipts from the petroleum product suppliers was correct, Y will contend that this obligation was an express condition precedent to his obligation to pay X anything (the contract states that the payments to X will be made **only** on proof that all lienable claims have been paid). W will contend in rebuttal that the language expresses a covenant (rather than a condition precedent), and that this covenant was substantially performed (since X gave Y proof that the workmen had been fully paid). However, (1) despite the judicial aversion to forfeitures, the language of the Y-X does appear to be language of condition; and (2) even if it were construed to be a covenant, X's failure to provide proof that the petroleum suppliers had been paid would probably be a material breach (since Y, in the absence of such receipts, would have no means of determining the potential liens against his land). Y should prevail on this issue.

Even if Y was in breach by wrongfully withholding payment from X, was this default waived by X?

A waiver is the voluntary relinquishment of a known right by the party in whose favor such right was to have operated. Y could contend that X waived any breach by Y by continuing work on Y's land after the latter had refused to pay for the initial one-half of the job. However, W can probably successfully argue in rebuttal that X would not have intended to relinquish such a significant term (i.e., his receipt of payment for the work), and that X probably proceeded on the premise that Y would soon recognize that X's position on liens was correct. If X stopped the work, his workers would probably leave for other jobs, so that it would become impossible for X to finish his performance even if Y changed his initial position. W should prevail on the issue of waiver.

Summary:

Based on the foregoing, W should (1) cease making any further payments to X, and (2) commence an action immediately against X for the prior loans and accrued interest. Suit against Y would probably be unsuccessful; but if it were brought and won, only one recovery for W's losses would be possible.

Answer to Question 17

Can Ace ("A") introduce evidence pertaining to the verbal agreement with Beta ("B")?

B can be expected to contend that since the contract with A states that it cannot be modified "*except by a writing signed by both parties*," A cannot introduce evidence with respect to the *post-agreement modification.* However, most states adhere to the view that such a clause can be waived (especially where the oral modification has actually been relied on, as was done by A in this instance by completing the job). Given the obvious increased cost of performance as a consequence of the earthquake, A will probably be permitted to introduce evidence of the verbal modification to the original agreement.

Was the modification valid?

B can be expected to contend that since A was under a *preexisting duty* to fulfill the contract for a total price of $100,000, there was no consideration for his promise to pay A an additional $45,000. However, A can assert three theories in rebuttal.

I. Promissory estoppel:

Where a promisee foreseeably relies, to his substantial detriment, on a promise made by the other side, the latter may be estopped from asserting a lack of consideration with respect to such promise. A can contend that since it was forced to spend $60,000 more than anticipated, B should be estopped from asserting lack of consideration for its promise to modify the original agreement. However, B can argue in rebuttal that (1) promissory estoppel, an equitable doctrine, should not be applied to permit A to recover an amount in excess of that agreed to under the original contract, and (2) it is unclear whether A would incur a "substantial" detriment from completing the contract for the originally agreed-on fee (i.e., would a $45,000 loss on this one transaction have a significant effect on A's overall business?). Nevertheless, A should probably prevail.

II. Unforeseen hardship:

In a minority of states, where, due to unanticipated circumstances, an obligor's original performance has become substantially more burdensome, a promise received in exchange for the obligor's agreement to complete the contract is enforceable, provided the modification is fair and equitable. It is unclear from the facts whether (1) earthquakes could be anticipated in this locale, and (2) the added expense would have a significantly detrimental effect on A's overall business operation. Assuming, however, that (i) the earthquake was not foreseeable, and (ii) the impact on A would be severe, A should prevail if this state adheres to this minority view.

III. Preexisting duty disputed in good faith:

Under the preexisting duty rule, performance of a duty that is neither doubtful nor the subject of honest dispute cannot be consideration. Rest. 2d §73. If A honestly believed that the earthquake excused its obligations under the original contract, then promising to finish the work would be consideration for B's promise to pay more for the work. The arguments below offer three reasons A might honestly have believed it was discharged from the original contract. Even if A cannot prevail on any of these defenses, as long as it honestly believe the defenses excused further performance, the preexisting duty rule will not preclude enforcement of the modification.

Had A been discharged from its prior obligations under the original contract? (If so, then there would be consideration for the modification, since A had ceased to be obligated to B under the original contract.)

There are three theories on which A could contend that it had been discharged from its obligations to B under the original contract because of the earthquake. If so, B's promise to A to pay the enhanced price for A's construction would be supported by consideration.

I. Mutual mistake:

Where *both parties are mistaken with respect to a fact* going to the essence of the contract and existing at the time the agreement is made, the adversely affected party can avoid the contract (assuming the risk of the mistake was not borne by that party). A might argue that since its officers had carefully explained to B the basis for its cost estimate, the failure to anticipate the effect of the earthquake on these calculations was a material mistake on which the contract was premised. However, B could contend in rebuttal that the mere fact that A explained to B the calculations on which its estimate was based does not suggest that B had implicitly agreed that the contract could be rescinded if A's estimates ultimately proved to be inaccurate. B will probably prevail on this issue.

II. *Implied condition subsequent:*

A **condition subsequent may be implied** into a contract where, had the parties contemplated such condition, they almost certainly would have agreed to it. A can contend that had the parties considered the occurrence of an earthquake, given its explanation of the basis for the price extended to B, they certainly would have agreed that A would be entitled to be paid the out-of-pocket expense caused by the earthquake. While B can contend in rebuttal that had the parties desired such a condition subsequent, they would have explicitly provided for it in their written agreement, A should prevail on this issue *if* earthquakes were not foreseeable within this locale. (If they were, then B might not have agreed to such a condition.)

III. *Impracticability:*

A few jurisdictions recognize the rule that where a **party's performance becomes impracticable** (due to no fault of its own) as a consequence of some unforeseeable post-contract occurrence, that party is discharged from its prospective obligations under the agreement. If this view was followed in this jurisdiction, A could contend that his performance became impracticable (financially unfeasible) as a consequence of the earthquake. Again, however, if an earthquake should have been anticipated, then this risk would probably be deemed to have been borne by A. Additionally, it is unclear from the facts whether performance by A was made impracticable by the earthquake. If, as a consequence of performing the agreement under its original terms, A would still show a reasonable profit for the year, performance by A probably would *not* be deemed impracticable. It is difficult to resolve this contention without additional facts.

Summary:

If (1) A was discharged from his original contractual obligation to B by reason of the earthquake, *or* (2) A honestly believed a defense excused further performance of the contract, *or* (3) A prevails on the promissory estoppel issue, *or* (4) the minority view that recognizes the "unforeseen hardship" doctrine is followed in this state, A can probably enforce the modification against B and recover the additional $45,000 as stipulated.

Answer to Question 18

Bert ("B") will contend that he had no obligation to supply Walt ("W") with the containers under the initial agreement, and that there was consideration for his promise to pay W the $2 difference for each gallon furnished to W by Gray ("G"). The success of this contention will depend on resolution of the following issues.

Was B's statement to W an offer?

A *quotation is ordinarily deemed to be an invitation, rather than an offer*. However, where a reasonable offeree would construe the statement as an offer, it is capable of acceptance. B will initially contend that he simply "quoted" W a price, but did not make an offer. W, however, will probably successfully argue that since B was specific as to price, number of gallons a month, and length of time, he was reasonable in taking B's statements as an offer.

Was the offer accepted by W?

B may next contend that W never accepted his offer since W insisted that the price include the cost of the container (and therefore W made a rejection and counteroffer). However, where an offeree's acceptance is made conditional on *additional terms which were implicit in the offer*, the offeree's response will usually be deemed to be an acceptance. Thus, W can probably successfully argue in rebuttal that inherent in B's offer of $7.00 a container was the fact that B would also furnish the container (and therefore W's response was simply a verification of that fact). Since both B and W would probably be considered merchants, W's addition of a term to the contract will result in the integration of that term into the agreement (assuming it doesn't materially alter the contract), and W's response therefore constitutes acceptance, in view of B's silence on the matter. UCC §2-207.

In a state that has adopted the 2003 revisions to article 2, the analysis of UCC §2-207 will differ slightly. Assuming W's response was an acceptance with an additional term (under UCC §2-206(3)), the additional term would become part of the contract only if both parties agreed to it — even if it was not a material change — or if the term was supplied by the UCC. UCC §2-207. Thus, the issue turns on whether B, by beginning performance, effectively agreed to W's additional term.

Even if W's response was a counteroffer, did B accept it by fulfilling W's orders?

While *acceptance must ordinarily be unequivocal*, it may be implied by the offeree's conduct. W may contend that even if his response was a rejection of the original offer and a counteroffer, B accepted it by filling his orders for two weeks. While B can argue in rebuttal that he simply accepted a few particular orders made by W (rather than agreeing to be bound for a year), W would probably prevail on this issue in light of B's agreement to pay W the $2 difference during the remainder of the one-year period.

Thus, B and W entered into a one-year agreement for the purchase and sale of the containers of solvent.

Was the original B-W agreement unenforceable under the UCC's Statute of Frauds ("SOF")?

The UCC's SOF under §2-201 would seem to require a writing since this is a contract for sale of $500 or more (or $5,000 or more under the 2003 revisions to article 2). (The expected value of the contract is $420,000 — $7 a gallon times 5,000 gallons a month times 12 months). As to the original agreement, UCC §2-201(3)(c) provides an exception to the requirement of a writing where part performance is accomplished; B's right to payment for his first two weeks of production would not be defeated for lack of a writing. However, because the original agreement may not have been enforceable beyond the goods received and paid for, B could argue (probably successfully) that he had no further obligation to W; therefore, there was no consideration for the subsequent agreement. Assuming there was consideration, B would contend that a writing was required for the subsequent agreement. UCC §2-201(3)(b), however, provides an exception to the writing requirement if the party to be charged admits in his pleading, testimony, or otherwise under oath that a contract was made. Thus, if B were to admit his agreement to pay the $2 a gallon difference (for example, in response to a claim of higher liability by W), the lack of a writing would be cured, at least for the quantity B admitted. If W did not prevail on the writing requirement and consideration issues, he could assert promissory estoppel (though this would be a weak argument), claiming that in relying on B's promise to pay him the $2 difference, W incurred substantial obligations or expenditures regarding his anticipated use (resale) of the solvent.

Was B relieved of any obligations to W under the original agreement by reason of the impossibility of performance doctrine?

Under the impossibility of performance doctrine where, as a consequence of an unforeseeable, post-contract event, one party (through no fault of his own) cannot possibly perform his contractual obligations, that party is relieved of his prospective obligations under the agreement. B can contend that since he could not possibly pay the $50,000 necessary to acquire the purification equipment, he was relieved of his obligations under the original contract. Thus, there was no consideration for his promise to pay W $2 per gallon. W can contend in rebuttal, however, that: (1) in some jurisdictions, the event constituting the impossibility must be objective in nature (i.e., no one can possibly perform it), and in that case, this defense would not be available to B (since someone with adequate funds could acquire the purification equipment); and (2) the event causing the impossibility was a consequence of B's own actions (polluting the nearby river). W should prevail on this issue.

Was B relieved of his obligations under the original agreement by reason of the commercial impracticability doctrine?

Under UCC §2-615, where the performance of a supplier has become *impracticable as a consequence* of some post-contract contingency that was unforeseeable at the time the contract was made, she is relieved of her prospective obligations under the agreement. B could contend that performance of his obligations under the original agreement became impracticable as a consequence of the order requiring him to obtain the purification equipment. Thus, having no obligation to W under the initial contract, there was no consideration for his promise to pay W the $2 difference for each gallon ordered from G. However, the Official Comments to §2-615 state that where the supplier should have foreseen the contingency and could have prevented it, the commercial impracticability defense is not available. Since B should have realized that he might be compelled to cure the pollution for which he was responsible, W should again prevail.

Assuming W prevailed on each of the foregoing issues, was B relieved of his obligations when G's plant burned down?

Contractual provisions will ordinarily be interpreted in accordance with their plain meaning. B will argue that the three-party agreement stated that B was obligated only to pay the difference between B's and G's prices for each gallon manufactured by G; thus B was relieved of any obligations when G ceased furnishing W with the containers. W can contend in rebuttal that the overall intention of the three-party contract was that W would receive the difference between the original contract price ($7 a gallon) and whatever W's cover price (now $10 a gallon) would be. However, W will probably be deemed to have accepted the risk that G might ultimately cease doing business (if W intended otherwise, he could have so provided in the agreement with G and B). Thus, even if the three-party agreement was enforceable by W, B was probably relieved of any liability when G ceased supplying containers to W.

Answer to Question 19

Manor ("M") v. Valley ("V"), V v. M.

If M were to sue V, the following issues would probably arise.

Is the contract sufficiently definite?

A contract must be definite as to all material terms to be enforceable. V may contend that the contract was not definite as to the following terms: (1) when the additional $2,000 was to be paid, (2) whether the entire $13,000 principal and accrued interest were to be paid at the end of the five-year period proved in the note or amortized over the five-year period, (3) what the term "good and clear title" means, or (4) by what date the transaction had to be completed. M will argue in rebuttal that it is **implicit in real property sales** that (1) the down payment is paid when the deed is tendered; (2) the mortgage and interest would be due at the end of the five-year term unless otherwise provided specifically, (3) "good and clear title" means that no adverse interest in the land would be disclosed by a title report, and (4) where no time is specified, a reasonable time will be implied. M should prevail on this issue.

Was V relieved of his obligations under the contract by reason of the anticipatory repudiation ("AR") doctrine?

An AR can occur by voluntary conduct that clearly evidences an intention by a party not to perform a material contractual obligation. Where such conduct has occurred, the aggrieved party is relieved of her duties. V could contend that M's act of placing a mortgage against the land, at a time when M was already contractually obliged to convey "good and clear title" to him, constituted an AR (thereby relieving V of his obligation under the agreement). However, M can probably successfully argue in rebuttal that V should have realized that it would be entirely possible for M to repay (and thereby discharge) the mortgage prior to delivery of the deed to V. Thus, M's conduct in obtaining the mortgage constituted merely a potential inability to perform (i.e., an action that makes the required prospective performance appear dubious), a consequence that ordinarily suspends (but does not discharge) the other party's obligation to perform the agreement. However, in most states, where the innocent party has materially changed her position as a consequence of the other side's apparent inability to perform, she is discharged from her prospective duties. Thus, V would contend that since he had already entered into a contract with Smith to buy a new home, V was relieved of his performance under the contract with M.

V should prevail (unless, possibly, it can be shown that Smith would have agreed to release V of his obligation to purchase Smith's home).

Was the two-month delay between the time the contract was made and M's tender of the deed to V a material breach by M?

Where nothing has been stated, it is usually implied that each side must render his performance within a reasonable time. V could contend that M's two-month delay in tendering the deed constituted a *material breach*, relieving V entirely of his obligations. M will argue that persons moving from their homes will usually require at least two months to pack their belongings and make certain their new dwelling is habitable. Either party might rely on custom in the region: if the time between contract formation and closing commonly is 45-60 days, this will favor M; if 30 days or less in customary, V should prevail.

Summary:

Since V will probably prevail on the prospective inability-to-perform or material-breach issues, it is unlikely that M could successfully sue V. Additionally, V should be able to recover the $1,000 deposit paid to M under an unjust enrichment theory (i.e., M would be unjustly enriched if he were to retain the deposit since V has no liability to M).

Assuming, however, that M prevailed on the foregoing issues, what are his remedies against V?

Where a *contract for the sale of land* is breached by the vendee, some states permit the vendor to obtain specific performance against the buyer (i.e., the seller obtains a judgment for the purchase price against the vendee; the deed is delivered to the court for transfer to the buyer on payment or collection of the purchase price). In other jurisdictions, the vendor can recover only the out-of-pocket costs incurred in making the agreement (since there is a presumption that the value of the land being retained by the seller is exactly equal to the purchase price). Finally, other states permit the aggrieved party to recover only the difference between the contract price and market price (which is often zero since the contract price should reflect the market price). Finally, since there is no indication that the V-M agreement contained a liquidated damage clause, M would have no right to retain the $1,000 deposit except as applied on account of one of the other recovery theories (out-of-pocket costs or damages).

Broker v. M:

If Broker ("B") were to sue M, the following issues would probably arise.

Has B's commission been earned?

M would contend that consummation of the sale was a condition precedent to B's becoming entitled to the commission, and the sale was never completed. B could argue in rebuttal, however, that a party is excused from the **occurrence of a condition** precedent where the performance is prevented by the other party; here, M, in effect, prevented the sale by his conduct in placing a mortgage on Blackacre.

Assuming B prevails on the preceding issue, when did M's obligation to pay B the commission arise?

M might also contend that in no event could the sale be "consummated" until the price was fully paid. Under the agreement with V, this would not have occurred for an additional five years. Thus, M would not be liable to B until that time. However, B could probably successfully contend in rebuttal that when nothing else is said, a commission is ordinarily deemed to be earned when the buyer's consideration for the deed is delivered (i.e., the $2,000, plus the note), and that, but for M's breach, this would have occurred on May 1. B should prevail on this issue and thus be immediately entitled to $800 from M.

Answer to Question 20

Owner ("O") v. Byer ("B"):

Before it can be determined if O can compel B to specifically perform the original agreement, it must first be decided if O has a substantive right to sue B for breach of contract.

Did a novation occur?

A **novation** occurs where an obligee agrees to release the obligor from his duties under the contract and to substitute a new party in his place; and the latter agrees to assume the obligor's duties. B might contend that O impliedly accepted a novation since (1) O accepted the $5,000 down payment from Ellis ("E"), and (2) B had advised O that (i) the contract had been assigned to E, and (ii) B no longer considered himself bound by the original agreement (a statement to which O did **not** reply). However, there would probably have to be more affirmative conduct by O indicating his release of B and his acceptance of E as the sole obligor, so a novation probably did not occur.

Can B successfully assert the mutual mistake doctrine?

Where there is a **mutual mistake** going to the essence of the contract, the adversely affected party may avoid the agreement (assuming the risk of the mistake was not borne by that party). B can possibly contend that since the assumption of both parties that a 50-acre square parcel was being sold and purchased was incorrect, he can avoid the agreement. However, O can probably successfully assert in rebuttal that the mistake as to ownership of the 3-feet wide strip bordering Greenacre ("G/A") does not go to the essence of the contract. There is no indication from the facts that this relatively small area was of some special importance to B. Unless the 3-feet strip had some obvious import (e.g., was vital for access to highway or beach), O should prevail on this issue also.

Can B successfully assert the Statute of Frauds ("SOF")?

Contracts pertaining to the transfer of an interest in land must be memorialized in *a writing that contains the essential terms and is signed by the party against whom enforcement is sought.* The facts indicate that O "contracted in a signed writing" to sell G/A to B, but not that B signed the agreement. However, B's signed assignment to E, assuming it adequately described G/A, would probably satisfy the SOF.

Can B successfully assert the material breach doctrine?

Where one of the parties to an executory contract has committed a **material breach,** the aggrieved party can rescind the agreement. The factors to be weighed in determining whether a breach is material are described in the Rest. 2d §241. They include the extent to which (1) the aggrieved party would be deprived of the benefit that she reasonably expected; (2) the breaching party acted in good faith; (3) the injured party can be compensated for the breach; (4) the breaching party would suffer a forfeiture; and (5) there is a likelihood of cure. B could contend that since O did not own (and therefore couldn't convey) the westerly 3-feet wide strip of G/A, O had materially breached. Cure (such as O acquiring the strip and conveying it) does not seem likely since O tendered a deed without offering to cure. However, O could probably successfully contend in rebuttal that since the 3-feet wide strip was, in relation to the entire contract for 50 acres, a very minor aspect of the agreement, his innocent breach (there is no indication that O was aware of the problem when he entered into the transaction) should not be deemed material. In addition, B can probably be adequately compensated; B can buy the strip from its owner and seek damages in that amount (or in the amount of the market value of the strip) from O. On the other hand, O would not suffer forfeiture (he can resell the land if B is discharged from his duty to purchase). These factors seem relatively balanced, but unless the strip is vital for some reason not mentioned in the facts, the small difference between the promised lot and the lot delivered seems likely to allow O to prevail on this issue.

Assuming O prevailed on the previous issues, can he obtain specific performance ("SP") against B?

Some states permit an aggrieved seller of realty only to recover his out-of-pocket expenses. We'll assume, however, that this jurisdiction permits the seller of realty to obtain SP (i.e., the vendor may obtain a judgment for the contract price, but must give the buyer a deed to the property when he has been paid in full). This remedy puts the vendor in the position he would have been in if the buyer had performed. B, however, would be entitled to damages caused by the failure to deliver the 3-feet strip.

O v. Ellis ("E"):

While E and O are not in privity of contract, *O could probably successfully contend that he is a third party beneficiary* ("3PB") of the E-B agreement since E specifically agreed with B that E would pay O (apparently for B's assignment of his rights under the contract to E). Additionally, where one party assigns all of her rights under a contract to another party, the latter is ordinarily deemed to have assumed all of the assignor's duties under the agreement. Since E does not appear to have any counterarguments to these contentions, and assuming O prevailed with respect to the issues described under *O v. B* (E would also be able to assert those contentions against O since a promisor can assert any defenses against the 3PB that he could have asserted against the promisee), O should also be able to obtain a judgment against E. O, of course, will be permitted only one aggregate recovery.

E v. O:

If E is successful (1) with respect to any of the issues (except novation) raised by B under *O v. B*, or (2) in showing his contract with B was unenforceable, he will be entitled to rescind the contract and recover the $5,000 previously paid to O.

Answer to Question 21

If B were to sue O for breach of contract, O would probably raise the following issues.

Did the contractual anti-assignment clause prevent A's delegation of duties to B?

Contractual clauses absolutely prohibiting the assignment of rights or delegation of duties are ordinarily given effect. O will contend that the agreement clearly states that the "contract may not be assigned"; therefore the assignment to B (including any work done by him) is **not** enforceable. B may reply that the contractual prohibition gives O an action for damages against A, but does not prevent the assignment from conveying rights to B. Rest. 2d §322(2)(b). O will argue that the parties manifested a different intention, though it does not appear in the text of the contract. Given the variability of taste in architecture, it seems likely that A understood O would rather choose its own replacement if A could not perform the work. If so, O may prevail on this point.

Even assuming that the assignment was not absolutely prohibited contractually, was A's performance too personal in nature to be delegated?

Where performance of a contractual duty is **highly personal in nature**, it cannot be delegated. O will argue that he retained A's unique expertise and architectural genius (A had won many awards and was nationally acclaimed), and therefore A's obligations were too personal in nature to be delegated. B can contend in rebuttal that any difference in their abilities was insignificant since (1) B's reputation was of virtually equal prominence with A's, and (2) B had worked for A on numerous occasions. Nevertheless, O would probably prevail on this issue.

Even if A's duties were highly personal in nature, did O waive his rights by failing to object to A's delegation of duties to B?

A waiver may be found from conduct that is so inconsistent with an intent to enforce the right in question as to induce a reasonable belief that such right was not meant to be enforced. B can contend that he had commenced performance of the contract with O's obvious knowledge that he (rather than A) was working on the hotel's design (B met with O and thereafter called to discuss various aspects of the emerging design). In fact, it was not until B tried to deliver the design that O expressed his disapproval by refusing to accept or pay for it. O might argue in rebuttal that he never actually realized that B had assumed the contract, but (assuming O knew that B had worked with A on prior projects) presumed that B was merely assisting A with the hotel design. Thus, no waiver could have occurred since the aggrieved party — O — did not know about the breach. Nevertheless, B will probably prevail on this issue since O should have realized that something had happened to A since A had never communicated with him.

Is O relieved of liability to B by reason of the frustration of purpose doctrine?

Where the **basic purpose of a contract**, recognized as such by both parties, is **permanently frustrated** by an **unforeseeable** post-agreement event, the party whose basic purpose has been frustrated by such event is discharged from his prospective contractual obligations. O will contend that O's liability under the agreement is discharged since (1) the hotel was obviously intended to accommodate people desiring to use the airport (a fact that must also have been known to B), and (2) that purpose has been frustrated by closure of the airport. However, B can argue in rebuttal that since the decision to close the airport was preceded by a year of mounting public protest that had been featured prominently in the news media, the shutdown of the airport was **not unforeseeable**. Assuming the public displeasure with the airport was of sufficient magnitude to suggest the possibility that the facility could be closed, B should prevail on this issue.

Was O relieved of liability to B by reason of the failure of a constructive condition precedent?

Where one party's performance will take a lengthy period of time and the other side's duties can be completed quickly (i.e., the payment of money), performance of the former is ordinarily deemed to be a constructive condition precedent to performance of the latter. O could conceivably contend that B's failure to deliver the design to him on May 1 constituted the **failure of a constructive condition precedent**, thereby discharging O from any obligations to B. However, performance of a condition is relieved where the other party has deliberately made the occurrence of such performance impossible. Since O refused to accept B's plans, the constructive condition of delivery on or before May 1 would be deemed to have been satisfied by B.

To what damages is B entitled?

If B is successful on the foregoing issue, he can recover the entire $300,000 prescribed by the contract.

However, if O is able successfully to assert the frustration of purpose doctrine, B can still recover a portion of his compensation under quasi-contract principles. Under this theory, when Party X has rendered services to Party Y with the expectation of payment, and those services were received by Party Y with knowledge that Party X expected payment, Party X can recover the reasonable value of the services rendered to Party Y. Since O knew that B was working on the project with the expectation of receiving compensation, a court will probably permit B to recover the value of the plans that had been completed as of March 31 (when the purpose of the contract was frustrated). O may reply that it received no benefit from these services since undelivered partial plans did not enrich O. B may point out that some courts have found enrichment when requested services are performed, even if the work is never completed or delivered. Since it is not clear from the facts what portion of the work had been completed by B on that date, it is difficult to determine what B's likely recovery will be in this instance. B may seek recovery for the all work done, even after March 31, because O failed to inform B (or A, it seems) promptly of the claimed excuse. Notice to stop work also would have eliminated any uncertainty regarding how much work was done before March 31.

Answer to Question 22

In Betty's ("B") suit against Art ("A") the following issues will probably arise.

Is A relieved of his obligations to B under the mutual mistake doctrine?

A will contend that since **neither side was aware of the rock that caused the drill to break** (thus making it impossible for him to complete the job by June 1), he can avoid the agreement. B would argue in rebuttal, however, that (1) the risk of the rock's existence was borne by A since he could have made the necessary subsoil investigation, and (2) the incident that prevented A's performance (the collision with the rock) occurred **subsequent** to the time the contract was made. A will reply that the rock was there from the time the contract was made, so the mistake did not involve a subsequent event. In addition, A was a novice well-driller, as B knew, not an expert in subsoil conditions. Even if A was negligence, that should not preclude the defense of mistake. Rest. 2d §157. A may prevail on this issue.

Was A discharged from his obligations by reason of the impossibility or impracticability of performance doctrines?

Where, as a consequence of an unforeseeable, post-contract event, one of the parties (through no fault of his own) **cannot possibly perform** his prospective obligations, that party is relieved of his obligations until the impossibility ceases to exist. A will contend that as a consequence of the drill's unexpectedly breaking after it struck the rock, his performance by the June 1 due date **became impossible, and thereafter A's obligation was completely discharged** when B advised him that he would not be permitted to finish the contract. However, B can argue in rebuttal (as many states hold) that it must be objectively impossible for the obligor to perform (i.e., no one in the obligor's position could have rendered the requisite performance), and that one with unlimited funds could (presumably) have acquired new equipment that could have drilled to a depth of 600 feet by June 1. A's defense will probably **not** be successful.

However, some jurisdictions follow the rule that where a **party's performance is made impracticable as a consequence** of an unforeseeable, post-contract event (which occurred through no fault of his own), that party is relieved of his obligations until the impracticability ceases to exist. If this jurisdiction adheres to this view, A will contend that his obligation was suspended when the drill unexpectedly broke as a result of striking the rock, and that A's obligation discharged entirely when B advised him that she would not permit him to finish the drilling. It is unclear from the facts whether A should have foreseen that a subsurface rock would be hard enough to break his drill. If a rock formation had previously been encountered by persons in the area, it would be difficult for A to satisfy the "unforeseeability" element. Unless A can demonstrate that the rock and its effect on the drill were unforeseeable, B should prevail with respect to this contention too.

Did B materially breach the agreement when she refused to permit A to complete the drilling?

Where a **material breach** occurs, the aggrieved party is relieved of any further obligations under the agreement. A could argue that when B advised him that he could not commence another well, she materially breached the contract. It is an implied obligation in all contracts that neither party will undertake any conduct that prevents the other side from performing his obligations under the agreement. B can assert the **anticipatory repudiation doctrine** in rebuttal. An anticipatory repudiation ("AR") occurs where one party unequivocally advises the other that her performance will not be forthcoming. Where an AR has occurred, the aggrieved party can treat the agreement as terminated and sue for damages. Thus, B will contend that when A advised her that performance was unlikely prior to July 1 (a full month subsequent to the contractual due date), his statement constituted an AR (thereby discharging B from the obligation to permit A to complete the drilling). While A can claim in rebuttal that he advised B only that he "could not promise" that the drilling would be completed before July 1 (not that he absolutely couldn't perform by June 1), A's acknowledgment that performance could not be assured, even one month after the date agreed on for completion, would probably constitute an AR. Thus, B probably did not materially breach the agreement by refusing to permit A to recommence the drilling.

B can probably **not** contend successfully that A materially breached the agreement when his drill struck on the rock and broke. The facts indicate that this occurrence was unavoidable, and therefore B's annoyance with A's failure to complete the job expeditiously would not support the argument of a material breach by A.

Assuming B prevails on the foregoing issues, to what damages will she be entitled?

B will assert that the damages sought in her complaint are necessary to put her in the position she would have been in had A performed in a timely manner.

A will initially argue that the $15,000 loss reflecting the ruined apple crop is not recoverable since it was *not foreseeable at the time* the contract was made. B had advised A that the new well was for the purpose of obtaining better drinking water (rather than for cultivation) and the likelihood of the dam's failing could not be anticipated. Additionally, A could contend that the *loss was avoidable.* Had B permitted A to finish the contract, the well would presumably have been completed by July 1 (in fact, it took Carlos ("C") only 30 days to complete the job). B may reply that it is reasonable to refuse a modification with a party who just breached a contract. Because B appears to have no effective means of countering this foreseeability argument, the $15,000 apple crop loss is probably *not* recoverable.

Whether B can recover the remaining $8,000 claimed as damages will depend on whether the fee charged by C was reasonable. Where one side fails to complete a personal services agreement, the aggrieved entity is permitted to retain another to finish the original obligor's performance. Thus, B would be entitled to recover the $3,500 advanced to A, *plus* $1,000, the difference between the fee paid to Carlos (assuming the $4,500 fee is reasonable) and the advance paid to A ($3,500). B cannot recover *both* the advance paid to A and the fee paid to C; otherwise, she would wind up with a windfall. A again might argue that the loss was avoidable if B had been willing to allow A to finish the work by July 1. B's decision to hire another contractor for more money and a later due date might be unreasonable; it seems motivated by pique rather than business considerations. However, A's breach might justify B's decision to seek a contractor whom she trusted more.

Answer to Question 23

If P were to sue D, D would probably raise the following issues.

Is the contract sufficiently definite?

While D may argue that the contract is not sufficiently definite as to a material item (i.e., the term "prevailing price" is ambiguous), P can probably successfully contend in rebuttal that since the parties had been dealing with each other for approximately three and one-half years, they had obviously agreed on a mutually acceptable basis for determining the prevailing price.

Is there lack of consideration (illusoriness)?

D may also contend that the original agreement is unenforceable because of a lack of consideration in that P never promised to utilize his best efforts to sell D's chairs. The contract is therefore illusory (P could unilaterally avoid his obligations by failing to make any effort to sell D's chairs). However, P could probably successfully contend in rebuttal that there is adequate consideration because UCC §2-306(2) explicitly imposes a duty on a buyer with the exclusive rights to a seller's product to use reasonable efforts to sell the product.

Was there a material breach of the agreement?

Where one of the parties has **materially breached**, the other side is relieved of his prospective obligations. D might contend that since P was 12 days behind in his payment on 30 previously ordered chairs, P had materially breached the contract. P, however, can probably successfully contend in rebuttal that substantial performance had occurred since (1) the impact of 30 chairs on the entire transaction was minimal, and (2) the contract still had one and one-half years to run. Also, P can contend that if P did breach, D waived his right to sue on the contract by acknowledging that P could have an additional two weeks to make his payment.

P can argue that he was relieved of his obligation to pay for the 30 chairs when he was advised by D that no more chairs would be supplied (i.e., this unequivocal statement constituted an anticipatory repudiation by D since D's refusal to supply additional chairs was wrongful). D might reply that, pursuant to UCC §2-306, a buyer under a **requirements contract** is not permitted to demand an amount that is "unreasonably disproportionate to any stated estimate or in the absence of [any such] estimate to any normal or otherwise comparable . . . prior requirements." D will contend that since the largest prior annual order was 330, P's requirements had become unreasonably disproportionate (P had already ordered 625 chairs for the year). P can contend that the agreement did not place any limitation on orders that P could make. D will probably be successful on this argument, at least as a justification for delivering no more chairs this year. If so, D's refusal to supply more chairs would not be a breach. D would have *no* liability to P and would be entitled to recover for the chairs delivered to P and to A.

Assuming, however, P prevailed on each of the foregoing issues, can P obtain specific performance?

Under UCC §2-716, an *aggrieved buyer may obtain specific performance* where the goods are unique or other appropriate circumstances exist. It is unclear from the facts whether the goods are unique in the sense that only D sells the particular type of chair involved. If similar chairs are unavailable or in very short supply, P may be able to contend successfully that "other appropriate circumstances are present" because he cannot purchase substitute chairs. It may be impossible for P to establish with reasonable certainty the damages arising from D's breach. P cannot be expected to obtain orders he cannot satisfy since that would destroy his business reputation. Thus, the number of chairs P could have sold but for the breach will be speculative. If P could cover (i.e., buy from another manufacturer at wholesale), he would be entitled to recover as damages the difference between the contract price and the cover price (assuming the cover price is reasonable), minus any expenses P saved because of D's breach.

D vs. A:

If D sued A based on A's guaranty, A would probably raise the Statute of Frauds ("SOF") as a defense (a promise to pay a creditor the obligations that may become owing to him by another party must be embodied in a writing that contains the essential terms and is signed by the party against whom enforcement is sought). Since A's promise to pay P's obligations to D was made telephonically, the SOF argument appears to be applicable.

However, under the "*principal purpose*" rule, as embodied in Rest. 2d §116, where the principal purpose of the party making the guaranty was to benefit itself (rather than the debtor), the *guarantor's promise* is enforceable despite the lack of a writing. Since it appears that A's concern was primarily to acquire the chairs for itself (rather than to facilitate a business transaction for P), D would probably be successful in his claim against A.

A can additionally contend that there was a lack of consideration for his guaranty promise since D was already under a ***preexisting duty*** to fulfill P's orders. Thus, A actually received nothing in exchange for its promise to D. Even if D was under a preexisting duty, in some jurisdictions a promise made by someone other than a party to the contract to induce performance is enforceable. Another exception to the preexisting duty rule ordinarily exists where the party receiving the promise reasonably believed (albeit erroneously) that she was ***not*** obligated to perform the promise. Since D believed he was not required to deliver additional chairs because P had exceeded his annual quota, there is probably consideration for A's guarantee.

D should prevail on these issues and therefore be able to enforce A's guaranty promise.

Multiple-Choice Questions

1. Allen decided to play a joke on his classmate, Paul. He told several of his friends that he would make Paul an offer of $3,000 for his used car. The vehicle had a fair market value of $1,500. The next time Allen and Paul met, Allen offered Paul $3,000 for his vehicle. Paul immediately said, "I accept your offer. I will deliver the transfer papers to you tomorrow." Allen said nothing. When Paul presented Allen with the "pink slip" the next day, Allen and his friends burst into laughter. Allen said, "It was all a big joke, and you fell for it." Paul was very upset and walked away.

   Based on these facts, it is most likely that

   A. A contract occurred because Paul was reasonably entitled to believe that Allen's offer was seriously made.

   B. A contract occurred under the doctrine of estoppel because Paul was subjected to the ridicule of his friends.

   C. No contract occurred because Allen's offer was not seriously made.

   D. No contract occurred because Allen had previously told his friends that the offer would not be serious.

2. Seller verbally offered to sell her home to Buyer for $100,000. The offer was later confirmed in a writing prepared and signed by Seller. The written offer stated, "I hereby offer to sell my home at 202 Neptune Street to you for $100,000, all cash." In response to the written offer, Buyer said: "I'll think about it." Seller responded: "All right, but please let me know within two days." The next day, Buyer called Seller and said simply, "I accept your offer." Seller now refuses to go ahead with the sale.

   Based on these facts, it is most likely that

   A. The agreement was unenforceable because no writing was signed by Buyer.

   B. No contract was formed because Buyer's promise was unenforceable, and thus Buyer gave no consideration for Seller's promise.

   C. No contract was formed because Seller had a right to revoke her offer since Buyer gave no consideration for the promise to keep the offer open for two days.

   D. A valid contract exists between Seller and Buyer.

3. Seller is a major distributor of pens on which inscriptions are engraved. Seller sends a *pro forma* letter to several hundred potential customers, including Buyer. Neither the letter nor the envelope recites the Buyer's name. The letter states that Seller is offering his pens with any inscription at 50¢ per item. It further states that orders must be

for a minimum of 1,000 pens with an inscription of no more then 25 letters each. Buyer telegraphs Seller, "Send me 2,000 pens, at 50¢ each, with the following inscription. . . ." The inscription contains 22 letters. The next day, Seller wires Buyer and advises him that the purchase price for 2,000 pens is now $1,150, due to an unforeseen increase in the cost of production.

On these facts, if Buyer sues Seller, it is most likely that

A. Buyer will prevail because Seller's letter was accepted by Buyer's telegraph.

B. Buyer will prevail unless the increase in production costs will make Seller's performance impracticable.

C. Seller will prevail because the telegraph does not bear the buyer's manual signature.

D. Seller will prevail because his letter to Buyer did not constitute an offer.

4. In September 1986, Joe Smith, 23 years old and unmarried, was beginning his third year of law school. He entered into a written lease with Landlord for an apartment near campus for the nine-month school year ending on May 31, 1987. The rent was $150 a month payable in advance on the first day of each month. Joe paid the rent through December 1, but did not pay the rent due on January 1, nor has he paid any rent since.

On January 15, 1987, Landlord threatened to evict Joe if he did not pay the rent. That night Joe called his father, Henry, and told him that he did not have the money for the rent nor did he have the money with which to pay his tuition for the second semester. Henry told Joe that if he agreed not to marry until he finished law school, Henry would pay his tuition, the $150 rent that was due on January 1, the rent for the rest of the school year, and $100 a month in spending money until he graduated. Joe, who was engaged to be married, agreed that he would not marry until after he graduated.

On January 16, Henry wrote Landlord the following letter, which Landlord received on January 17: "Because of the love and affection which I bear my son, Joe, if you do not evict him, I will pay the rent he now owes you and will pay you his $150 rent on the first day of each month through May 1987. If I do not hear from you by January 25, I will assume that this arrangement is all right with you. (Signed) Henry Smith."

Landlord did not reply to Henry's letter and he did not evict Joe. Henry died suddenly on January 26. Joe continued to live in the apartment through May 31, 1987, but paid no more rent. He did not marry and graduated from law school. Before his death, Henry paid Joe's tuition for the spring semester, but he paid no money to either Landlord or Joe.

Joe asked Henry's executor for the $400 in spending money, but the executor refused to pay it. Joe brought suit against the estate, asking for a judgment of $400 ($100 spending money for each of the four months, February through May). In this action, Joe will be

A. Successful.

B. Unsuccessful, because his contract with Henry was illegal.

C. Unsuccessful, because Henry's death terminated the offer.

D. Unsuccessful, because his contract with Henry was not in writing and signed by Henry.

5. Buyer and Seller (both merchants) agree over the phone that Seller will sell the Buyer 500 metal tubes at $5 each. Buyer informs the Seller that the tubes will be incorporated into one of his products. The parties do not discuss Buyer's remedies in the event of Seller's default. The next day, Seller sends a "Confirmation" to Buyer. The confirmation recites the quantity and price, but states that in the event of a breach by Seller, the Buyer's only remedy is to return the defective goods and recover the purchase price. Seller ships the tubes to Buyer, which accepts delivery and incorporates the tubes into one of its products. Subsequently, Buyer finds that the tubes are defective and the products are unsaleable. Buyer sues and seeks to recover damages.

Which of the following is correct?

A. Buyer can recover its damages because the remedies limitation in the Confirmation was a material alteration of the oral agreement.

B. Buyer can recover its damages because the default terms of the UCC apply unless the parties' writings agree on a different term.

C. Seller will prevail because the limitation on remedies in his Confirmation was a condition that Buyer accepted by accepting delivery.

D. Seller will prevail because Buyer did not object to limitation on remedies within a reasonable time.

6. Paul, a job printer, called Seller and asked for the price of "two tons of 50 lb. white paper." Seller told Paul he would calculate the price and then responded, via a signed letter dated April 1, "our price for the next three weeks will be 52¢ per pound." One week later, Seller sent another letter to Paul. It stated that because of a devastating forest fire,

the price of the paper would be raised to 80¢ per pound. One week after Seller's second letter, Paul sent a signed letter to Seller stating, "I accept your offer of paper at 52 cents in your April 1 letter. Please ship two tons ASAP."

If Paul attempts to enforce the original offer against Seller, it is most likely that

A. Paul will prevail because Seller's April 1 letter was a firm, nonrevocable offer.

B. Seller will prevail if his performance has become commercially impracticable.

C. Seller will prevail unless Paul has committed printing jobs in reliance on Seller's April 1 offer.

D. Seller will prevail because the April 1 letter was not an offer but a price quotation.

7. Neff and Owens owned adjoining residences in Smithville. In May, they hired a contractor to lay a continuous sidewalk running in front of both their homes. Each man was to pay the contractor for that part of the work measured by the width of his property. After he had paid the bill that the contractor submitted to him, Neff reasonably (but erroneously) became convinced that the contractor had mistakenly charged him for labor and materials that were used for that part of the sidewalk in front of Owens's home. Neff asked Owens to reimburse him for the amount that he thought he had erroneously paid the contractor. After a lengthy discussion, and although he believed that he owed Neff nothing, Owens finally said: "I want to avoid trouble, so if you agree to forgo the money, I'll hire a caretaker to keep our sidewalks free of ice and snow this winter." Neff orally agreed.

Owens decided to go to Florida for the winter. He left without hiring anyone to remove snow and ice in front of either property. When the first snow fell and the sidewalk was not cleared, Neff cleaned his own sidewalk and then kept it clean the rest of the winter. Was Owens's promise to hire a caretaker supported by consideration?

A. Yes.

B. No, because Owens did not believe that Neff had a valid claim.

C. No, because Neff's claim was groundless.

D. No, because the agreement between Neff and Owens was not in writing.

8. Buyer and Seller are both merchants. Buyer sends Seller a Purchase Order for 100 9″ clamps. Seller responds with its *pro forma* "Acknowledgment," stating that it will fill Buyer's order with 100 assorted 9 to 9½″ clamps. Most of the time, 9½″ clamps can be used in lieu of 9″ clamps. Seller ships the clamps, and Buyer accepts them, assuming that the clamps will be adequate for his job. However, Buyer finds that only clamps measuring exactly 9″ will fit the job. He returns the clamps and sues Seller. Which of the following is the most likely result?

   A. Buyer will prevail since Seller's Acknowledgment was not part of the contract.

   B. Buyer will prevail because Seller's Acknowledgment materially altered the contract.

   C. Seller will prevail because Buyer accepted the terms of Acknowledgment by accepting the goods.

   D. Seller will prevail because the difference in the size of the clamp did not constitute a material alteration of the Buyer's original offer.

9. On February 1, Oliver sends a signed letter to Bill. In the letter, Oliver offers to sell his home on Linington Street for $100,000. The letter goes on to include all other material terms. The letter closes, "I must have your notice of acceptance no later than March 1." On the morning of March 1, Bill mails a letter of acceptance to Oliver, along with a certified check for $100,000. Bill's letter states, "I accept your offer and enclose my check. You must convey clean title." Oliver receives the letter on March 3. Oliver does not respond to Bill's letter or deposit the check. On March 10, Bill decides he doesn't want the house after all and advises Oliver in writing that his acceptance is revoked and that he has stopped payment on his check. Oliver sues Bill for specific performance. The court is likely to decide in favor of

   A. Bill, because his acceptance was untimely.

   B. Bill, because requiring clean title made his letter a counteroffer.

   C. Oliver, because Bill accepted his unconditional offer in writing without adding a material change.

   D. Oliver, because Bill's letter of revocation was not sent in a timely manner.

10. Axel wrote to Grant: "Please ship 175 Model X Hearing Aids at catalog price. . . ." Grant shipped 175 Model Y Hearing Aids, which are superficially similar to Model X but have different working parts. Model Y is an obsolete model with no market demand. On tender of delivery, Axel discovered the discrepancy and demanded that Grant deliver Model X Hearing Aids. Grant refused.

    If Axel sues for breach of contract, what result?

    A. Grant wins, because there was no meeting of the minds.

    B. Grant wins because his shipment was a counteroffer that Axel rejected.

    C. Axel wins, because the offeror is master of his offer.

    D. Axel wins, because Grant's shipment of Model Y Hearing Aids constituted an acceptance of Axel's offer to buy.

11. Seller and Buyer agree by phone that Seller will sell Buyer 450 widgets at $1.00 each. The widgets will be delivered by Seller to Buyer within one month. One week later, Seller learns that a strike at the processing plant will result in a price increase to him. Seller phones Buyer and demands $1.25 per widget to perform the contract. Buyer agrees to pay the increase. The Seller delivers, and Buyer accepts delivery. Seller invoices the Buyer at the new price, but Buyer sends a check for $450. With his check, he sends a note reading, "We had a deal, and you had no right to change it. I agreed only because I had to have the widgets and you left me no choice." Seller sues Buyer for the difference.

    Based on these facts, it is most likely that

    A. Seller will prevail because performance of the contract at the original price became commercially impracticable.

    B. Seller will prevail because he had a good faith reason for the price increase.

    C. Buyer will prevail because he received no consideration for the increased price.

    D. Buyer will prevail because the contract as modified fell within the Statute of Frauds, but no writing signed by Buyer records the modification.

12. Jack loaned $1,000 to his friend Lawrence. When the loan became due, Jack did not ask for the money and Lawrence did not offer it. Neither spoke of the loan again. Five years later, after the statute of limitations had expired, Jack died. The executor of Jack's estate found the promissory note among his papers and wrote a letter to

Lawrence, demanding payment. Lawrence replied that he would not only pay the entire loan, but also all the required interest (3% per annum) within six months. The letter was signed by Lawrence. On the designated payment date, Lawrence wrote to the executor, "I've consulted with a lawyer and he tells me I don't have to pay the note because the statute of limitations had run when Jack died. After all, Jack never asked me to pay it."

If Jack's executor sues Lawrence, the most likely result is that

A. The executor will prevail because he is not bound by the statute of limitations.

B. The executor will prevail because Lawrence acknowledged his debt in the letter.

C. The executor will not prevail because there was no new consideration for the promise of repayment.

D. The executor will not prevail because the statute of limitations on the debt had expired prior to Jack's death.

13. Paul walks past a building that is under construction. Dan is about six feet behind Paul when he notices a loose brick falling from the top of the building. Dan rushes at Paul and pushes him in the back to get him out of the brick's path. The brick misses Paul but shatters Dan's hand and forearm. Grateful for Dan's help in avoiding a blow that might have killed him, Paul comforts Dan as he lies on the sidewalk, writhing in pain. He says, "You saved my life. I'll never be able to repay you, but I will pay all your hospital and medical expenses. And I'll pay whatever income you lose while you're mending." In too much pain to speak, Dan nods.

Under the Restatement (Second) of Contracts, it is most likely that

A. Dan will prevail because it would be unjust not to enforce Paul's promise.

B. Paul will prevail because he did not request Dan's assistance.

C. Paul will prevail because there was no consideration for his promise to Dan.

D. Paul will prevail because Dan did not unequivocally accept his offer.

Questions 14–15 are based on the following fact situation:

On December 20, Carl, the owner of Carl's Coffee Shop, entered into a written contract with Dan, owner of Dan's Doughnut Factory, under which Carl agreed to purchase from Dan all his doughnut requirements for the next calendar year. The contract provided that "Carl shall have no obligation to accept any specified quantity of doughnuts, but only all his daily requirements" and that Dan "agrees to supply your requirements" at a fixed price per dozen specified in the contract, "cash on delivery." During the year, Carl's requirements of doughnuts averaged approximately 50 dozen per week.

14. The parties renewed the contract for a second year. After three months, Dan experienced a rise in his costs and decided he could no longer afford to supply Carl's requirements at the price fixed in their agreement.

    If Dan asserts that the agreement is not binding on him because of lack of consideration, will Dan prevail?

    A. Yes, because requirements contracts lack mutuality of obligation.

    B. Yes, because the provision that Carl had no obligation to accept any specified quantity made the contract illusory.

    C. No, because requirements contracts do not need consideration to be enforceable.

    D. No, because Carl's agreement to buy his requirements was sufficient consideration for Dan's agreement to supply those requirements.

15. Assume instead of the facts in Question 14 that six months into the second year of the contract, Carl opened "Carl's Coffee Shop No. 2" in a new office building. In the previous four months, Carl had ordered an average of 50 dozen doughnuts per week from Dan. The first week after the opening of the second shop, he ordered 75 dozen doughnuts, explaining that he needed the larger quantity for the two shops. Dan refused to supply any more than 50 dozen at the price fixed in the agreement.

    Is Dan justified in his refusal?

    A. Yes, because Carl demanded an unreasonably large increase over the prior needs.

    B. Yes, because the opening of Carl's Coffee Shop No. 2 was an unanticipated occurrence that excused Dan from his contract with Carl.

    C. No, because the agreement provided that Dan would supply Carl's requirements of doughnuts at the fixed price.

    D. No, if in opening Carl's Coffee Shop No. 2, Carl relied on his requirements contract with Dan.

16. Joan (a consumer) purchased a three-piece living room set from Norton, Inc., a local dealer. Norton presented Joan with a three-page agreement, signed by Norton's president at the foot of the document,

above a signature line under which his name was typed. Joan signed the contract on a line parallel to the president's after her name was typed underneath. On page 2, the contract contained a clause that stated that it could not be modified, except in a writing signed by both parties. Joan did not place her signature or her initials alongside this clause. Joan paid for the set by paying $200 down and agreeing to pay an additional $500 in five monthly installments. She paid the first two installments and then noticed a long tear in the back of a sofa. She went to the store and demanded a refund. Norton suggested instead that they reduce the remaining payments to $50 per month instead of $100. Joan agreed but refused to make any further payments. Norton sued for $300.

Based on these facts, what is the likely result?

A. Norton will prevail because the agreement to reduce the price was not in writing.

B. Joan will prevail because she was not bound by the no-oral-modification clause.

C. Norton will prevail because Joan signed the agreement.

D. Norton will prevail because there was no consideration for its agreement to reduce the price.

17. Ben applied to ABC Bank for a loan to expand his florist business. ABC agreed in writing to make the loan. The writing specified that the loan would be repaid within six months, at interest of 10% per annum, a legal rate in that state. The writing was countersigned by Ben. Before the closing and delivery of the funds, however, the loan officer indicated that ABC might need the guarantee of Joe Smith, Ben's wealthy uncle. Ben verbally assured the officer that the guaranty would be "no problem." The loan closed without the guarantee. The next day, the officer called Ben and informed him that Joe Smith's guarantee was necessary after all. Ben approached Joe with ABC's standard guarantee form and requested his signature. Joe signed the guarantee and Ben delivered it to ABC. Despite the infusion of funds, Ben's business has failed, and he is unable to repay the loan. ABC asks Joe to honor his guarantee. Joe refuses to pay, and ABC sues.

If we construe these facts under the Restatement (Second) of Contracts and the Uniform Commercial Code:

A. ABC will prevail because of the relationship between Joe and Ben.

B. ABC will prevail because no consideration was necessary for the execution of the guarantee.

C. Joe Smith will prevail because there was no consideration for the guarantee executed by him.

D. Joe Smith will prevail because ABC closed the loan before asking for the guarantee.

Questions 18–22 are based on the following fact situation:

Anna, the owner of a nightclub, booked Sam, a famous entertainer, for the week beginning July 1. His surgeon advised that Sam would not be able to perform until August 1. On June 21, Anna sent the following telegram to Ella, Bella, and Stella, three other famous performers.

> Sam too ill to perform during the July 1 week. Desperately need replacement act. You must arrive no later than June 29 to give the band time to rehearse with you. Money no object as all performances already sold out. /s/ Anna.

18. Assume that Ella received her wire on June 22 and immediately wired back: "On my way. Hope I get a better room than you provided last time. /s/ Ella." After Ella sent her wire, but before Anna received it, Anna learned from Sam's surgeon that Sam had recovered and could perform July 1 after all. Anna immediately telephoned Ella and told her she was not needed because Sam had recovered.

    If Ella asserts a claim against Anna and Anna defends on the ground that there was no effective acceptance of her offer, who will prevail?

    A. Ella, because her acceptance was dispatched prior to Anna's revocation of her offer.

    B. Ella, because Anna's revocation was not communicated in the same form as Anna's offer.

    C. Anna, because Ella's response failed to state any performance fee.

    D. Anna, because Ella's response added a new term to the offer, which Anna was free to reject.

19. Assume the same facts as in question 18. Anna defends on the ground that her wire was not intended as an offer because it was sent to three people and she needed only one replacement act. Will this defense succeed?

    A. Yes, because Anna did not intend to hire more than one performer.

    B. Yes, if Anna did not intend to make an offer.

    C. No, because Anna assumed the risk that more than one person might accept.

    D. No, if Ella was the first person to respond to the wire.

20. Assume the same facts as in question 18. Anna defends on the ground that Sam's recovery was a changed circumstance that excused her from liability to Ella. Will this defense succeed?

    A. Yes, because Sam's continuing illness was a condition to Ella's employment.

    B. Yes, because illness in personal service contracts operates to excuse performance.

    C. No, because Anna's contract with Ella superseded the agreement with Sam.

    D. No, because Anna did not condition her offer to the others on Sam's continued incapacity and, therefore, the risk of his recovery was assumed by her.

21. Assume for this question that a valid contract was formed between Ella and Anna, and that Sam recovered and insisted on performing. Assume further that Anna refused to allow Ella to perform on the same bill as Sam, but, instead, offered to employ Ella, at a salary of $3,000 for the week, to perform in a less prestigious nightclub that Anna also owned. Ella's usual salary for a one-week engagement is $5,000, and this is the sum she would have demanded for replacing Sam. Ella refused to perform in Anna's other nightclub and was unable to obtain another booking for the week. Anna paid Sam $10,000 for his one-week performance.

    How much is Ella entitled to recover for Anna's breach?

    A. $3,000

    B. $5,000

    C. $10,000

    D. Nothing

22. Assume that Stella, one of the other performers, received one of the three wires sent by Anna. Without communicating with Anna, Stella canceled a previous booking for the week of July 1 and appeared personally at the door of Anna's nightclub on June 29, stating: "Here I am. You knew you could count on me to help you out." Anna told Stella that Sam had recovered and was scheduled to perform. Anna said, "When I didn't hear from you, I decided you weren't coming." If Stella sues Anna, who will prevail?

    A. Stella, because she could reasonably interpret Anna's wire as an offer permitting acceptance by performance.

    B. Stella, because she canceled her previous booking.

C. Anna, because her wire should reasonably have been understood as requiring a communication before Stella's appearance.

D. Anna, because an offer can only be accepted by a return promise.

23. Corey has just graduated from high school and is about to take a job at a beer factory. Corey's grandfather, Alex, tells Corey that he wants him to go to college. He says, "If you'll go to college instead of taking that no-end job at the beer factory, I'll pay your tuition, and, if you get all A's, I'll buy you a new car." Corey enrolls at the local college, where he gets a B average. When Corey asks Alex for the tuition and the car, the older man says, "I never meant to give you the money or the car. But think what I've done for you. You know now that you can get good grades and a decent education. That's my gift to you."

    Corey consults you and asks whether he has a cause of action against Alex. You will advise him:

    A. You can recover your tuition payments, but not the purchase price for a new vehicle.

    B. You can recover the purchase price of a new vehicle, but not your tuition expenses.

    C. You have no cause of action because there was no consideration for your grandfather's promise.

    D. You have no cause of action because your grandfather's promise was not in writing.

24. Two years ago, Paul made a loan of $10,000 to Frank. The purpose of the loan was to enable Frank to expand his restaurant business. After six months, the business failed and Frank himself was having difficulty paying his debts. When Paul threatened to sue Frank to collect the outstanding principal and interest, Frank told Paul that he was virtually insolvent but would pay Paul 60% of the amount due if Paul would agree to release the balance of his claim against Frank. Paul agreed to accept Frank's offer. Paul prepared a document confirming the offer, and Frank and Paul both signed it. Paul has asked Frank for the money several times, but he has failed to pay any part of it. Paul consults you about his rights. You would advise him:

    A. You may disregard the agreement to accept 60% of the debt and sue for the full amount because there was no consideration for your agreement.

B. You may sue only for the 60% set forth in the settlement agreement because it did not require consideration.

C. You may sue for the full amount because you did not receive any security from Frank under the new agreement.

D. You may sue only for the 60% in the settlement agreement because Frank is insolvent and can file for bankruptcy.

25. Bob sells radios. His friend and neighbor of more than ten years, Arthur, is a C.P.A. Bob puts a note in Arthur's mailbox. It reads, "You've asked me if I'll sell my '87 Volvo. I'll sell it to you for $2,000. I'll keep this offer open for two weeks." A week later, Bob has not heard from Arthur, so he puts another note in Arthur's box. It reads, "I have to cancel my offer on the Volvo. My Toyota's transmission is gone, so I need the Volvo." Arthur immediately knocks on Bob's door and says, "You can't go back on your offer. You said it was good for two weeks, and I want the Volvo. Here's your $2,000." Arthur tenders a check for $2,000 to Bob and demands the car.

On these facts, if Arthur commences an action for specific performance of the transaction, it is most likely that

A. Bob will prevail because he revoked his offer for good reasons.

B. Bob will prevail because there was no consideration for his promise to keep the offer open for two weeks.

C. Arthur will prevail because Bob's offer was binding as an option contract.

D. Arthur will prevail because Bob's offer was a firm offer not subject to revocation.

Questions 26–28 are based on the following fact situation:

Tom is a teacher of numismatics. He is an acknowledged expert in coins and their value. His collection is worth thousands of dollars. Tom regularly buys and sells coins. Jim, who had no prior experience with coins, inherited a sizable coin collection. Jim opened "Coin Shop" in a local shopping center.

26. Assume that on June 1, Jim advertised in the local newspaper as follows: "Special sale. Coins on sale at 10% over their face value." In response to this ad, Tom visited Jim's shop and saw in a display case a 50-cent coin that Tom recognized as having a value of $100. Tom tendered 55 cents to Jim, but Jim refused to sell the coin. Jim said that the coin had already been sold to Zeke for $100 prior to the start of the special sale, but that Jim had forgotten to remove it from the display case.

Tom sued Jim for damages. What result?

A. Jim wins because the ad was not an offer.

B. Jim wins because 55 cents was not sufficient consideration for a coin worth $100.

C. Tom wins because he relied on the ad in traveling to Jim's shop.

D. Tom wins because Jim's ad was an offer that Tom accepted when he tendered the 55 cents to purchase the coin.

27. Assume that Tom telephoned Jim and learned that Jim owned 50 silver dollars minted in 1937. Jim agreed to sell them to Tom for $1,000, which sum Tom agreed to pay in advance of shipment. Following the conversation, Jim sent Tom this letter: "This confirms your purchase of 50 silver dollars. On receipt of your check for $1,000, the coins will be shipped to you as agreed. /s/ Jim." Tom received the letter, but did not respond to it and did not pay the $1,000. A month later, Jim sued Tom, who asserted the Statute of Frauds as a defense. Will this defense succeed?

A. No, because the letter signed by Jim satisfies the writing requirement against Tom.

B. No, because the face value of the coins is less than $5,000.

C. Yes, because there is no writing signed by Tom.

D. Yes, because a memorandum signed after the contract is made does not satisfy the Statute of Frauds.

28. Assume the same facts as in question 27. Tom defends on the ground that there was no legally sufficient consideration for his promise to pay $1,000. Will this defense succeed?

A. Yes, because a court will not enforce a promise to pay $1,000 for coins with a face value of $50.

B. Yes, because Jim did not change his position in reliance on the promise of Tom to pay $1,000.

C. No, because Jim's promise to sell the coins was sufficient consideration.

D. No, because both Tom and Jim are merchants, and contracts between merchants do not require consideration.

29. Landlord hires Painter to paint the outside of his office building. Painter agrees to accomplish the task within one month. A week later, Painter becomes ill and asks his friend, Arthur, to finish the work. When Landlord visits the premises, he sees Arthur painting the

building. Landlord has seen Arthur paint other buildings in the area and he assumes that Arthur is an employee of Painter. After the job is finished, Landlord visits the premises and finds that a large section is not painted, that the color in some places is wrong, and that part of the surface is peeling. Landlord suspects that Arthur is judgment proof and wants to sue Painter. He asks for your advice. You review the facts and conclude:

A. Landlord will prevail against Painter because Painter is still liable under the original contract.

B. Landlord will prevail because Painter was not authorized to delegate his duties to Arthur.

C. Painter will prevail because construction and repair contracts are delegable.

D. Painter will prevail because Landlord accepted a novation of duties when he saw Arthur at work and did not complain.

30. Joe and Bill live on the same street. One day, Joe notices a deep dent in his car door. Checking around, he notices that Carl, Bill's teenage son, has a dent in his car as well. Joe concludes that Carl struck Joe's car when he drove out of his driveway. Joe confronts Bill with his suspicions. Bill tells Joe that he will pay to have Joe's car repaired at a body shop. Joe agrees. Later that night, Bill questions Carl about the dents. Carl insists that the dent in his car occurred when he hit a pole in his employer's parking lot. He shows Bill the accident report he submitted to his employer and establishes that the dent was caused by a car with a different paint color. In the meantime, Joe takes his car to the body shop and has the dent repaired. Bill now refuses to pay for Joe's repairs.

If Joe sues Bill for the cost of the repairs, it is most likely that

A. Joe will prevail because Bill's promise is enforceable.

B. Bill will prevail because both parties mistakenly believed Carl caused the dent.

C. Bill will prevail for lack of consideration because Carl did not cause the dent.

D. Bill will prevail because his agreement with Joe was oral.

31. Builder and Owner verbally agreed that Builder would install a driveway leading to Owner's garage for $5,000. The job was to be completed in one month, at which point Owner would pay Builder in full. Builder asked Jonathan to supply him with the cement he

needed for $1,000. Jonathan agreed, and Builder wrote a memo to Owner, instructing him to pay $1,000 of the sum due him directly to Jonathan. Builder completed the job on schedule, but the work was defective and unacceptable to Owner. Owner refuses to pay either Builder or Jonathan.

If Jonathan sues Owner, the likely result is that

A. Jonathan will prevail even if Builder did not perform his work in a reasonably competent manner, as long as Jonathan supplied concrete in a competent manner.

B. Owner will prevail if Builder did not perform his work in a reasonably competent way.

C. Owner will prevail because Builder could not assign his right to payment before the work was finished.

D. Owner will prevail because the contract involves land and there was no writing.

Questions 32–35 are based on the following fact situation:

Youth is a 17-year-old boy who has been buying and selling bicycles since he was 11. Teller is a 25-year-old bank teller who has never bought a bicycle before. Teller asked Youth if he had a bicycle to sell. Youth showed Teller a bicycle with a slight crack in the frame. Teller asked if the slight crack would impair the bicycle's utility, and Youth said, "Not a bit." In fact, the crack would probably cause the frame to collapse after very little use. Youth knew this, but Teller did not. Teller said, "Very well, I'll pay you $100 for the bicycle and pick it up tomorrow." They both signed a writing, prepared by Youth, which purported to memorialize the terms of their agreement. Later that day, Teller learned that the crack would probably cause the frame to collapse after little use.

32. If Teller tells Youth he will not accept the bicycle and Youth asserts a claim against Teller for damages for breach of contract, who will prevail?

A. Teller, because Youth is a minor and lacks capacity to contract.

B. Teller, because he relied on a material misrepresentation.

C. Youth, because the contract is voidable only at Youth's election.

D. Youth, because Teller's reliance on Youth's statement was not reasonable.

33. Assume that Teller says to Youth, "I know the crack can cause a problem, but that's all right. I can have it welded and it will work well enough." Teller demands the bicycle, but Youth refuses, saying he has changed his mind about selling. Teller asserts a claim against

Youth for damages for refusing to deliver the bicycle. Who will prevail?

A. Teller, because he has waived his right to avoid the agreement.

B. Teller, because even a minor is responsible for his misrepresentations.

C. Youth, because as a minor he can avoid liability on an executory contract.

D. Youth, because Teller could not waive his right to avoid the agreement.

34. Assume the writing prepared by Youth purports to describe the bicycle by serial number, but Youth mistakenly inserts serial number 100B, the number of another bicycle in his possession, instead of number 100A, the number of the bicycle at issue. No one notices the error until the time of delivery. The bicycle designated by serial number 100B is the same model as the one Teller agreed to buy, but it does not have a cracked frame. Youth delivers the bicycle with the cracked frame, the one bearing the serial number 100A, but Teller refuses to accept it. Youth then tenders the sound bicycle, with serial number 100B, but Teller also refuses to accept it.

    If Youth asserts a claim against Teller for damages for breach of contract to accept the bicycle with serial number 100B, who will prevail?

    A. Youth, because the parol evidence rule bars evidence that the bicycle identified in the writing is not the one Teller agreed to accept.

    B. Youth, because the bicycle identified in the writing is a fair exchange for $100, while the bicycle with the cracked frame was not.

    C. Teller, because parol evidence is admissible to show that he never agreed to accept the bicycle identified as 100B.

    D. Teller, because the writing was not a sufficient memorandum to satisfy the Statute of Frauds.

35. Assume the same facts as in question 34, except that at the time the writing was signed, Teller knew that the wrong serial number was contained in the writing. Teller demands the bicycle identified in the writing as 100B, but Youth refuses to deliver it.

    If Teller asserts a claim against Youth for damages for breach of contract for refusing to deliver the bicycle with serial number 100B, who will prevail?

    A. Youth, because there was a mutual mistake.

B. Youth, because there was no agreement to sell the bicycle identified in the writing as serial number 100B.

C. Teller, because the mistake was Youth's unilateral mistake.

D. Teller, because the parol evidence rule bars evidence that the bicycle identified in the writing as number 100B is not the one Youth agreed to sell.

36. Seller entered into a written agreement with Buyer. Seller agreed to provide 5,000 widgets to Buyer at a price of $7,500. A few days later, Seller assigned in writing to Bradley "all of my rights under my contract with Buyer for the sale of widgets." Bradley was another widget distributor with an excellent business reputation. The assignment did not contain an assumption by Bradley of Seller's obligations under the contract. Bradley failed to deliver the widgets to Buyer on time, and Buyer was unable to complete a job requiring the widgets.

    If Buyer sues Bradley, the result will be:

    A. Bradley will prevail because he never expressly agreed to assume Seller's duties under the Buyer/Seller agreement.

    B. Bradley will prevail because he was not in privity of contract with Buyer.

    C. Buyer will prevail because Buyer is a third party beneficiary under the agreement between Seller and Bradley.

    D. Buyer will prevail because Bradley indemnified Seller.

Questions 37–38 are based on the following fact situation:

Buyer was in the business of selling home furniture. Recognizing the increase in home offices, Buyer decided to add office desks and chairs to his catalog. He entered into a one-year agreement with Seller. Seller agreed to fill all orders submitted by Buyer at a cost 10% below the wholesale price quoted in Seller's catalogue. Buyer prepared and distributed flyers and brochures offering the chairs and desks at the prices listed, but before Buyer could submit his first order, Seller notified Buyer in writing that the contract was "canceled." Buyer now had several orders for the desks and chairs and was forced to purchase them from another wholesaler at a considerably higher price.

37. In an action by Buyer against Seller, the most likely outcome is that

    A. Seller will prevail because there was no consideration for its promise to deliver.

    B. Buyer will prevail because he relied on a constant source of supplies in advertising and promoting his new inventory.

    C. Seller will prevail because the desks and chairs had not previously been sold by Buyer and his future sales could not be calculated or estimated.

D. Seller will prevail because Buyer has found another source of goods and can adjust his price to his customers to avoid any loss or damage.

38. Assume the same facts as in question 37, except that Buyer is the party canceling the contract instead of Seller.

What result?

A. Seller will prevail because the contract is sufficiently definite as to its material terms.

B. Seller will prevail because Buyer has an obligation to use his best efforts to sell the desks and chairs.

C. Buyer will prevail because it is impossible to determine its requirements with reasonable certainty.

D. Buyer will prevail because a crucial element of a purchase contract, the price, cannot be fixed with certainty.

39. Joe was a highly successful tire manufacturer. He sold most of his production to Rubberco. When Rubberco's requirements increased, it suggested to Joe that he expand his facilities. Joe asked ABC for a loan to finance the expansion. ABC reviewed Joe's earning records and decided it could not make the loan without a supporting guarantee. Joe asked Rubberco to act as guarantor. Rubberco called ABC, where it had a substantial account, and told the bank officer, "Don't worry, we'll be responsible for Joe's loan." Without asking for a written guarantee, ABC made a loan to Joe of $100,000.

If Joe is unable to repay the loan, can ABC recover the loan from Rubberco?

A. Yes, if it can show that it would not have made the loan but for Rubberco's statement.

B. Yes, because Rubberco guaranteed payment of the loan.

C. No, because Rubberco did not guarantee the loan in writing.

D. No, because Rubberco's words were not the language of guarantee.

40. Seller and Buyer entered into an agreement providing for the sale of Seller's home at 2000 Westbury Court. Seller and Buyer had orally agreed that the sales price of $100,000 would include all of the furniture at the premises. The written agreement between the parties was prepared by Seller's attorney and reviewed by Buyer's attorney. Among other provisions, the contract read: "This agreement constitutes the entire agreement of the parties, there being no other agreements or

understandings pertaining to the purchase." Title closed, and Buyer paid the purchase price. When he arrived at the premises, he found that all the furniture had been removed.

Buyer sues to recover the reasonable value of the furniture. What result?

A. Seller will prevail because the written agreement makes no reference to the furniture.

B. Seller will prevail because the Buyer is estopped under the quoted provision from introducing any evidence as to the furniture.

C. Buyer will prevail because furniture is generally assumed to be included in the sale of a private residence.

D. Buyer will prevail because extrinsic evidence is always admissible to prove a mistake in a written agreement.

Questions 41–45 are based on the following fact situation:

Daniel and Paul were involved in an automobile accident. Paul sued Daniel for $10,000, alleging that Daniel was negligent. Each party claims to have had the green light. Of the two other witnesses, one was prepared to testify that Paul had the green light. Before trial, Daniel offered Paul $5,000 to settle all claims arising from the accident. Paul accepted the offer.

41. Assume that before payment of the $5,000 and before dismissal of the suit, Daniel repudiates his promise to pay Paul $5,000. Paul amends his complaint to ask for $5,000. What result?

A. Paul wins because the agreement was an enforceable compromise of a disputed claim.

B. Paul wins because Daniel's promise to pay $5,000 was enforceable without consideration.

C. Daniel wins because his promise did not specify when payment was to be made.

D. Daniel wins because his promise was void as against public policy.

42. Assume the same facts as in question 41, except that, instead of amending his complaint to sue for $5,000, Paul prosecuted his $10,000 negligence action. Daniel defended on the ground that his liability, if any, has been replaced by his promise to pay $5,000. What result on this defense?

A. Paul wins because the promise to pay $5,000 was void from the outset.

B. Paul wins because, after Daniel repudiated his promise, Paul had the option to sue on that promise or on the original claim.

C. Daniel wins because there is a presumption that the parties intended a substituted agreement.

D. Daniel wins because his promise to pay $5,000 is enforceable without consideration.

43. Assume that after Daniel promises to pay $5,000 but before the payment is made, Paul dismisses his negligence suit. Paul's witness then admits to Daniel that the traffic light was green in Daniel's favor. Paul does not learn that the witness lied until Daniel tells him. Daniel now refuses to pay Paul, and Paul sues Daniel for $5,000. What result?

A. Daniel wins because his promise was conditioned on his belief that he was liable to Paul.

B. Daniel wins because the new evidence constitutes a failure of consideration for Daniel's promise to pay $5,000.

C. Paul wins because the settlement was an accord and satisfaction.

D. Paul wins because he did not know the witness was lying when he accepted Daniel's offer in settlement of his claim.

44. Assume that after Daniel promised to pay the $5,000, Paul dismissed the negligence suit. When Daniel suffered a large business reversal and was unable to pay the $5,000, Paul threatened to sue Daniel. On learning these facts, Ted told Paul, "Daniel is an old friend of mine. If you will not sue him, I will pay you the $5,000." Paul said, "Okay," and did not file suit against Daniel. A week later, Ted repudiated his promise to Paul. Paul sued Ted for $5,000. What result?

A. Ted wins because there was no consideration for his promise.

B. Ted wins because Paul must recover against Daniel before he can sue Ted.

C. Paul wins because his agreement not to sue Daniel is sufficient consideration for Ted's promise.

D. Paul wins because Ted's friendship with Daniel is sufficient consideration for Ted's promise.

45. Assume the same facts as in question 44, except that Ted defended on the ground of the Statute of Frauds. What result on this defense?

A. Ted wins because his promise was to pay an amount in excess of $500 and was not evidenced by a writing signed by Ted.

B. Ted wins because his promise was to pay the debt of another and was not evidenced by a writing signed by Ted.

C. Paul wins because Ted's promise was not one required to be evidenced by a writing signed by Ted.

D. Paul wins because his forbearance to sue Daniel constituted part performance.

46. ABC Co. and XYZ Corp., both dealers in hardware, agree over the phone that XYZ will purchase 500 couplings from ABC at $4.00 per coupling. The parties exchange the usual Purchase Order and Confirmation confirming the terms of sale, including price and delivery date. There is no mention in either document of payment terms except for the usual "net 30 days." ABC delivers the couplings on time. Two days later, XYZ issues a check in payment of the price less a 10% discount "for early payment." ABC calls immediately and demands payment of the remaining balance ($200). XYZ replies, "What are you talking about? All we did was take the discount the whole industry takes for early payment. We're not required to pay for 30 days." It is, in fact, the custom in the industry to take a 10% discount if payment is made in the first 10 days after delivery.

    If ABC sues XYZ for the discounted amount:

    A. XYZ will prevail because a buyer of goods can always take a discount for early payment.

    B. XYZ will prevail if it is the custom in the hardware industry to permit a 10% discount for payment within 10 days after invoice.

    C. ABC will prevail because the parol evidence rule precludes XYZ from introducing evidence of industry payment practices.

    D. ABC will prevail because the parties never discussed an early payment discount.

47. Buyer, a wholesale distributor, enters into a requirements contract with Universal Power. The agreement provides that, for one year, Buyer will supply all of the metal tables and chairs needed by Universal. Buyer usually purchases its tables and chairs from Metalco, a local manufacturer. Buyer calls Metalco and learns that Metalco's plant has been destroyed by fire. Buyer immediately calls Steelco and orders the goods he needs for Universal's first order. He agrees to pay Steelco 50% of the first order immediately, and the other one-half when Universal pays Buyer (30 days later). Buyer picks up the goods and delivers them to Universal. Before Universal can pay Buyer, it files for bankruptcy and cannot pay Buyer.

    If Steelco sues Buyer for the balance, it is likely that

    A. Buyer will prevail because payment to him by Universal was a condition precedent to his payment to Steelco.

B. Buyer will prevail because Universal's inability to pay excuses his performance.

C. Steelco will prevail because the provision for payment by Universal controlled only the time of payment and was not a condition precedent.

D. Steelco will prevail because the second payment was merely an installment of the price that Buyer confirmed by paying the first installment.

48. Autocorp is a manufacturer of auto parts. Transco sends Autocorp a Purchase Order for 500 cables at $10 per cable. The last paragraph of the order reads, "If this order is acceptable, please sign and fax a copy back to us today. We need to know you have goods." Autocorp countersigns the order and puts it in the night's mail. Before the mail reaches Transco, it finds the cable in its own warehouse and telegraphs a notice to Autocorp canceling the order of cables. The telegraph reaches Autocorp before its mail reaches Transco. On receipt of the wire, Autocorp calls Transco and says, "We confirmed your order and are holding you to the deal." Transco replies, "We don't have a deal. I wired you my cancellation before I got your acknowledgment of my order."

In a lawsuit between the parties, what result?

A. Transco will prevail because its telegram reached Autocorp before it received Autocorp's letter.

B. Autocorp will prevail because it accepted Transco's order before the cancellation.

C. Transco will prevail because Autocorp deviated from the specified mode of acceptance.

D. Autocorp will prevail because the means of communicating an acceptance is not a material element of a contract.

49. Pubco is a publisher of travel guides. Filberts is a general bookstore. Filberts orders 5,000 copies of *Travel in France* at $8.50 per guide. Pubco acknowledged the sale in writing. Later, Pubco learned that Filberts does not intend to sell the guides in its store for $19 each (the usual domestic markup), but, instead, to sell them in Paris at $100 per guide. Pubco tells Filberts that the price of each guide is raised from $8.50 to $15.00. Filberts knows that it can buy the guides from a competitor at $10 per guide, but in its rush to fill the Paris order, it agrees to pay Pubco $15. Pubco ships the guides and Filberts accepts them but sends a check calculated at $8.50 per guide.

On these facts, if Pubco sues Filberts, it is likely that

A. Filberts will prevail because Pubco secured the modification in price in bad faith.

B. Filberts will prevail because there was no consideration for its agreement to pay the increase in price.

C. Pubco will prevail because both parties are merchants and no consideration for the modification is necessary.

D. Pubco will prevail because a seller is entitled to change the price if the buyer's margin of profit changes.

50. Owner and Builder agreed in writing that Builder would construct an additional room on Owner's home. The agreement contained a "no-oral-modification" clause. During the course of the work, Owner asked Builder how much it would cost to add one foot to the length of the room. Builder told him it would cost $1,000. Owner replied, "That sounds fine. Go ahead with the work as soon as you can." Builder calculated that he would net $300 on the extra work. That evening, Builder decided to surprise his wife by buying a new TV set. The set cost $280. The next morning, Owner met Builder on the job and advised him that he had changed his mind about lengthening the room. Builder threatens to sue Owner for $300, his lost profits.

If Builder goes ahead with his suit:

A. Builder will prevail because the oral agreement regarding the extra work was valid and enforceable.

B. Builder will prevail because he relied on the agreement to his detriment by purchasing the TV set.

C. Owner will prevail because proof of the oral agreement is barred by the parol evidence rule.

D. Owner will prevail because the written agreement barred oral modifications.

Questions 51–53 are based on the following fact situation:

Carl and Homer entered into a valid written contract under which Carl agreed to build a house on Homer's lot. Homer agreed to pay $150,000 for the house. The contract stated: "Homer's duty to pay shall not arise unless and until the house is constructed in full compliance with the attached specifications."

51. Assume that shortly after commencing performance Carl called Homer and said that the ½″ rods for the foundation required in the specifications were in short supply, but that ¼″ rods were readily available. Homer replied: "Go ahead and use the ¼″." One day later,

before Carl had bought or installed the rods, Homer called and stated that Carl must use the ½" rods. Carl refused to do so.

The best analysis of the parties' legal rights is that

A. Homer waived his right to demand ½" steel, and his waiver cannot be retracted.

B. Homer and Carl modified their contract, and Carl may use ¼" rods.

C. Homer waived his right to demand ½" rods, but he has retracted the waiver, and Carl must use ½" rods.

D. Homer's statement, "Go ahead and use the ¼"," is not effective either as a modification or a waiver because Homer did not expressly agree to modify or waive the contract.

52. Assume that the specifications required installation of a hot water heater but failed to specify the size of the heater. Carl installs a 20-gallon heater. The size of the house would reasonably require a heater of at least 40 gallons. After the house is completed, the smaller heater proves inadequate, and Homer refuses to pay the last installment due on the contract amounting to $20,000.

Carl is entitled to recover from Homer

A. Nothing because his failure to install the 40-gallon heater allows Homer to treat the contract as discharged.

B. The full contract price because the agreement did not specify the size of the water heater.

C. The full contract price because he substantially performed the contract.

D. The full contract price minus the difference in cost between a 20-gallon heater and a 40-gallon heater.

53. Assume that the contract provided that Homer's payment for the house would be due only on receipt of the architect's certification that the house was built in strict accordance with the specifications. The architect refused to issue such certification "because the fireplace was not constructed in a workmanlike manner as required by the specifications." Homer refused to pay the contract price.

If Carl insists that the fireplace was constructed in a workmanlike manner and sues for the full contract price, who will prevail?

A. Homer, unless other architects would have been satisfied with the fireplace.

B. Homer, if the architect's refusal was in good faith.

C. Carl, unless the architect's refusal to certify was both reasonable and in good faith.

D. Carl, if a reasonable person would conclude that the fireplace was constructed in a workmanlike manner.

54. Peartree Partridge agreed to pay Artist $5,000 for an oil painting of his family. He told Artist he intended to hang the portrait in his parlor "for all to see and admire." He added, "But you won't get a dime unless I'm satisfied 100%." Artist scheduled a series of sessions with the family and worked six weeks to complete the painting. While the work was in progress, Partridge made no effort to look at it. When Artist announced that the work was finished, Partridge examined it carefully and said, "This is completely unacceptable. You've made me look like a dried-up apple and my wife like a swollen pumpkin. Take it away." The other members of Partridge's family thought the portrait was accurate and a great work of art, and they urged him to keep it. Partridge refused. Artist debated whether to sue and sought the advice of his colleagues. They all agreed that the work was a masterpiece and urged him to sue.

If Artist decides to sue, the likely outcome is that

A. Artist will prevail because Partridge's dissatisfaction is unreasonable.

B. Artist will prevail because Partridge waived his right to insist on satisfaction by failing to view the work in progress.

C. Partridge will prevail because the contract provided that he be satisfied with the work.

D. Partridge will prevail because a portrait is a personal thing that cannot be forced on the subject.

55. Peter Piper is a leading auctioneer. He retains Litho to typeset and print 5,000 glossy brochures promoting an auction to be held on August 1. The price for the brochures is $5,000, to be paid on delivery of the brochures. When Seller delivers the brochures, they contain a typo showing the date for the auction as August 3. The auction is still 30 days off, and Piper asks Litho to correct the date and reprint the brochures. Litho replies that it will correct the error if Piper will pay an additional $1,000 "to cover the cost of paper." Piper refuses to pay the additional sum and tells Litho that he must have delivery of the brochures "in one week" if he is to get them out in time for the sale. Piper fails to hear from Litho within the week. Desperate to get the mail out, Piper contacts Printco, which agrees to print the brochures in six days for $7,000. Two days later, Litho

delivers corrected brochures to Piper and demands $5,000. Piper refuses the brochures, mails the brochures delivered by Printco, and pays Printco its invoice for $7,000.

In a suit between Piper and Litho:

A. Piper will prevail and recover $2,000 in damages.

B. Piper will prevail and recover $7,000 in damages.

C. Piper will prevail and recover $2,000 plus any damages resulting from the late mailing of the brochures.

D. Litho will prevail and recover $5,000.

56. Builder was building a three-story office building. He entered into an agreement with Seller, a window supplier, to deliver a specified number of windows "as needed" to the construction site. The term "as needed" was defined as "within 24 hours after notice by fax or phone." Attached to the contract was a schedule of nine separate deliveries. Builder faxed his order for the first delivery, which was late by one day. On the second order, Seller delivered windows with the wrong measurements, causing Builder to miss a construction deadline and incur a large penalty. The correct windows were delivered the following day and accepted by Builder. Fearing further costly delays, Builder notified Seller that their agreement was canceled.

If Seller sues Builder for damages, the likely result is that

A. Seller will prevail because Builder's cancellation was premature.

B. Seller will prevail because Builder waived a claim for breach by accepting both deliveries.

C. Builder will prevail because Seller's failure to make timely delivery and to deliver conforming goods were a material breach of the agreement.

D. Builder will prevail because his cancellation was proper under the "perfect tender" rule.

Questions 57–59 are based on the following fact situation:

On March 1, Seller and Buyer entered into a written contract under which Seller agreed to sell his home to Buyer, and Buyer agreed to purchase the home for the sum of $60,000. The contract specified July 1 as the closing day on which Seller was to deliver the deed and Buyer was to pay the price.

57. Assume that on April 1, Seller conveys his home to a third party. Buyer learns of the sale from a friend the following day and wants to cancel his contract with Seller and buy another home. May he do so without any risk that he will be obliged to perform his contract obligation to Seller?

A. Yes, but only if he first demands assurance from Seller that Seller will perform on July 1, and Seller is unable to provide such assurance.

B. Yes, if Seller, in connection with the sale to the third party, did nothing to preserve Buyer's rights to acquire the property.

C. No, because Seller's performance is not due until July 1 and Buyer must remain in a position to perform his contract obligation up to that time.

D. No, because there is a possibility that Seller could buy back the property and tender a deed to Buyer on July 1.

58. Assume that on April 1, Seller tells Buyer that he (Seller) has changed his mind and will not convey his home to Buyer. May Buyer immediately maintain an action for damages for breach of contract?

A. Yes, but only if Seller has sold or contracted to sell the home to another party.

B. Yes, because Seller's statement constituted a repudiation, giving rise to an immediate cause of action for breach of contract.

C. No, because Seller's performance is not due until July 1 and thus there can be no breach of contract until that date.

D. No, because Seller might retract his repudiation before July 1.

59. Assume that on July 1, Seller fails to deliver or tender the deed. May Buyer successfully maintain an immediate action against Seller for damages for breach of contract?

A. Yes, if Buyer tendered payment on July 1.

B. Yes, but only if Buyer actually made the payment on July 1.

C. Yes, whether or not Buyer tendered payment or actually paid on July 1.

D. Yes, because payment of the price by Buyer was a condition subsequent to Seller's duty to tender the deed.

60. Erik and Myron agreed in writing that Myron would build an additional room on to Erik's home. The contract required a payment of $10,000, $5,000 on the commencement of the work and the balance "on completion of the work and delivery of a completion certificate by a licensed architect." An addendum to the agreement,

signed by both parties, named Mitch Vander Hoffe as the architect. Erik paid the first $5,000 and Myron completed the work. Mitch inspected the work and refused to issue the certificate, citing numerous imperfections in the work. He estimated that $2,250 would be required to correct the imperfections. Furious with Mitch, Myron had the work inspected by Frank Paul Right, another architect, who certified that the work conformed to the contract.

In an action by Myron to recover the balance of $5,000, what result?

A. Myron will recover $5,000 because Frank certified that the work conformed to the contract.

B. Myron will recover $2,750, representing the balance of $5,000 less the amount estimated by Mitch to correct the work.

C. Myron will recover nothing because Mitch refused to issue a completion certificate.

D. Myron will recover $5,000 less the amount actually paid by Erik to another builder to correct the imperfections.

61. Bob owns a small shopping mall in Eureka. One winter's day, there is a big snowfall and the sidewalk and parking area are soon covered with snow. Bob sends his maintenance crew out to shovel the snow. Because he thinks that the law of Eureka requires him to clear both the sidewalk and the parking area, he tells his men to clear both. It's getting dark and the men clear both areas as well as they can in the dim light. Sally Smith walks on the sidewalk, slips on a piece of ice and breaks her leg. Also under the belief that Bob is responsible to clear the sidewalk, Sally threatens to sue Bob, who is uninsured. He agrees to pay Sally's medical bills. Sally's bills come to $15,000 and Bob refuses to pay her. He consults his lawyer, who advises him that the law in his state places the responsibility for clearing sidewalks on the municipality, not the property owner. Bob calls Sally and tells her, "We were both mistaken about the law. I'm not liable for your accident. You'll have to sue the City."

Sally sues Bob for damages. Who will prevail?

A. Bob will prevail because his promise was not in writing.

B. Bob will prevail because his promise was based on a mutual mistake of law.

C. Bob will prevail because there was no consideration for his promise.

D. Sally will prevail because Bob's promise was binding and enforceable.

62. Builder was hired to reconstruct a garage behind Owner's home. The agreement was in writing. After the work was completed, Owner claimed a $2,000 adjustment because the siding used by Builder was wood and not vinyl as specified in the contract. The Builder argued that wood was longer lasting and easier to maintain, and that, if anything, Owner owed him an adjustment. Their disagreement remained unresolved until Owner learned that Builder was a fellow lodge member. He called Builder and said, "Let's call it quits." Builder submitted a written release that Owner signed and delivered. Now Owner has learned that Builder is not a lodge brother after all. He reasserts his demand for an adjustment of $2,000.

What result if Owner sues Builder for $2,000?

A. Owner will prevail because he received no consideration for the release.

B. Owner will prevail because he signed the release under the mistaken assumption that Builder was a lodge brother.

C. Builder will prevail because the release is enforceable against Owner, who signed it.

D. Builder will prevail because the release was evidence that Owner no longer claimed an adjustment.

63. Orville owes Bradford $2,500 on a note which is now due. Orville has no money and is out of a job. He approaches Bradford and tells him that the only asset he has is a seven-year-old station wagon. He offers to turn the title over to Bradford if Bradford will accept it in full payment of the note. Bradford agrees. A week goes by, and Orville has not delivered the station wagon or the title. When Bradford calls Orville, Orville says, "That was a bad deal for me. I need the wagon. You'll have to wait until I can put the money together."

Bradford asks for your advice. You will probably tell him:

A. You can sue for the $2,500 but not the value of the car.

B. You can sue for the $2,500 and the value of the car.

C. You can sue for the reasonable value of the car but not the principal of the note.

D. You can sue in the alternative for payment of the note or payment of the reasonable value of the car.

Questions 64–66 are based on the following fact situation:

Barney owned a hardware store in New York. Wishing to move to a warmer climate, he entered into a written contract to buy Sampson's hardware store in Florida. The contract stated that Barney would buy Sampson's store for $125,000 "provided Barney finds a purchaser who will buy his present business for $100,000." Prior to signing the agreement, the parties had a conversation during which they agreed that because Barney would need the money, Barney's buyer would have to pay all cash. No mention of these conversations or of the all-cash understanding is contained in the written agreement. The written agreement recites that Sampson rents the building in which his store is located, under a lease with one more year to run.

64. Assume Sampson repudiates the contract soon after signing it and before Barney has made any effort to find a buyer for his present business.

    Barney sues Sampson for breach of contract and Sampson defends on the ground that his promise to sell was not supported by consideration. Will this defense succeed?

    A. Yes, because Barney's promise to buy was subject to a condition within Barney's complete control and was therefore illusory.

    B. Yes, because Barney's promise to buy was still executory.

    C. No, because the court will interpret the condition of Barney's promise as requiring Barney to make a good faith effort to find a buyer for his present business.

    D. No, because Barney's promise to sell his present business was consideration for Sampson's promise to sell his business to Barney.

65. Assume that Barney makes a diligent effort to find a buyer for his business, but the only willing buyer has only $20,000 in cash and wants Barney to take back an $80,000 mortgage. Barney calls Sampson and says, "I've got a buyer but I can't buy your business because I won't have enough cash. I'm sorry, I tried to find an all-cash buyer as we agreed orally, but no one has come forward. I won't be able to close our deal." Sampson reminds Barney that the conversations about an all-cash buyer were not incorporated in the written contract and that since Barney has found a willing buyer, he's got to go ahead with the deal. Barney refuses and Sampson sues Barney. What result?

    A. Sampson wins because the written agreement was a total integration of the parties' agreement.

    B. Barney wins because the written agreement was only a partial integration of the parties' agreement.

C. Sampson wins if the judge decides that the written agreement was a partial integration of the parties' agreement.

D. Barney wins if the judge decides that the written agreement was a partial integration of the parties' agreement.

66. Assume the agreement makes no mention of Sampson's lease. Barney refuses to perform his promise to buy Sampson's business and Sampson sues. Barney defends on the ground that after the contract was signed the parties orally agreed that Barney's obligation to buy was conditioned on Barney's obtaining a five-year extension of Sampson's lease, and that Sampson has been unsuccessful in his efforts to obtain an extension from the landlord. Sampson objects to the admission of any evidence about the oral agreement.

    Which of the following arguments can Barney make to support his evidence?

    A. The evidence is offered to clear up an ambiguity in the writing.

    B. The evidence is offered to show a subsequent modification of a written contract.

    C. Without the modification, the written agreement would be unconscionable.

    D. The evidence is offered to establish a constructive condition to Barney's performance of the agreement.

67. Jill Mills was anxious to improve the landscaping on her palatial estate. She consulted with Jack Sprat, a local landscaper who agreed to plant three large beech trees on her property. Jill agreed to pay Jack $10,000 on completion of the work. When the work was finished, Jill inspected the trees and complained that they were planted too deep and would not survive. She refused to pay Jack. After much argument, Jack agreed that he would wait for payment for 12 months. In the meantime, he would water and feed the trees regularly to make sure they lived through the year. After two months, Jack agreed to do all the landscaping for a large local golf course and stopped looking after Jill's trees.

    What result if Jack sues Jill?

    A. Jack will recover nothing because the original agreement was supplanted by the compromise agreement.

    B. Jack's suit will be dismissed as premature.

    C. Jack will recover $10,000, less the cost to Jill of maintaining the trees for the balance of the year.

D. Jack will recover nothing because he breached the compromise agreement.

68. Scents, Inc. contracts with Aroma Corp. to supply all of Aroma's oils for one year at $25 a container. Scents delivers in the first month and then sends a letter to Aroma advising it that it has assigned all rights and obligations under the contract to Parfumco, which joins in the letter and confirms the assignment. Aroma consults you as its attorney and asks you what steps it can take to protect itself.

What is the best advice you can give Aroma?

A. Notify Scents that you do not accept the assignment and will continue to look to it for performance.

B. Notify Scents that it has breached the agreement by making the assignment.

C. Send a copy of the agreement to Parfumco and ask it to reconfirm the terms.

D. Write to Parfumco demanding assurances of its ability to perform.

69. OSI is in the business of supplying live plants and flowers to decorate office building lobbies and atriums. Peckendorf owns 40 large office buildings in Manhattan and contracts with OSI to supply all its needs for live flowers for one year at $25,000 per month. OSI delivers on schedule for two months. At the end of the second month, it receives a notice from Iris Nurseries, its source of live flowers, advising OSI that Iris must suspend all deliveries because of a storm that has wiped out its flower beds. OSI can get the flowers from a nursery in Holland for $7,500 per month more than it would pay Iris. At that price, OSI will lose $7,500 per month, a loss that may cause it to fail. OSI notifies Peckendorf that it cannot make any further deliveries without an increase of $9,000 per month. Peckendorf refuses to adjust the contract, and OSI makes no further deliveries. Peckendorf purchases the flowers from another supplier and sues OSI.

What result?

A. Peckendorf will prevail because OSI can order the flowers from Holland.

B. OSI will prevail because the subject matter of the contract was destroyed.

C. Peckendorf will prevail because OSI breached the agreement.

D. OSI will prevail because the loss to it was extreme and unforeseeable.

70. Homeowner and Contractor agree in writing to the construction of a new free-standing garage on Homeowner's property. The finished price is $15,000, payable in four progress installments of $1,000 each; the balance of $11,000 is payable on completion. Contractor builds the garage, receives the four installments, and demands the balance of $11,000. On final inspection, Homeowner's architect advises him that some of the material on the roof of the garage does not meet local requirements. The cost to remove and replace the material is $4,000. Homeowner asks Contractor to do the repair work, but Contractor refuses, insisting on the full sum.

If Contractor sues Homeowner, the most likely result is that

A. Contractor will recover judgment for $11,000.

B. Contractor will recover judgment for $7,000.

C. Contractor will lose because the construction did not conform to local requirements.

D. Contractor will recover nothing until he his removed and replaced the defective material.

71. On December 20, Carl, owner of Carl's Coffee Shop, entered into a written contract with Dan, owner of Dan's Doughnut Factory, under which Carl agreed to purchase his doughnut requirements from Dan for the next calendar year. The contract provided that "Carl shall have no obligation to receive any specified quantity of doughnuts, but only all his daily requirements" and that Dan "agrees to supply such requirements" at the fixed price per dozen specified in the contract, "cash on delivery." During the year in which the contract was made, Carl's requirements of doughnuts for his coffee shop averaged approximately 50 dozen per week. In May of the next calendar year, Carl sold Carl's Coffee Shop to Ed, assigning his rights and delegating his duties under the contract with Dan to Ed. Ed has several coffee shops and has a history of increasing the volume of business wherever he goes. When Dan was notified of the sale, he refused to supply doughnuts to Ed for Carl's Coffee Shop.

What are Ed's rights, if any, against Dan?

A. Ed has no rights against Dan.

B. Ed is entitled to have Dan supply Ed's requirements of doughnuts for Carl's Coffee Shop, but not in a quantity unreasonably disproportionate to Carl's normal requirements before he sold to Ed.

C. Ed is entitled to have Dan supply whatever quantity of doughnuts Ed may order for Carl's Coffee Shop, but Ed is free to buy doughnuts elsewhere.

D. Ed is entitled to have Dan supply whatever requirements of doughnuts Ed may have for Carl's Coffee Shop.

72. Roland wishes to build the finest yacht in Largo Harbor. He contracts with Harpo, who agrees to build the yacht for $125,000. Harpo expects to make a profit of $25,000. He buys all the materials he needs for $40,000 and stores them at the yacht basin. The storage cost is $5,000. Roland calls Harpo one morning before the work begins and tells him he's changed his mind and is going to buy a plane instead. Harpo ponders his alternatives and discusses them with you. He tells you that if he sells the materials, he will recover only $30,000, but if he finishes the yacht, he is likely to sell it for $120,000. He asks you for your advice as to the course of action that will put him in the best position to recover his losses from Roland.

    What should you advise Harpo?

    A. Sell the materials and sue Roland for expectation damages.

    B. Sell the materials and sue Roland for reliance damages.

    C. Sell the materials and sue Roland in restitution.

    D. Build and sell the yacht and sue Roland for consequential damages.

73. Subdivider has received approval to subdivide a plot in Hiawatha County and to build ten two-story colonials. All the houses are exactly the same except for minor details in exterior decoration. He contracts with Builder to build all ten houses at a total cost of $750,000. Subdivider pays $150,000 to Builder on execution of the contract and an additional $10,000 on satisfactory completion of each house. Builder completes five houses and is paid $50,000. Subdivider and Builder have a violent argument, and Subdivider throws Builder off the job. Builder says, "You owe me $375,000 for five houses and you've paid me $200,000. Please give me a check for $175,000." Subdivider replies, "I won't pay you anything until I build the other five houses and see how much they cost me."

    Builder retains you, and you ask your associate to write you a memo outlining the best theory on which to sue. What theory is your associate most likely to recommend?

    A. Material beach by subdivider

    B. Divisibility of contract

C. Promissory estoppel

D. Quantum meruit

74. Delwood has just won the Nobel Prize for literature. His books have been distributed and read all over the world. He agrees to speak at the annual International Convention of Kiwanis Clubs in Queen City. Twenty thousand people are expected for his talk. The Agreement between Delwood and Kiwanis calls for a handsome speaker's fee plus lodging for three days in the Embassy Room of the Harriot Hotel. Anticipating a large turnout and the resulting consumption of food and spirits, the Hotel spends $5,000 in a general mailing to the registrants at the Convention. Delwood arrives in Queen City and taxis directly to the Anniversary Inn, where he registers and stays. The Harriot nets less than half of its anticipated revenue from the convention while the Anniversary cleans up.

If the Harriot sues both Delwood and the Kiwanis Clubs, what result?

A. The Harriot will recover against the Kiwanis Clubs, but not against Delwood.

B. The Harriot will recover against Delwood but not against the Kiwanis Clubs.

C. The Harriot will recover from both Delwood and the Kiwanis Clubs.

D. The Harriot will not recover from either the Kiwanis Clubs or Delwood.

Questions 75–78 are based on the following fact situation:

On January 1, Joe and Bob entered into a written contract. It was agreed that on January 30, Joe would deliver to Bob his 1968 Edsel, in good condition, and that Bob would simultaneously pay $5,000 to Arthur, to whom Joe owed $5,000; provided, however that Jack, a used car expert, would certify that the Edsel was worth at least $5,000.

75. Until Arthur becomes aware of the agreement, Joe can, without penalty,

A. Revoke the offer to sell the Edsel, provided Jack has not yet examined it.

B. Repudiate the agreement because Bob's promise is illusory.

C. Rescind the agreement if Bob consents.

D. Rescind the agreement provided he gets Bob's consent and requests and obtains Arthur's consent.

76. Assume (1) a valid contract has been entered into between Joe and Bob, (2) Arthur is told the terms of the contract, and (3) Jack certifies the Edsel is worth $5,000. Assume also Joe sells the car to Bob for that amount but that Bob makes payment to Joe instead of Arthur. Arthur would probably be successful in an action against

A. Joe, but not Bob.

B. Bob, but not Joe.

C. Both Joe and Bob.

D. Neither Joe nor Bob.

77. Assume that the writing is held to be a valid contract. If Arthur learned of the contract on January 30, and on the next day, filed suit against Bob for $5,000, which of the following circumstances, if true, would provide Bob with a valid partial defense?

I That prior to signing the contract, Joe and Bob had agreed on a purchase price of $4,000, but the contract nevertheless mistakenly listed a price of $5,000.

II That on January 15, following Jack's appraisal, Joe and Bob agreed to reduce the Edsel's price to $4,000.

A. I only.

B. II only.

C. Both I and II.

D. Neither I nor II.

78. Assume that on January 15, Bob repudiated his agreement with Joe. Which of the following circumstances, if true, would provide Bob with the best defense in a suit against him by Arthur filed on January 20?

A. That Bob's performance was not due until January 30.

B. That Joe told Bob on January 16 that the agreement was irrevocable.

C. That Arthur told Bob on January 16 that he would hold him to the agreement.

D. That the car was destroyed on January 18.

79. Fabrico, the area's largest manufacturer of ski outfits, looks for a supplier of zippers and finds Zippro, a medium-sized plant nearby. Fabrico offers "to buy all the zippers we need for the next ten years, and we'll pay you $2 for each zipper." Zippro knows, from reading trade reports and other sources, that Fabrico uses between 500,000 and 600,000 zippers a year. Zippro's annual production is 300,000, but it has the plant capacity to gear up, and it agrees in writing to supply all of Fabrico's needs for ten years as proposed by Fabrico. The agreement does not specify a fixed annual production or purchase quantity. For three years, Fabrico orders and Zippro manufactures and delivers 595,000 zippers annually. In the fourth year, Skisuit, Inc. announces the production of an all-weather ski suit at half the price charged by Fabrico, and Fabrico's sales plummet. Fabrico orders only 200,000 zippers from Zippro. Zippro notifies Fabrico that it can no longer honor their agreement and signs an agreement with Skisuit instead. Fabrico is unable to find another source of zippers.

In the resulting lawsuit by Fabrico against Zippro, what is the likely result?

A. Zippro will prevail because it expanded its facilities in reliance on a reasonably constant level of orders from Fabrico.

B. Zippro will prevail because it is required to mitigate its damages.

C. Fabrico will prevail because the agreement did not specify a minimum requirements level.

D. Fabrico will prevail because Zippro could have delivered 200,000 zippers to Fabrico and the balance of its production to Skisuit.

80. Farmer Brown needs a new well and asks Digger White to drill it for him. Brown says, "You can't start until I bring the sheep in from the field for the winter on Labor Day, but I'll need the well soon after that." Digger agrees to dig the well for $5,000. Digger shows up at Farmer Brown's on the day after Labor Day and wants to begin drilling. Farmer Brown says, "I'm sorry, but we haven't been able to bring the sheep in yet. Come back in ten days. Digger replies, "Sorry, farmer man, but I've got other jobs. You'll have to wait until spring." Farmer Brown can't find anyone else to dig the well, and some of his prize sheep die of thirst over the winter. Farmer Brown wants to sue Digger for the value of his sheep. What do you advise Farmer Brown?

A. You will win because the contract did not specify a specific date for performance.

B. You will lose because you did not bring the sheep in before Labor Day.

C. You will lose under the "perfect tender" rule.

D. You will lose because the contract involved land and was not in writing.

81. Raoul Massenet is impresario of a summer opera festival in the White Mountains. He sends a circular to several singers, describing the program, the dates, and the roles to be filled. Sue Solo, leading soprano of the Pittsburgh Opera, sends a letter offering to appear in *Turandot* and *La Boheme*, for a fee of $20,000, "my usual fee." Mark responds, "Your fee is too high for my budget. I can offer you $10,000." Solo replies, "I'm sorry, but its $20,000 or nothing. If you want me to perform, send a contract for my approval." Mark wires Sue, "I accept your terms. A contract follows. Please sign it and send it back pronto." The next day, before the contract arrives, Solo receives an offer to sing at the New York Met for $35,000. She immediately writes to Mark, "I cannot sign your contract. I've been offered a role at the Met on the same nights." Mark responds, "You can't renege now. We've got a deal for $20,000, and I'm going to hold you to it."

Mark sues Sue. What is her best defense?

A. The negotiations between Sue and Mark were preliminary only and were intended to be merged in a written agreement, which was never executed.

B. Mark's offer of $10,000 was a counteroffer that was never accepted by Sue.

C. The correspondence between the parties did not cover all the material terms of a performance agreement.

D. There are many sopranos qualified to perform in Puccini's operas and Mark suffered no damage.

Questions 82–83 are based on the following fact situation:

Oscar had two large identical elm trees in his front yard. He hired Felix to prune the trees for $500.

82. Assume that Felix arrived to begin work with three men and all the required gear. When Oscar came out to meet him, Felix demanded payment in advance. Oscar refused because he had never hired Felix before and didn't know if his work would be satisfactory. If Felix brings suit against Oscar for breach of contract, who will prevail?

A. Oscar, because he was entitled to see if Felix's work was satisfactory.

B. Oscar, because when an agreement is silent about the order of performance, payment is not required until the work is performed.

C. Felix, because no order of performance was specified in the contract and he has as much right to first performance as Oscar.

D. Felix, because he had rented the equipment necessary to perform under the contract.

83. Assume that Felix pruned one of the two trees satisfactorily, but then refused to prune the other. Oscar hired Murray to prune the second tree for $150. Felix is entitled to

A. Nothing, because he willfully breached the contract.

B. Nothing, because the contract required pruning of two trees.

C. $150, as the reasonable value of his services.

D. $350, as the difference between the contract price and the cost of completion.

84. Albert sold his used Alfa Romeo to Bart for $7,000. They agreed that $3,000 would be paid on transfer of title and the remaining $4,000 "in 30 days." Bart knew that he would be unable to pay the balance. He said to his friend Otto, "Look, I need to pay $4,000 to Albert in 30 days. You need your house painted. If I paint your house, will you pay $4,000 to Albert?" Otto replied, "That sounds look a good deal to me. I agree." Bart diligently and efficiently painted Otto's house, but Otto now refuses to pay Albert. Albert sues both Bart and Otto. What result?

A. Albert can recover against Bart but not against Otto.

B. Albert can recover against Otto but not against Bart.

C. Albert can recover against both Otto and Bart.

D. Albert cannot recover against either Otto or Bart until Bart sues and recovers a judgment against Otto.

85. Maples, Inc., a distributor of trees and shrubs in the Northeast, enters into a five-year contract with Viburnum Corp., a grower of shrubs, to supply Maples with all its requirements of viburnums and hollies for five years. Viburnums and hollies represent 35% of Maples's and 75% of Viburnum's business. There is no mention in the contract of the right of either party to assign. The parties enjoy a model relationship for the first two years. In the third year, Maples receives an irresistible offer for its business and sells all its assets to Poplar Nurseries, the nation's largest distributor of plants. Among the assets assigned is the contract with Viburnum. Viburnum is concerned that Poplar's requirements will be too much for it to handle and that Poplar will be slower to pay its invoices than Maples.

It notifies Maples and Poplar that it will not honor the assignment and will not sell to Poplar. In its notice, it states, "We bought the credit, payment record, and requirements of Maples. We do not believe that Poplar will be able to pay our invoices on time or that we can satisfy Poplar's needs." To satisfy its needs for viburnums and hollies, Poplar goes into the market and is unable to find another grower with the production capacity of Viburnum. Poplar sues Viburnum for damages and for specific performance.

What result?

A. Poplar will recover damages but not an order of specific performance.

B. Poplar will recover both damages and an order of specific performance.

C. Viburnum will prevail because the contract is not assignable.

D. Viburnum will prevail unless Poplar can prove that its credit is as good as Maples's and its requirements about the same.

86. The Sunset Hotel, a weekend retreat with 95 rooms, wrote to 500 of its former guests offering them a special July 4 three-day holiday at $95 per person per day, meals included. Sunset's usual weekend rate is $175 per person per night. Mac Maxwell wrote back immediately, "My wife and I will be there for July 4 holiday. Reserve a large double. Deposit check for $100 enclosed." When the Sunset staff counted the Hotel's reservations, they found that they had 107 reservations for the holiday. They immediately wrote a letter to the last 12 guests. Maxwell was among the 12. The letter said, "Sorry, all sold out for July 4 holiday. Suggest you try the Sunrise instead." Anxious to see the autumn leaf display, Maxwell reserved a room at the Sunrise for $145 a night. Maxwell demanded that the Sunset return his deposit and reimburse him for the difference in rates between it and the Sunrise. The Sunset agreed to return the deposit, but refused to pay the reimbursement.

Maxwell sues Sunset in the local small claims court. What will the court decide?

A. Sunset will prevail because its offer anticipated acceptance not by a letter and deposit but by the use of its facilities.

B. Sunset will prevail because it notified Maxwell that it was sold out before it confirmed his reservation.

C. Maxwell will prevail because he accepted Sunset's offer and was forced to pay more than the special Sunset rates.

D. Sunset will prevail because, as a former guest, Maxwell should have known that Sunset had a limited number of rooms.

Questions 87–90 are based on the following fact situation:

In early January, Farnsworth and Jones entered into a contract whereby Farnsworth would sing in Jones's club for a period of 24 months, beginning on February 1, at $1,500 per month.

87. Assume that on January 25, Farnsworth phoned Jones and told him, "I still haven't finished moving all my belongings into my new apartment. It's going to take me a while to get settled and I may not be ready to start singing until February 10."

Can Jones bring an immediate suit against Farnsworth?

A. Yes, because Farnsworth's telephone call was a repudiation.

B. Yes, if Jones interpreted Farnsworth's telephone call as a repudiation.

C. No, because Farnsworth's telephone call did not constitute a repudiation.

D. No, because a repudiation must be in writing to be given effect.

88. Assume that Jones had no communication with Farnsworth between January 1 and January 31. On January 31, Jones received a telegram from Farnsworth stating:

Cannot get passage to US from China. Unable to start singing engagement at your club until February 10. I'm sorry for any inconvenience this causes you. Suggest you get temporary performer.

On the morning of February 10, as promised, Farnsworth appeared at Jones's nightclub, ready to sing that night.

May Jones cancel the contract?

A. Yes, because Farnsworth failed to appear when he contracted to do so.

B. Yes, because Farnsworth's actions constituted a material breach.

C. No, because Jones was not materially prejudiced by Farnsworth's failure to appear on February 1.

D. No, because Farnsworth notified Jones of his delay in a timely fashion.

89. Assume that Farnsworth failed to appear at Jones's nightclub on February 1. That same morning, Jones read in *Variety* that Farnsworth had been injured in a traffic accident caused by a

drunken driver on January 15 and was hospitalized with extensive head injuries. The article said he was in a coma and was expected to remain in the hospital for two months. Jones hired Young to sing in his nightclub for two months at a salary of $2,000 per month. When Farnsworth recovers and appears at the club, can Jones deduct from Farnsworth's fee the additional $1,000 he was forced to pay Young?

A. Yes, because Jones was not responsible for Farnsworth's injury.

B. Yes, because impracticability does not apply where Farnsworth's injury was his own fault.

C. No, because Farnsworth was not permanently injured.

D. No, because Farnsworth's disability established an impracticability defense.

90. Assume that Farnsworth failed to appear at Jones's nightclub because he received a better offer to sing at Kent's nightclub. He did not notify Jones that he would not appear. Anticipating that Farnsworth would eventually appear, Jones hired Stone to sing. Jones insisted on a contract at $1,800 for the entire month of February. At the end of February, Jones learned the reason for Farnsworth's failure to appear and hired Stone to sing at his nightclub for the remaining 23 months of Farnsworth's contract at $1,800 per month. On the same day Jones filed suit against Farnsworth. How much can Jones recover from Farnsworth?

A. $300 damages for the month of February only.

B. $300 damages for the month of February plus the present value of the difference between the Farnsworth fee and the Stone fee for 23 months.

C. The full contract price to be paid by Jones to Stone.

D. Nothing, because Jones failed to notify Farnsworth that he was hiring Stone at a higher fee.

91. Multiplex owned a vacant parcel of land. It contracted with Construct, Inc. to build a shopping center on the land. Multiplex paid Construct an "advance" of $850,000 under a complicated written agreement that prohibited assignment by either party. The work continued over many months without complications. One day, the treasurer of Construct called Multiplex and said, "We've got a big shipment of paving stones coming in next month. Can we get an advance on the next payment?" Multiplex replied, "Sorry, but we're tight ourselves. Why don't you ask your bank?" The Construct treasurer said, "We can't do that under the contract." Multiplex then

told the treasurer that it would be OK to arrange an assignment to the bank "this one time." Construct assigned the payment to the bank and received the loan. Bank notified Multiplex of the assignment, but on the due date of the next payment, Multiplex refused to pay the bank, citing the no-assignment clause in the original contract. The bank sued Multiplex for the payment. What result?

A. Bank will prevail because Multiplex consented to the assignment.

B. Bank will prevail because the parties to a written agreement can enter into a subsequent oral modification.

C. Multiplex will prevail because contracts involving land must be in writing.

D. Multiplex will prevail because integrated written agreements cannot be varied or amended orally.

92. Lord Northchild wishes to give his wife a gift on the couple's 25th anniversary, which will come in eight months. He asks Nick Casso, an up-and-coming portrait painter, to paint her portrait for $25,000. Northchild says, "I want it to be a surprise for all of us, even me. You'll work from a series of her photographs. I want you to deliver it to my castle on June 21st at 9:30 p.m. We're going to give a big ball that night. You should be able to do a great job; after all, you have eight months to finish it." Realizing that a portrait for Lady Northchild will lead to bigger and bigger commissions, Nick agrees and labors every day for eight months. When Nick delivers the portrait on the night of the ball, Lady Northchild is horrified. "You've made me look like a cross between a hippo and an elephant!" she cries. Northchild says, "Take this thing away," and refuses to pay Nick anything. Nick retains you and asks you to describe his remedies. You reply:

A. You will recover $25,000, the price Northchild agreed to pay you.

B. Your recovery will be limited to the market value of the portrait.

C. You cannot recover because you were foolish enough not to reduce your agreement to a writing.

D. You cannot recover because Northchild found your portrait unacceptable.

Additional Questions for Siegel's
Questions 93–97 are based on the following fact situation:

Shelly sells candles over the Internet. Terry purchased a scented candle from Shelly's website. The candle was so good that Terry decided to purchase a large supply, in part to avoid running out, in part to give as gifts, and in part to sell at her booth in a local farmer's market. Terry logged on to Shelly's website, clicked on the goods she wanted, filled in the quantity (100), and went to the checkout screen. That screen showed the total price and asked Terry to select shipping terms. As a special that week, Shelly's site offered free standard shipping (which the webpage said would arrive in 7-10 business days via a ground delivery service). Expedited shipping would have cost at least $300 on an order this size, so Terry elected the free shipping. Terry gave credit card information for the payment and then clicked to confirm the order. A final page appeared with all the information Terry had supplied (quantity, price, delivery, credit card, billing and shipping address, etc.). It asked Terry to review the page and confirm the information, and to then click a button to submit the order. Terry clicked the confirmation button without reviewing the information. The website gave Terry a confirmation number and emailed a confirmation of the receipt of her order, promising a second email when it had been shipped. All of these messages were generated automatically by the web engine running the page; no human being saw the order until the next day.

93. Shelly had only 30 candles of this type in stock. Shelly can get 45 more in two weeks and another 25 in a month, both after the delivery date mentioned by the website. Shelly sent Terry an email stating that the goods had been backordered and offered Terry three options: (i) to wait until the full order could be shipped at one time, which would involve no additional shipping charges; (ii) to receive 30 candles in 7-10 business days and the rest as they arrive, but multiple shipments would require additional shipping charges; or (iii) to cancel the order if neither of these terms were acceptable. If Terry insists on the original terms and sues for damages caused by Shelly's failure to perform, what is the likely outcome of the suit?

    a. Shelly will prevail because Terry's order was only an offer and Shelly's email a counteroffer.
    b. Shelly will prevail because acceptance requires a response from a person, not a machine.
    c. Shelly will prevail because the agreement is not evidenced by a signed writing.
    d. Terry will prevail because the confirmation email from Shelly's website accepted Terry's offer in writing.

94. In addition to the facts of the preceding question, Shelly's checkout page included the following language directly above the button labeled "Confirm Order and Continue with Checkout": "By clicking Confirm Order you agree to be bound by all the terms and conditions of this website. Click here to read the terms and conditions." "Click here" was a different color; clicking on it would take the user to a page containing numerous terms, including this one: "All orders are subject to availability. Shelly reserves the right to

reject any order for any reason or no reason at all." Terry did not click this button (not this time and not the first time, when she ordered one candle) and, thus, did not see this language. With these additional facts, how will Terry's claim against Shelly be resolved?

    a. Shelly will prevail because the order is an offer that she can reject.
    b. Shelly will prevail because the Statute of Frauds is not satisfied.
    c. Terry will prevail because the terms were not displayed in a manner reasonably calculated to call them to a user's attention.
    d. Terry will prevail because the offer was accepted.

95. Consider the general facts, but not the facts of the preceding two problems. Immediately after submitting the order, it dawned on Terry that there were too many zeros in the numbers just confirmed: the order was for 1,000 candles, not 100, for a price of $20,000, not $2,000. She immediately clicked "Contact Us" and emailed a revocation of the offer, explaining that she intended to order 100 candles, not 1000. Just after she clicked "Send," she heard the sound announcing incoming mail. Opening her inbox, Terry saw the confirmation of a 1,000 candle order from Shelly's website. Assume Terry's email, sent from Shelly's website to Shelly's website, arrived immediately in Shelly's inbox, but that no one checked the email until the next morning. Shelly's acceptance was dispatched almost immediately after Terry submitted the order, but Terry's computer checked for email only every 20 minutes, so the confirmation probably was dispatched before Terry sent the email canceling the order (as the time stamps on the messages confirm), even though it arrived after Terry sent the email. If Shelly has enough candles and wants to enforce Terry's order, what is the likely result?

    a. Shelly will prevail because the acceptance was dispatched before the revocation was dispatched.
    b. Terry will prevail because the revocation was received before the acceptance was received.
    c. Shelly will prevail because the acceptance was dispatched before the revocation was received.
    d. Terry will prevail because the revocation was dispatched before the acceptance was received.

96. On the facts of the preceding problem, what is Terry's best argument to avoid the contract?

    a. The contract is not enforceable for lack of a writing.
    b. The contract should be rescinded for unilateral mistake.
    c. The contract should be reformed for mistake of integration.
    d. The contract is unconscionable.

97. Suppose Terry did not recognize her mistake, but thought she had ordered 100 candles and never read the email confirmation that

revealed the error. Shelly bills Terry's credit card and ships 1,000 candles. Shelly was busy and decided to ship the order in ten boxes, each containing 100 candles, sent over a period of several days. (This allowed Shelly to do other work, instead of focusing on Terry's order exclusively for an extended period.) Terry received the first box of 100 candles eight business days after the order was placed and accepted delivery. On the ninth business day, one more box arrived. Terry accepted the box, but emailed Shelly for instructions on how to return the double shipment. On the tenth business day, no boxes arrived, but Shelly's reply email alerted Terry, for the first time, to the mistake in the order. On the eleventh business day, the other eight boxes arrived. Terry rejected the boxes. If Terry claims that late delivery justifies rejection of the candles, will Terry prevail?

   a. Yes, Terry can reject the eight late boxes because late delivery is a defect within the perfect tender rule, but must keep the two boxes already accepted.

   b. Yes, Terry can reject all ten boxes because late delivery is a defect within the perfect tender rule and allows rejection of the entire shipment, not just the portion that was late.

   c. No, because this was an installment contract and the one-day delay did not substantially impair the value of either this shipment or the entire contract.

   d. No, because the goods delivered were not defective in any way, just late.

98. Sean, a wholesale food salesman, phoned Compco to order a laptop computer. Compco's sales agent discussed the configuration Sean wanted and quoted a price, including the special discounts available that week. Sean agreed to that price. Compco took Sean's credit card information and said the computer would arrive in five business days. Compco billed Sean's credit card when it shipped the computer. When the computer arrived (on time), Sean opened the box and began setting up the machine, discarding various papers that were inside the box. Among these papers was one labeled "Terms of Sale." This paper said that all sales were subject to the terms on that page. The lengthy terms included provisions limiting Sean's remedy for breach of warranty to repair or replacement, at Compco's option, and excluding any consequential damages that result from breach. The Terms of Sale also specified that if the buyer was unwilling to be bound by these terms, it should return the computer to Compco within 30 days for a full refund, including shipping both ways. Sean kept the computer more than 30 days. Sean then went on a business trip with the laptop, but was unable to use the wireless connections

anyplace. Ultimately, Compco determined that the integrated wireless function was defective and replaced the laptop with one that worked. In the meantime, Sean lost considerable time trying to make the wireless work and can point to at least two business opportunities lost as a result of the defective wireless. Under the Uniform Commercial Code, if Sean seeks damages against Compco, will the limited remedies in Compco's Terms of Sale be enforceable against Sean?

- a. No; the Terms of Sale, though accepted by Sean, never became part of the contract because the modification lacked consideration.
- b. Yes; the Terms of Sale were a counteroffer, which Sean accepted by keeping the computer instead of returning it within 30 days.
- c. Yes; the Terms of Sale were proposals to modify the contract, which Sean accepted by keeping the computer instead of returning it within 30 days.
- d. No; the Terms of Sale were proposals to modify the contract, which Sean never accepted.

99. On the facts of the preceding problem, if the Terms of Sale do not limit Sean's remedy, is Sean likely to recover consequential damages for the lost sales?

- a. Yes, because a computer seller should foresee business use of a laptop will occur in the ordinary course of events.
- b. Yes, but only if Sean informed Compco while ordering the computer of his needs, including the need for wireless access for business purposes.
- c. No, because the lost sales were easily avoided by buying a dial-up cord and accessing the Internet that way.
- d. No, because the losses were not foreseeable by Compco at the time of contract formation, even if they were fully aware of Sean's business uses.

Multiple-Choice Answers

Note: An asterisk (*) indicates a possible correct answer.

1. A The law does not expect people to be mind-readers. For this reason, if a party *says* that he's making an offer, we assume that he means it. The offeree is entitled to respond to the offeror's actions and *manifestations,* so long as they appear to be reasonable. An offer to buy a $1,500 car for $3,000 is not so unreasonable that the offeree should not be able to rely on it. The correct answer is **A**. Choice **B** is incorrect. The doctrine of promissory estoppel requires some action or forbearance by the offeree to his detriment. Rest. 2d §90(1). The facts do not indicate that Paul took any action in response to Allen's offer except to offer him the transfer documents. Choice **C** is incorrect because it begs the real issue. It doesn't matter whether Allen was serious or not. What matters is that he *manifested* seriousness. Choice **D** is incorrect because, again, although his statements to his friends confirmed that he intended a jest, he did not appear to Paul to be acting in jest.

2. D Buyer accepted the offer within the time specified. None of the defenses apply. Choice **C** is a correct statement of law, but does not fit the facts. Absent consideration (or an exception), Seller had a right to revoke, despite the promise to keep the offer open. But Seller did not revoke the offer before Buyer accepted; Seller refused to perform only after Buyer accepted. Choice **A** is factually correct, but legally insufficient. The agreement providing for the transfer of an interest in land is within the Statute of Frauds. Rest. 2d §125. This law requires a writing signed by the party to be charged — here, the Seller, who is resisting enforcement. Seller's written and signed offer was sufficiently definite to satisfy this requirement. Rest. 2d §131. Because Buyer's acceptance was communicated by phone and not in writing, the contract would not be enforceable against Buyer if Buyer raised the Statute of Frauds as a defense. Choice **B** suggests the unenforceable promise was not consideration for Seller's promise. That is wrong; even an unenforceable promise can satisfy the requirement of consideration. Rest. 2d §78

3. D Like an advertisement, a mass mailing to a general list of potential customers generally is not construed as an offer but as an invitation to negotiate a transaction. These facts tell us that Seller's letter was a *pro forma* letter and the Buyer's name did not appear on the envelope or the letter itself. Buyer's wire would not create a binding contract until confirmed by the Seller. Choice **A** is wrong for the same reason that Choice **D** is correct; Seller's letter was not an offer. Choice **C** is incorrect. Unless the offeror specifies the means of response, the acceptance of an offer may be communicated by any reasonable means. Although wires are not manually signed by the senders, they are nevertheless effective to communicate an acceptance. Buyer's name on the telegram, if put there to authenticate the writing, may satisfy the requirement of a signed writing. Choice **B** is wrong because the facts do not state a sufficient basis on which the Seller could claim impracticability of performance. On the contrary, the Seller merely confirmed the availability of the product, albeit at a different price.

4. **A** *A promise* to refrain from doing something that a party has a legal right to do constitutes adequate consideration for *another's promise*, even though the latter does not derive any direct benefit from the former's promise. Henry proposed a **bilateral contract** to Joe (Henry told Joe that if the latter would **agree** not to marry until he finished law school, Henry would pay him spending money). A **contract** enforceable against Henry and his estate was formed when Joe **accepted** the offer. Choice **B** is incorrect because there is nothing illegal about the Joe-Henry contract (it merely specified that Joe would not wed during law school, not that he would never marry). Choice **C** is incorrect because, while the death of an offeror will ordinarily terminate his offer, in this instance a bilateral contract had already been formed between the parties when Joe agreed to Henry's terms. Finally, Choice **D** is incorrect because the agreement involved in this instance was not within the Statute of Frauds.

5. **A*** A written confirmation of an oral agreement operates as an acceptance even if it states terms different from the terms of the agreement. UCC §2-207(1) (UCC §2-206(3) in the 2003 revisions to article 2). However, in transactions between merchants, the additional terms might become part of the contract unless they contain material alterations of the original terms. §2-207(2)(b) (deleted under 2003 revisions). Here, the language limiting the remedies of the Buyer on Seller's default was a sufficiently material alteration to be excluded from the bargain. * Choice **B** is not correct under existing law, but will become correct if the 2003 revisions become law. If the parties had not made an agreement at all, UCC §2-207(3) might produce the result in choice **B**. But if the term had not been material, Buyer's silence might have been deemed an acceptance, producing an agreement that would obviate recourse to UCC §2-207(3). Thus, choice **B** is true only if choice **A** already prevented the term from becoming

part of the contract. Choice **A**, then, is a better answer. Choice **C** is not correct. The limitation was not an express condition to acceptance of delivery, but a material change imposed by the Seller's form of Confirmation. Choice **D** is incorrect because an objection is unnecessary when the additional term materially alters the agreement.

6. **D** In commercial transactions, a buyer often asks a supplier for a price in advance of placing an order. He may wish merely to compare the price of one supplier against the price of a competitor. A price quotation is, therefore, not always an offer. The facts in this case would indicate that Seller was merely stating a price in anticipation of Paul's order. Since Paul did not respond until Seller changed the price after the forest fire, there was no agreement between the parties. Choice **A** is incorrect because the April 1 letter was not a firm offer but a price quotation. Choice **B** is not the best answer because the facts are not dispositive on the issue of practicability. We are not told what the impact of the fire on Seller will be. If he is able to sell his inventory at the increased price, there may be no impact at all. Choice **C** is not the right answer because Paul was not entitled to rely on the April 1 quotation, especially since his order was placed only after he had received notice of the price increase.

7. **A** When a party agrees to forbear from asserting a claim which he honestly (albeit mistakenly) believes to be valid in exchange for the promise of another, the latter's promise is ***ordinarily enforceable***; Rest. 2d §74. Even though Owens may have owed Neff nothing, his *promise* to Neff would still be enforceable by Neff, because Neff believed that Owens did owe him reimbursement for Neff's overpayment to the contractor. Choice **B** is incorrect because the fact that Owens did not believe Neff had a valid claim is not pertinent under the facts and the applicable rule of law (i.e., Owens' promise is enforceable because Neff believed that he had a claim against Owens). Choice **C** is incorrect because it doesn't matter that Neff's claim was in fact groundless: so long as he reasonably believed he had a valid claim, Owens' promise is enforceable. Finally, Choice **D** is incorrect because the agreement did not have to be in writing. It provided for performance by Owens over a single winter. If it had provided for his hiring a caretaker over a period longer than one year, it would have fallen within the Statute of Frauds and required a writing.

8. **D*** An acknowledgment can be an acceptance even if it states different or additional terms. UCC §2-207(1) (UCC §2-206(3) in the 2003 revisions to article 2). Here, the promise to fill the order accepted the

order of 9″ clamps, but proposed changing the description to assorted 9 to 9½″ clamps. That different term would become part of a
contract between merchants unless it materially altered the terms or
the offeror objected within a reasonable time. No objection is noted
until after the clamps have been received and used. Because 9½″
clamps usually work in place of 9″ clamps, the change does not
seem material. (Even if 9½″ clamps are nonconforming goods, shipping them without an acknowledgment would have been an acceptance under UCC §2-206(1)(b) — unless the Seller expressly negated
acceptance by notice that the shipment is offered only as an accommodation, a reservation not mentioned as part of the acknowledgment.) Choice **A** is incorrect because the acknowledgment was an
acceptance, a part of the contract between the parties. Choice **B** is
wrong because Seller's terms did not materially alter the terms. The
clamps shipped were a usual substitute for the goods specified in the
offer. Choice **C** is incorrect because merely accepting goods does not
necessarily assent to different terms. If the terms were materially
different, accepting the goods would not agree to the proposed modification of the contract.

   * Under the 2003 revisions to article 2 of the UCC, choice **C**
might be correct. The acknowledgment remains an acceptance, but
different terms no long become part of the contract by silence. Thus,
materiality will not matter to the outcome, making both choice **B**
and choice **D** incorrect. Choice **A** remains wrong since the acceptance is part of the contract, even though its specification regarding
size of the clamps may not govern. The problem is quite difficult
under the revisions. Because the writings differ, neither party's term
(9″ for Buyer, 9 to 9½″ for Seller) becomes part of the agreement
unless otherwise agreed. UCC §2-207(b). In this case, because the
default terms of the UCC cannot resolve the difference between 9″
clamps and 9½″ clamps, it seems likely a court would rule that
acceptance of the shipment constituted acceptance of the modification. Alternatively, a court might treat the shipment of nonconforming goods as an acceptance and a breach at the same time. If so, buyer
might prevail. This was not one of the choices and may be wrong
because it gives no effect to the acknowledgment.

9. A The basic rule is that the offeror is always the "master of his offer." If
his offer is definite as to such terms as the method and time of
acceptance, it will control, and the offeree may not deviate from
it. Under these facts, Oliver certainly specified the time and, in effect,
the method of acceptance. His requirement that he "have" the notice

of acceptance "no later than March 1" could not reasonably be satisfied by a letter mailed on March 1. It was necessary for Bill to make sure that his acceptance was actually in Oliver's hands on or before March 1. He could have accomplished this by hand delivery, by wire, or by any other means that would have ensured *receipt* by Oliver on or before the required date. There was no contract between the parties. Choice **B** is incorrect. Even if Oliver argued the requirement of clean title did not make Bill's acceptance a counteroffer (because that term was implicit in the original offer), Bill's acceptance was too late. Choice **C** is wrong because Bill did not accept Oliver's offer in a timely manner, according to its terms. Choice **D** is wrong. Bill's late acceptance could be treated as an offer to buy Oliver's house on the terms Oliver specified. Oliver probably could have accepted this offer. But Oliver did not respond to the offer until after it was revoked.

10. **D** *Under the UCC,* if nonconforming goods are sent in response to an offer for prompt shipment, and the offeree fails to advise the offeror that the shipment is merely an accommodation, the offeree is deemed to have concurrently accepted the buyer's offer and be in *breach of the contract.* UCC §2-206(1)(b). Grant's shipment of the Model Y Hearing Aids constituted an acceptance of Axel's offer (even though the goods were nonconforming) and also a breach of contract because Axel tendered nonconforming goods. Choice **C** is a true statement of a sound legal principle, but it is not the best answer because Grant did ship in response to Axel's order. Choice **B** is incorrect because a shipment of nonconforming goods in response to an order constitutes an acceptance if the shipper does not notify the buyer that the shipment is offered only as an accommodation. Finally, Choice **A** is incorrect because the facts do not state that Grant misunderstood Axel's order.

11. **B** Ordinarily, a substantial modification following the execution of a contract requires new consideration to be binding. In connection with the sale of goods, however, an agreement to modify a contract needs no consideration, as long at the modification was made in good faith. UCC §2-209. Seller was acting in good faith; he increased his price only after he learned of the strike at the processing plant and the resulting increase in price to him. Buyer accepted Seller's modification in price. He cannot now insist on the original price. Choice **A** is incorrect because the facts do not state that performance by Seller had become commercially impracticable.

Choice **C** is incorrect in connection with a sale of goods; consideration is not required for a modification in price if the buyer accepts delivery. Finally, Choice **D** is incorrect, even though the Statute of Frauds does apply. Buyer's note mentions his agreement to the modification and might be deemed signed since attached to the signed check. Alternatively, the goods were received and accepted, an exception to the UCC's Statute of Frauds. UCC §2-201(3)(c).

12. **B** Under certain circumstances, a debt or obligation that is barred or unenforceable by operation of law will be revived without consideration. The most common circumstances arise after a discharge in bankruptcy or the operation of the statute of limitations. The original debt will be revived either by a new explicit promise to pay or by a promise implied by the actions of the debtor. Rest. 2d §§82, 83. Here, the facts confirm Lawrence's promise to pay the loan. His new promise will be enforced. Choice **A** is wrong because the executor would be barred by the statute in the absence of the new promise. The executor has no greater rights than the deceased. Choice **C** is incorrect because no consideration is needed to support a promise to pay a debt barred by the statute of limitations. The promise to pay does not even have to be in writing but may be inferred from the acts or statements of the debtor. Rest. 2d §82(2). Choice **D** is wrong because the executor succeeded to Jack's interests. This included the right to remind Lawrence of the debt and to receive and enforce Lawrence's new promise to pay.

13. **A** The question requires us to construe the facts under the Restatement. The Restatement follows the minority view in cases involving promises to pay for past humanitarian acts. The majority view is that these promises are not enforceable for lack of consideration. The Restatement, on the other hand, follows the decision in *Webb v. McGowin* on the theory that the promisee received a material benefit and it would be unjust to allow him to avoid his promise. Rest. 2d §86(1). Under these facts, it's clear that Dan probably saved Paul's life, to his own detriment. Under the Restatement, his promise will be enforceable. Choice **B** is wrong because the Restatement does not require that the promisor request the services. In a case such as this one, the services arise under circumstances that make a request impossible. Choice **C** is incorrect because under the Restatement no consideration is required. Choice **D** is incorrect because no response by Dan was required. The facts indicate that he did nod, but the result would be the same even if he were unable

to respond at all. What makes Paul's promises enforceable under the Restatement view is the underlying notion that the contrary result would create an injustice.

14. **D** The modern view, as represented in the UCC, is that neither party to an output or requirements contract can evade obligation with impunity, but may avoid the obligation only if, in good faith, they have no requirements or output. UCC §2-306. Agreement to accept this limitation is consideration. Choice **A** is incorrect because mutuality of obligation is not required (as long as consideration exists). Rest. 2d §79(c). In addition, both parties have obligations to act in good faith. Choice **B** is incorrect because the facts tell us that Carl had an obligation to purchase all of his doughnuts from Dan. Carl cannot withdraw from the contract at will, but is committed to buy from Dan unless, in good faith, Carl has no requirements for doughnuts. The contract was not illusory. Choice **C** is not the best answer because it implies that consideration is not needed to support a requirements contract. The UCC rules create obligations that satisfy the requirement of consideration, but do not create an exception to the requirement.

15. **A** A requirements or output contract involving the sale of goods must meet the test of fairness and good faith, i.e., "no quantity *unreasonably disproportionate* to any stated estimate or, in the absence of a stated estimate, to any normal or otherwise comparable prior output or requirements, may be tendered or demanded." UCC §2-306(1). Since Carl's prior requirements had been 50 dozen doughnuts per week, the increase to 75 dozen doughnuts (a 50% increase) would probably be considered unreasonably disproportionate to the parties' prior dealings. Choice **B** is incorrect because there is no rule of law that permits the supplier to a requirements contract to refuse to perform because of an "unanticipated occurrence" external to and independent of the buyer's requirements. Choice **D** is incorrect because a buyer is not entitled to rely on a requirements contract to create new outlets and then insist on deliveries unreasonably disproportionate to his previous orders. Finally, Choice **C** is incorrect because price is not relevant to the issues raised in this question.

16. **B** A consumer who deals with a merchant is at a disadvantage when required to sign an agreement on the merchant's form. In recognition of this, the UCC frowns on contract clauses that prevent modification of contracts between merchant and customer except by a

writing. These are called no-oral-modification clauses. The clause will be ineffective unless it is separately initialed or signed by the customer. UCC §2-209(2). Under these facts, Joan did not sign or initial the no-oral-modification clause and was not bound by it. Her oral agreement with Norton to reduce the price is therefore effective against Norton's efforts to recover the full price. Choice **A** is wrong because the agreement to reduce the price did not have to be in writing. Joan was not bound by the no-oral-modification clause. Choice **C** is incorrect because, although Joan signed the agreement itself, she did not separately sign the no-oral-modification clause. Choice **D** is incorrect because contracts for the sale of goods are an exception to the general rule that contracts may not be modified if the modification benefits only one party; between seller and buyer, a modification needs no consideration. UCC §2-209(1). (**Note:** If the new agreement was deemed an accord rather than a modification, Joan's failure to perform the accord might permit Norton to sue on the original agreement. Rest. 2d §281. That is not one of the choices in this question, but might arise in your course.)

17. **B** If a guarantee is not given until the principal debt has already been created, there would appear to be no consideration to support the guarantee. This is the view of many jurisdictions. However, the more modern view is that if the guarantee is in writing, it will be enforceable. The Restatement requires that the writing make some references to a purported consideration, even if none is really paid. Rest. 2d §88(a). The UCC is even more liberal; it requires only that the guarantee be in writing — no recital of consideration is necessary. Under these facts, the written guarantee of Ben's Uncle Joe would be clearly enforceable by ABC Bank. Choice A is incorrect because, although it was clearly the motivating force behind the guarantee, the relationship between Ben and Joe is not necessary to support the guarantee; the guarantee of a friend would be treated in the same way. Choice **C** is incorrect because both the Restatement and the UCC dispense with the need for consideration. Choice **D** is incorrect because it is exactly in those cases in which the principal debt is incurred *before* the guarantee that both the Restatement and the UCC will support the subsequent guarantee.

18. **A** If an offer does **not** specify an exclusive mode of acceptance, **any reasonable mode** of acceptance is valid. An acceptance is ordinarily effective when it is dispatched. Anna's offer did not stipulate a

specific mode of acceptance, and, in any event, Ella used the same means as Anna — a wire. Because Ella's wire was sent before Anna's revocation was received by her, Ella's acceptance was valid. Choice **B** is incorrect because a revocation may be made by any reasonable means. In this instance requiring speed, a telephone call was certainly reasonable. However, the call came too late. Ella had already dispatched her acceptance. Choice **C** is incorrect because Anna would be presumed to know Ella's usual fee: the facts tell us that Ella had performed for Anna previously. Finally, Choice **D** is incorrect because Ella's response clearly indicated that Ella was accepting the engagement: "On my way." Her desire for a better room was a "hope," not a demand.

19. **C** Under some circumstances, a party will request a "quote" from a number of potential sources. A promoter, for example, might request quotes from several performers. Under these facts, however, Anna's wire was clearly not a request to quote a fee for performing. On the contrary, it was a desperate cry for help and required an immediate acceptance. Anna did not reserve the right to select only one of the three performers to whom she sent her wire. She knew, or should have known, that all three might accept. Choice **C** is the correct answer. Choice **A** is incorrect. If Anna had not intended to assume the risk of receiving more than one acceptance, she could have wired one at a time and waited for an answer, or she could have made it clear in her wire that she was soliciting three responses and that the first to accept would be hired. Choice **D** is incorrect because it doesn't matter who accepted first. All three would be able to recover if they accepted. Finally, Choice **B** is incorrect because Anna's objective manifestations govern, regardless of her secret intent. If a communication would appear to a reasonable person to constitute an offer, it is an offer. In addition, the facts suggest that Anna did intend to make an offer.

20. **D** When Anna wired her offer to Ella, she had no reason to believe that Sam would recover. On the contrary, his surgeon had advised that he would not. Sam's recovery was therefore a subsequent event unknown to either party at the time of contract. An offeree's rights are not affected by a supervening event that is not in the contemplation of either party. The correct answer is **D**. Because Anna did not suspect that Sam might recover, she did not condition her offer to Anna on his continued incapacity. Choice **A** is incorrect on the facts as stated. Anna's offer made no mention of the possibility that

Sam might recover; on the contrary, it cited Sam's illness as the reason for requesting Ella's appearance. Choice **B** is incorrect. Although illness will sometimes operate to excuse default in a personal services contract, Sam's illness was relevant only to Sam's performance, not to Ella's. Choice **C** is wrong. Although it is arguably a good answer, it is not the best answer. The fact that Ella's contract came after Sam's is not critical; if Ella's appearance had been conditioned on Sam's continuing illness, the order of contracts would not have mattered.

21. **B** If the parties to an agreement omit one of the four essential elements of a contract (parties, subject matter, time for performance, and price), the item will often be supplied by the court. If there is no agreement with respect to compensation in a personal services contract, the person performing the services is ordinarily entitled to her ***ordinary and reasonable compensation.*** Ella would be entitled to receive her usual and reasonable compensation from Anna, especially since she had previously performed for Anna and Anna is presumed to know her usual fee. Choice **C** is incorrect because the agreement did not provide for the same fee for Ella as for Sam. Choice **A** is incorrect because Ella had no obligation to accept employment in the less prestigious nightclub. This was not what she bargained for, and appearance there might damage her reputation and her career. Finally, Choice **D** is obviously incorrect because the parties had a contract and Ella is entitled to recover her normal and usual compensation from Anna. (**Note:** In saying money is no object, Anna may have agreed to pay whatever price Ella requested (within limitations of good faith). *Cf.* UCC §2-305(2). That option is not available in this question, but might arise in your class.)

22. **A** If it is not clear whether an offer is intended to solicit a promise or performance, the offer must be interpreted as inviting the offeree to accept **either** by promising to perform the act requested **or** by performing the act itself. Rest. 2d §32. Under these facts, Anna's wire could certainly be interpreted as soliciting either or both. She wanted to know if someone would appear, but she wanted even more to obtain an appearance. Stella was reasonable to conclude that she didn't have to wait to communicate with Anna but could just pack her bags and show up at the door. Anna had wired, "You must arrive no later than June 29," not "Let me know if you're coming." Choice **D** is incorrect because, as we have seen, some offers can be accepted either by a return promise or by performance.

Choice **B** is wrong because it is not Stella's best argument. Anna could not reasonably be charged with knowledge that Stella would cancel another engagement and, in any event, Stella can rely on her appearance as a valid acceptance entitling her to be paid her usual fee. Choice **C** is wrong because Anna's wire was at least ambiguous as to whether it expected a response other than performance (Stella's appearance).

23. **A** A promise to make a gift that anticipates that the promisee will either perform some act or refrain from performing some act in reliance on the promise is enforceable under the doctrine of promissory estoppel. Consideration is not required. The doctrine will be applied especially in the case of intrafamily relationships. Here, Corey gave up his job and enrolled in a college, all in reliance on his grandfather's promise. To the extent that Corey did these things, the grandfather's promise will be enforced. (**Note:** Because Corey went to college, as Alex requested, many courts would find Corey gave consideration.) However, Corey did not satisfy the condition Alex imposed — he did not get an all-A average. This condition limited the obligation to pay for a new car, but not the promise to pay tuition. Choice **A** is therefore correct, but Choice **B** is not. Choice **C** is not correct because consideration is not required in those cases in which promissory estoppel applies. Choice **D** is wrong, even though the agreement cannot be performed within a year. Once Corey has fully performed, the promise is removed from the Statute of Frauds. Rest. 2d §130. An exception for reliance under Rest. 2d §139 also would apply, but might limit Corey to recovery of the reliance interest. Because tuition was a reliance expense, the two provisions seem likely to produce the same result in this case.

24. **A** Creditors are often confronted with the need to renegotiate the terms of payment in response to the financial improvidence of their debtors. They are asked to reduce the obligation, to extend the period of payment, or both. The traditional view has been that even if a creditor agrees to these modifications, he is not bound by them for lack of consideration. Without an exception — a promise to change the duty (e.g., pay sooner), a dispute over the validity of the debt, reliance on the promise to forego part of the debt, or changed circumstances that make reduction fair and equitable — this agreement is not enforceable. Even if the agreement was enforceable as an accord, Frank's failure to perform the new agreement may permit Paul to insist on full payment. Rest. 2d §281.

Choice **A** is the best answer. Choice **B** is incorrect for the loan described here, but would be correct if the contract arose under article 2 of the UCC, where §2-209 permits good faith modifications without consideration. Choice **C** would be correct in some jurisdictions that are still trying to hold onto the old rule (*Foaks v. Beer*), but are permitting some inroads so long as the creditor gets something new to support his agreement. But choice C is not the best answer. Choice **D** is also not the best answer. It relies on a consideration — Frank's abstention from a filing in bankruptcy — that Frank did not agree to give. Nothing in the facts suggests Frank promised not to file for bankruptcy.

25. **B** Ordinarily, an offer is revocable by the offeror at any time. This is true even under these facts, which state that Bob's offer was "open for two weeks." Unless the offer created an option, it remains revocable. Choice **C** is wrong. Only the *recitation of a purported consideration* is required by Rest. 2d §87(1)(a). Bob's offer, however, does not state any consideration at all for the promise to keep the offer open, but merely states the price of the car. Thus, it is not an option. Choice **D** is wrong because Bob is not a merchant of cars. A signed, written signed by a merchant to buy or sell goods is irrevocable without consideration for the time stated. UCC §2-205. Choice **A** is wrong because Bob's reasons do not matter. If the offer created an option, it would be irrevocable despite good reasons; if not, it would be revocable even for bad reasons.

26. **A** Most mass-media advertisements are not offers to sell. Instead, they are an "invitation to the public to come and purchase." *Craft v. Elder & Johnson Co.*; Rest. 2d §26, cmt. b. The rationale is that the ads rarely contain precise information on price, availability, etc. The ad in this case was especially sketchy. It did not state what coins were being sold, the quantity of each kind of coin, or even that the special sales price applied to all the coins. Choice **A** is the best answer. Choice **B** is not a good answer because the law does not require adequacy of consideration. Rest. 2d §79(b). In any event, because there had never been an offer to sell the coin at any price, the parties were free to negotiate a price and Jim was free to reject Tom's offer. Choice **C** is incorrect because even if Tom's reliance satisfied the requirement of consideration, it would not overcome the absence of an offer. Choice **D** is wrong because, as we have seen, Jim's ad was not an offer but an invitation to Tom to come and examine Jim's merchandise.

27. A The facts of this question establish that both Jim and Tom were merchants (Jim operates a coin store and Tom deals in coins). The sale of goods between merchants is covered by several special provisions of the UCC. Between merchants, if a **written** confirmation of the contract is sent by the seller within a **reasonable time** after the sale, the Statute of Frauds is satisfied unless the purchaser objects in writing within ten days after receiving the confirmation. UCC §2-201(2). Choice **A** is therefore the correct answer. Choice **B** is incorrect because in the absence of a transaction between merchants and in other special circumstances, the UCC requires that all sales contracts for goods at a price greater than $500 be in writing. UCC §2-201(1). Even under the 2003 revisions of article 2, which increased the threshold value to $5,000, choice B would be wrong. The question will not turn on the face value of the coins, but on the coins, but on the price of the goods. The statute would not apply because the price is less then $5,000, but the reasoning offered in this choice is incorrect. Choice **C** is incorrect because the purchaser does not have to sign the memorandum. The seller's memorandum is sufficient if it is received by the purchaser and the purchaser does not object within ten days. Choice **D** incorrectly states the law. The seller's memorandum covered by the UCC always follows the sale.

28. C The facts of this question raise the issue of fairness in dealing between two parties to a contract. Can a party be forced to pay $1,000 for $50 in coins? The answer is yes. So long as the parties have freely agreed to the price, there is consideration. Consideration exists when the promisee gives up something of value and the promisor makes his promise in exchange. There is no requirement that the items exchanged be of equal value. The contrary view is obviously inapplicable in the kind of exchange between Jim and Tom. Who is to say that the 50 silver dollars are not worth $1,000? We leave the parties to their bargain. Choice **C** is the correct answer. Choice **D** is legally incorrect (contracts between merchants do require consideration). Choice **A** is incorrect because it is contrary to the facts: the courts will not ordinarily question the value of consideration in a bargain between two parties. Finally, Choice **B** is incorrect because it was not necessary for Jim to change his position. He was merely trying to enforce his bargain with Tom.

29. A A party's duties or obligations under a contract may be delegated and performed by the delagatee (Rest. 2d §318(1)) without the consent of the other party to the contract. This is true of all performance obligations except those that require special or unique skills, as in the case of an artist or professional (e.g., a particular tenor, surgeon, or defense lawyer). Rest. 2d §318, illus. 6. Choice **B** is therefore incorrect. Painter did not need any specific authority to delegate his duties to Arthur. There is nothing unique about the services required in the painting of a building and construction and repair duties are generally delegable. The correct answer is **A**. Although he could assign his duties to Arthur, Painter remained liable to Owner for the integrity of the performance. A delegator may transfer the duty, but he cannot escape the responsibility. The rationale for this rule is illustrated by the facts of this case: if Painter were released by the delegation to Arthur, Owner would be able to recover only from Arthur who appears to be less solvent. Rest. 2d §318(3). Choice **C** is wrong because it begs the issue — the delegation was valid, but Arthur remains liable. Choice **D** is incorrect because Owner could not be held to waive his claim against Painter simply because he saw Arthur doing the work and said nothing. His assumption that Arthur was Painter's employee was perfectly reasonable. In any event, the substitution of Arthur for Painter would require the specific consent of Owner before a true *novation* (release of Painter and assumption of duties by Arthur) could occur. Rest. 2d §318, cmt. d. The facts do not show that that happened.

30. A This question requires analysis of an agreement based on a mutual mistake concerning a basic assumption of the parties. Joe and Bill made their agreement on the mistaken assumption that Carl was responsible for the dent in Joe's door. Can Bill avoid his promises after he realizes that it was induced by a mistake? Many courts have held that in cases of mutual mistake, there is no contract at all and that either party may avoid it. The more modern view, however, is reflected in the Restatement, which will impose the obligation of performance under three circumstances: (1) the mistake must relate to a basic assumption, (2) the mistake must have a material effect on the agreement, and (3) the party seeking avoidance must not bear the risk of the mistake. Rest. 2d §152. These facts clearly revolve around a material mistake that was the underlying assumption of the agreement. The remaining issue is whether Bill bears the risk of the mistake. The answer under the Restatement would be yes. First of all, Joe relied to his detriment on Bill's promises. Second, and perhaps more importantly, Bill was "aware, at the time the contract was made that he had only limited knowledge with respect to the facts to which his mistake related but treated his limited knowledge as sufficient." This doctrine is called the doctrine of "conscious ignorance," Rest. 2d §154(b), illus. 1. Thus, choice **B** is wrong. Choice **C** is wrong because Joe waived his claim against Carl in exchange for Bill's promise. Even if Joe's claim was invalid, waiving it will be consideration as long as Joe honestly believed it was valid at the time the contract was made. Choice **D** is wrong because the agreement did not have to be in writing.

31. **B** A party to a contract may freely assign his rights under the contract. This principle makes an assignment of rights somewhat different from a delegation of duties. No consideration is required for the assignment, which operates as a present transfer. In this case, however, the delivery of cement by Jonathan constituted consideration. The assignment does not have to be in writing, but, here, Builder gave notice of the assignment to Owner. The assignment from Builder to Jonathan is a *partial assignment of payment* because Builder retained his rights to the balance. At common law, partial assignments were not permitted. These days, however, the courts generally allow partial assignments. The right to make a partial assignment is recognized in the Restatement. Rest. 2d §326(1). Generally, the partial assignee cannot sue the obligor without naming the assignor as co-plaintiff. In any event, the assignee "stands in the shoes of the assignor" and is subject to all the defenses, set-offs, and counterclaims that the *obligor* can assert against the *assignor*. The best answer is **B**. Because Builder did not perform his work in a reasonably competent manner, he cannot recover and Jonathan cannot recover. Choice **A** is wrong because any defense Owner has against Builder will also apply Jonathan. Builder cannot assign greater rights that it has. Choice **C** is wrong because Builder could *assign* the right to payment at any stage in the work; however, the Owner was not required to make payment until the work was completed. Choice **D** is incorrect. Although the contract relates to land, it does not involve the transfer of an interest in land. Only agreements to transfer or buy an interest in land are within the Statute of Frauds; contracts to build on or improve land are not.

32. **B** A party to a contract has the same defenses against the minor as against any other party. If a minor misrepresents a material fact on which the other party justifiably relies to his detriment, the latter has the option of rescinding the agreement or of asserting the defense of breach. Rest. 2d §164. Youth's misrepresentation of the condition of the bike entitles Teller to defend against Youth's claim. **A** is

incorrect. Although persons under 18 are classified as infants in most states, an agreement by an infant is voidable by the infant but enforceable by the infant against the other party to the agreement. Rest. 2d §14. Choice **C** would be correct if Teller asserted incapacity, but this has no bearing on the defense of misrepresentation. Because Teller will raise misrepresentation, this response is not the best answer. Choice **D** is incorrect because the facts indicate that Teller's reliance was reasonable. Many courts will not even inquire into the reasonableness of defendant's reliance if the plaintiff intended the misrepresentation, as is the case here.

33. C A minor who enters into a contract has the option of voiding the contract at any time until his majority (in most states, the age of 18). Rest. 2d §14. The correct answer is **C**. Choice **A** is incorrect because it's immaterial to our decision whether Teller waives the misrepresentation. If Youth voids the agreement, there's nothing Teller can do. Choice **B** is a valid statement of the law, but it is immaterial to the issue: Youth's right to avoid the contract. Choice **D** is wrong on all counts. Teller could waive his right to avoid the agreement, but he cannot enforce it either because of Youth's age and his decision not to perform.

34. C The parol evidence rule does not prevent the introduction of evidence that the parties made a critical mistake when they reduced their agreement to writing. The rationale is that the mistake vitiates the entire agreement. Teller will show that the bicycle described in the contract was not the one the parties intended to describe. Choice **C** is the correct answer. Choice **D** is incorrect because the transaction did not come within the Statute of Frauds (under UCC §2-201, only contracts for the sale of goods with an aggregate price of $500 or more are within the Statute of Frauds; the amount will increase to $5,000 or more if the 2003 revisions to article 2 are adopted). Choice **A** is incorrect because mistakes that are material to the agreement can always be proven. Finally, Choice **B** is incorrect because the fairness of a deal is no basis to require a party to accept goods she never agreed to buy. (**Note:** Youth could prevail by suing for the failure to accept bicycle 100A. The parol evidence rule will not preclude evidence that the writing incorrectly recorded the parties' agreement. If clear and convincing evidence shows that the parties agreed to the bicycle with the crack in the frame, the writing can be reformed to reflect the correct serial number and enforced accordingly — subject to other defenses, such as misrepresentation.)

35. B Reformation or a contract normally requires mutual mistake —
that both parties believed the writing correctly stated their agreement. But where one party recognizes the mistake and fraudulently
fails to disclose it, courts often allow reformation for unilateral
mistake. Once reformed to reflect the serial number of the bike
on which the parties actually agreed, Teller has no claim to damages
for failure to deliver a different bicycle. No agreement to sell that
bicycle ever existed. Choice **A** is wrong on the facts. There was a
unilateral mistake, not a mutual one. Choice **C** is wrong because
unilateral mistake will justify either rescission or reformation,
where the other party had reason to know of the mistake. Here,
Teller actually knew of the mistake, which probably amounts to
nondisclosure sufficient to establish fraud. Rest. 2d §161. Teller
might argue that Youth bore the risk of the mistake. Negligence
by Youth, however, is not sufficient to establish mistake. Rest. 2d
§157. Whatever Teller's options to avoid the contract, he cannot
enforce a contract Youth never made. Choice **D** is wrong on the law.
The parol evidence rule does not bar evidence of mistake.

36. A The best answer is **A**. A transfer of one's rights under a contract is an
assignment. A transfer of one's duties under a contract is a *delegation*. A "general assignment" of the entire contract operates both as
an assignment and a delegation. UCC §2-210(4); Rest. 2d §328(1).
These facts tell us that Seller "assigned all my rights under my
contract" to Bradley. This language ordinarily means both an assignment of rights and a delegation of duties. UCC 2-210(5) (UCC
§2-210(3) under the 2003 revisions to article 2). But the facts also
state that "the assignment did not contain an assumption by Bradley of Seller's obligations." This negates a delegation of duties. Thus,
when Bradley did not perform, he was not liable either to Seller or to
Buyer. Choice **B** is not as good an answer as **A**. The concept of
privity is a complicated one that applies generally when there is a
succession of interests between one party and another (e.g., assignor
and assignee, or testator and beneficiary), or when there is a mutuality of interest in a contract or property right. If Bradley
had agreed to the delegation, he would have been liable to Buyer
regardless of privity, so **A** is the better answer. Choice **C** is wrong. A
delegation to Bradley would make Buyer a third party beneficiary
of the contract. Because Bradley did not promise to perform
Seller's duties, there could be no third party beneficiary of a promise. Choice **D** is wrong because it is contrary to the facts. No

indemnification agreement is mentioned; nor would indemnification of Seller affect Buyer's rights.

37. **B** Contracts in which one party agrees to buy all his requirements for a stated period from another party at an agreed price are called requirements contracts. Before the UCC, many courts declared these contracts unenforceable for lack of consideration. Under the UCC, these contracts are enforceable. UCC §2-306. Choice **A** is incorrect. While Buyer is not committed to order any office furniture if he needs none, Buyer must determine his needs in good faith and cannot simply back out of the deal on a whim. Buyer has given up the right to order from any other supplier for a year — a legal right Buyer was under no obligation to relinquish. That is consideration for Seller's promise. Choice **B** is the best answer. Although the Buyer could have enforced the Seller's agreement even without reliance, his reliance under these facts is another reason to bind the Seller. Choice **C** is wrong. Even though Buyer had no purchase or sales history, the Court would impose a standard of good faith in the absence of a minimum or estimated quantity. There is nothing in the facts to indicate that Seller was unable to meet Buyer's needs, especially prior to his very first order. Choice **D** is incorrect because Buyer's ability to get his needs elsewhere is immaterial to Seller's obligation. Because Buyer was forced to pay more for his desks and chairs, Seller will be liable for Buyer's damages.

38. **A** The obligation of a seller to supply all the requirements of a buyer for a stated period at an agreed price is one-half of a requirements contract (the other half is the agreement of the buyer to purchase all its requirements exclusively from the seller) and is enforceable. UCC §2-306. By its very nature, a requirements contract is lacking several terms of an ordinary sales contract (i.e., the quantity to be purchased and the dates of performance). Under these facts, however, the contract is sufficiently definite to satisfy the UCC requirements: it fixes the term by which the quantity is to be measured (i.e., one year), the price to be paid by Buyer (i.e., 10% below listed wholesale), and the commodity to be sold (i.e., office desks and chairs). Choice **B** is wrong; in the absence of a "best efforts" clause, Buyer would be expected to use only reasonable efforts to sell the desks and chairs. Choice **C** is wrong because it is not necessary to know Buyer's needs in advance of his orders. *McMichael v. Price.* Choice **D** is wrong on the facts. The price was fixed at 10% below

the Seller's *quoted wholesale price*. (**Note:** If Buyer placed no orders because it changed its mind, in good faith, about entering this new product line, no breach would occur because Buyer's needs would be zero. The cancellation would be ineffective, however, where Buyer does have orders from customers, as stated in the facts to the previous problem.)

39. B In the case of a guaranty given simultaneously with the creation of the debt, as in this case, there is consideration to support the guaranty — the detriment incurred by the creditor in making a loan to a debtor it would not otherwise accept. The correct answer is therefore **B**. Choice **A** is incorrect because ABC does not have to prove reliance. The mere fact that Rubberco gave the guaranty will be sufficient to support its claim. Choice **C** is incorrect. Ordinarily, a guaranty needs to be in writing. Rest. 2d §110(b). Because Rubberco's guaranty seems to be motivated by its own advantage (obtaining more tires from Joe), the promise falls outside the Statute of Frauds. Rest. 2d §116. Choice **D** is wrong. The words "we'll be responsible for" will be given their conventional meaning of assurance or commitment, making them equivalent to the word "guaranty."

40. A If the parties to a written agreement intend that the agreement operate as a final expression of their agreement, the written agreement is said to be an *integration* of their agreement. A *total integration* is an agreement that contains all the details of the agreement. Such an agreement forecloses the introduction of any evidence of prior or contemporaneous agreements or negotiations that would contradict or add to the agreement. The operative rule is the parol evidence rule, which bars from the factfinder's considerations all evidence of prior agreements not recited in the written agreement. The written agreement in this question contains an integration clause that helps to support application of the rule and the exclusion of any evidence as to the furniture. Rest. 2d §213, illus. 4. Because this agreement contains this clause, it will be considered "integrated," and the oral agreement concerning the furniture will be inadmissible. Choice **B** is incorrect because **A** is the better answer. Evidence as to the furniture will be excluded not because of the application of estoppel but by the parol evidence rule. Choice **C** is wrong on the facts. Furniture is not generally included in the purchase of a home, although it may be included. Choice **D** is incorrect because there is nothing in the facts to indicate that the exclusion of any reference to the furniture was the result of a mistake.

41. **A** Because the law encourages the compromise of disputes, agreements of settlement will be enforced unless the party waiving a claim has no good faith belief that the claim might succeed. This policy extends to the settlement of tort actions. Obviously, society benefits if the actions can be kept out of our crowded courtrooms. Even if one witness offers to testify for one of the parties, there is no certainty of outcome, and neither party would be considered unreasonable to insist on trial. The correct answer is **A**. Choice **B** is incorrect. In the settlement of a *bona fide* dispute, both parties are giving up the possibility of a larger recovery in exchange for the certainty of their agreement. Daniel's promise was supported by Paul's promise to release all claims arising from the accident. Choice **D** is incorrect because public policy supports (rather than rejects) the compromise of legal disputes. Finally, Choice **C** is incorrect because the court will supply the missing term and impose a reasonable period for payment.

42. **C** The facts require us to distinguish between an accord and satisfaction and a substituted agreement or novation. If we look to the intent of the parties, we will probably conclude that we are dealing with a substituted agreement. The distinction is important. In an accord and satisfaction, one performance is substituted by the obligor for another. Until the substituted performance is given, the first performance is not discharged. If there is a failure of performance, the obligee can sue for the first performance or the second, but not both. Rest. 2d §281(2). In a substituted agreement, the second performance replaces the first one, which is discharged. An agreement settling a tort action is a substituted agreement. Neither party is bound to give any performance until the compromise. Paul is limited to $5,000, the amount promised by Daniel. Choice **C** is the correct answer. Choice **D** is incorrect because Daniel's promise to pay $5,000 was supported by consideration: the agreement of Paul to release his tort claim. Choice **A** is incorrect because Paul's promise to pay only $5,000 was not void. It was given to resolve and compromise a *bona fide* dispute, and the law encourages compromises. Finally, choice **B** is incorrect because the agreement between the parties was not, as we have seen, an accord and satisfaction.

43. **D** When there is a *bona fide* dispute and it's not clear whether one or the other party will win and, also, what the amount of recovery, if

any, will be, a compromise agreement offers each party an acceptable alternative to litigation. It's irrelevant to the validity of the agreement whether a party's position will prevail or not, so long as the party acts in good faith. Since Paul *asserted his claim in good faith,* Daniel will be bound by Paul's acceptance of his compromise offer. (It should be noted that even if *both* witnesses supported Daniel's contention that the light was green, he could still lose: a jury could still believe Paul's version of the accident.) Choice **D** is correct because it establishes that Paul was acting in good faith in asserting his claim. Choice **C** is incorrect because the settlement was *not* an accord and satisfaction (i.e., the parties did not intend to return to their unsettled dispute; they intended to enforce payment of $5,000 in exchange for Paul's release of claim). In addition, Paul has performed the accord, eliminating any right to reassert the original duty even if this was an accord and satisfaction. Choice **B** is incorrect because all that is required for a valid compromise of a tort claim is that each party believe in good faith that his position is valid against the other. Rest. 2d §74(1), (2). Finally, choice A is incorrect because Daniel's promise was not explicitly or impliedly conditioned on the validity of Paul's claim. On the contrary, each party to a tort settlement knows that the outcome of the trial cannot be relied on.

44. **C** If a party agrees not to enforce a valid claim, her promise is sufficient "detriment" to qualify as consideration. Here, when Paul agreed not to sue Daniel, he gave up his right to recover $5,000. In exchange, he received Ted's promise of payment. The fact that Paul's promise was made to Ted does not alter the result. Rest. 2d §73, illus. 11. The correct answer is **C**. Choice **D** is incorrect because Ted's friendship would not be sufficient consideration in the absence of Paul's reliance. Choice **A** is incorrect because, as we have seen, there was consideration for Ted's promise to Paul. Finally, choice **B** is incorrect because there is no requirement that Paul sue and recover against Daniel before suing Ted. The contrary result would be economically wasteful and unreasonable.

45. **C** The Statute of Frauds covers *suretyship agreements,* promises to pay another's debt if they default. Rest. 2d §110. The agreement in question is not a suretyship agreement. Ted did not promise to perform in Daniel's place, but rather created an independent obligation: a promise to pay Paul if Paul would perform a service for Ted. The service was not to sue Daniel on the prior default. This is

an independent service to Ted, despite the fact that it has the effect of erasing Daniel's debt. Thus, it does not fall within the Statute of Frauds. Thus, choice **B** is incorrect. Choice **A** also is incorrect because the provision requiring a writing in contracts involving more than $500 applies only to the sale of goods. Rest. 2d §110(2)(a); UCC §2-201. Choice **D** is incorrect because forbearance does not constitute part performance, and part performance may not be insufficient to establish an exception if the Statute of Frauds applied. Rest. 2d §139.

46. B Ordinarily, a written agreement that qualifies as a *total integration* (i.e., it reflects the intent of the parties to confirm their final agreement) cannot be varied by the introduction of evidence of any prior or contemporaneous agreement or of a term contradicting the language of the agreement. The operative rule is the parol evidence rule. Rest. 2d §213. However, a party is permitted to introduce evidence of certain items to help the court in interpreting the terms of the contract. These terms deal with course of performance, course of dealing, and usage of trade. UCC §2-202(a) (UCC §2-202(1)(a) under the 2003 revisions to article 2). In interpreting these facts, we are concerned with XYZ's claim of trade usage. UCC §1-205 (UCC §1-303(c) under the 2001 revisions to article 1). Evidence of trade usage may be admitted not only to help interpret a particular phrase but also to add or subtract terms. In this case, XYZ is claiming to act under a trade custom that permits a 10% discount if payment is made within 10 days after discount. Evidence to prove this custom will be admitted. The term "net 30 days" used in the Confirmation is not inconsistent with this custom, which supplements the agreement but does not contradict it. UCC §2-208(2) (UCC §1-303(e) under the 2001 revisions to article 1). Choice **A** is not correct. In the absence of an express provision in the purchase documents or a trade custom, a buyer is not entitled to a discount for early payment of an invoice that specifies payment terms. Choice **C** is wrong because it is contrary to the general exception that permits evidence of trade usage, including usage as to payment terms, to interpret or supplement a written agreement. Choice **D** is wrong because whether or not the parties agreed on the discount terms, trade usage will operate to control their agreement.

47. C Courts are often called on to determine whether a particular provision in an agreement creates a promise or a condition. They will look to the intent of the parties as manifested in their choice of words. Here, Buyer agreed to pay Steelco "when" he was paid, not "if" he was paid. The correct answer is **C**. Choice **A** is wrong because it is the antithesis of **C**. Choice **B** is incorrect. Universal's bankruptcy did not excuse Buyer's obligation to pay for the tables and chairs. Again, the ability or willingness of Universal to pay Buyer was not a condition precedent to Buyer's liability to Steelco and did not excuse his performance. Choice **D** is not the best answer because, although it correctly states the facts, it is not the best reason to compel payment by Buyer.

48. C Under these facts, Transco's Purchase Order was an offer that Autocorp could accept only by confirming both the order and the immediate availability of goods. Because the offeror is "the master of his offer," Transco was able to specify the method of acceptance — fax. This ensured a prompt written acceptance that would also confirm the immediate availability of goods. Because Autocorp deviated from the specified mode of acceptance, there was no agreement between the parties. Choice **A** is not correct because it ignores the "mailbox" rule, which is followed by most courts. In the absence of Transco's insistence that acceptance be by fax, Autocorp's acceptance would have become effective when it *mailed* its acceptance to Transco, not when Transco *received* the letter. Rest. 2d §63(a). Transco's telegraph would have been ineffective because it came after the acceptance was mailed. Choice **B** is wrong only because Autocorp did not comply with the method of acceptance specified by Transco. Choice **D** is wrong on the law. The means of communicating an acceptance can be, and often is, a material element of a contract.

49. A In general, a contract between two parties cannot be modified without consideration if the modification benefits only one party. Here, the change in price would benefit Pubco but hurt Filberts. Because we are dealing with the sale of goods, however, the modification needs no consideration to be binding. UCC §2-209(1). But the UCC does impose restrictions that are meant to operate in circumstances like those reflected in these facts. It imposes the requirement of good faith, designed to prevent acts of extortion or duress by one party against the other. UCC §1-203. It also recognizes the courts' right to refuse to enforce a contract that is unconscionable. UCC §2-302. Under these facts, choice **A** is the best choice. Choice **B** is wrong because lack of consideration is not the central issue in these facts. If the modification had not been unfair to Filberts, it would have been enforceable without consideration. Choice **C** is incorrect because there is no difference between the treatment of merchants and others in the general application of the modification-without-consideration rule. The difference in treatment between the two arises only when there is a written agreement that contains a no-oral-modification clause and the merchant attempts to enforce the clause against a customer who asserts that an oral modification exists and should be enforced. UCC §2-209(2). Choice **D** is wrong because it misstates the relationship between buyer and seller and ignores the sanctity of contracts.

50. **D** A written agreement that contains a no-oral-modification clause will ordinarily be enforceable according to its terms. This is true even if the existence of a modification can be proved by irrefutable testimony and even if the modification benefits both parties. UCC §2-209(2). The only exception to this rule occurs when the customer of a merchant fails to initial or sign separately the no-oral-modification clause itself. That exception obviously does not apply in this case. The oral agreement between Builder and Owner for the extra work on the room is therefore unenforceable. The correct answer is choice **D**. Choice **A** is wrong because, as we have seen, the no-oral-modification in the signed agreement precluded modification by a subsequent oral agreement. Choice **C** is wrong because the purchase of a TV set is not the kind of a reliance detriment that the law will recognize. The result might have been different if, following the discussion with Owner, Builder had purchased more materials or hired another worker. In that event, the oral modification might be enforceable under the doctrine of waiver. UCC §2-209(4). Choice **B** is wrong because the parol evidence rule deals with agreements and negotiations that *precede* the written agreement, not those that arise as modifications *after* the written agreement.

51. **C** The contract between the parties made compliance with the building specifications by Carl an express condition of Homer's promise to pay for the house. If a party manifests his willingness to waive a condition after the contract is executed, consideration is normally required for the waiver. However, courts are willing to recognize a waiver without express consideration if *either* the condition was not an important part of the original contract *or* the other party changes his position in reliance on the waiver. If the other party has not changed his position or relied on the waiver to his detriment, the

waiver may be retracted so long as no consideration has been given for the waiver. Rest. 2d §84(2). Under these facts, the correct answer is **C**. Choice **A** is wrong because Homer was free to retract his waiver until Carl changed his position in reliance on the waiver. Choice **B** is wrong because the parties did not modify the contract in the sense that they both became bound to use of ¼″ rods. Choice **D** is wrong on the facts. Homer's statement would certainly have served as a waiver if Carl had purchased and installed the ¼″ rods.

52. D If the parties clearly intend a contract but omit a term, the courts will almost universally apply the term. Rest. 2d §204. Here, the parties provided for a water heater but forgot to specify the size. It will be a simple matter for the court to conclude that what was intended was a heater large enough for the house, especially since the difference in cost between the smaller and larger heater will be insignificant for a $150,000 house. Once the omitted term is supplied, it's clear that the measure of damage is exactly the difference in cost between the two heaters. Since Carl has substantially performed (i.e., built the entire house), Homer is permitted to deduct the damages resulting from Carl's failure under the agreement. The correct answer is **D**. Choice **A** is incorrect because a party is not entitled to avoid an entire agreement by reason of a minor breach that can be corrected or reimbursed. Choice **B** is incorrect because the court will supply the missing term. Finally, choice C is incorrect because although Carl substantially performed he must be charged with the difference in cost to compensate Homer for Carl's breach.

53. B Building contracts often contain provisions requiring the express approval of a designated architect before final payment. Obviously, this creates a circumstance in which the subjective judgment of a single person controls the liabilities of the parties. Because the courts are unwilling to substitute their own interpretation of what may be reasonable for the parties' faith in another's judgment, they will generally respect these provisions. Rest. 2d §228, cmt. b. However, they will also require that the architect act in good faith. *Rizzolo v. Poysher*. The correct answer is therefore **B**. Choice **A** is incorrect because the judgment of other architects is not relevant. The parties have determined between themselves whose standards they will apply. Choice **C** is incorrect because the court will not normally inquire into the reasonableness of the architect's judgment unless one of the parties can show that he acted in bad faith. Choice **D** is wrong because the judgment of the ordinary reasonable person is hardly the best measure of the builder's performance. It certainly will not be substituted for the judgment of the designated architect.

54. **C** The requirement that Partridge be satisfied "100%" became an express condition of the parties' agreement when Artist undertook to work on the portrait. Rest. 2d §226. The correct answer is therefore **C**. Artist could have increased the chance of satisfying Partridge's express condition by showing him the work at various stages to make sure he was on the right track. When the recipient of performance insists on his personal satisfaction, it would be unfair to impose the standards of others on him. Choice **A** is wrong because there is no requirement that Partridge's judgment be reasonable. If Artist could show that Partridge was acting in bad faith — that he pretended not to like the painting, but really thought it was satisfactory — that might justify an award to Artist. But the standards and tastes of others are not what he bargained for. Choice **B** is wrong because there was no requirement that Partridge approve the work in stages. On the contrary, the test was whether he would be satisfied "100%" on its completion. Choice **D** is wrong. In the absence of an *express condition* requiring 100% satisfaction by the subject, the court would impose a *constructive condition,* which would require only that Artist render *substantial performance.* This would be measured by reasonable objective standards instead of the arbitrary satisfaction of the subject. Rest. 2d §226, cmt. c.

55. **C** A buyer of goods is entitled to receive goods that conform to his requirements. If the goods are defective, he is entitled to reject them. UCC §2-601(a). The facts tell us that Litho was responsible to typeset the brochure and that the mistake in dates was material. Once the goods were rejected by Piper, Litho could remedy its breach only by correcting the error in type, reprinting the brochure, and redelivering to Piper in time to avoid any damage to Piper. Litho not only failed in this duty but also affirmatively drove Piper to "cover" by demanding an increase in price. Once a buyer rejects the goods in good faith, he may resort to the remedy of "cover" (i.e., he may purchase substitute goods from another supplier). UCC §§2-711, 2-712(1). That's exactly what Piper did here. Once a buyer has covered, she is entitled to recover as damages "the difference between the cost of cover and the contract price together with any incidental or consequential damages as hereinafter defined (Section 2-715)...." UCC §2-712(2). UCC §2-715(2) defines consequential damages

in language that includes facts such as these, in that Litho had reason to know that the date of the auction was material. The best answer is therefore **C**. Piper is entitled to recover $2,000, the difference between the $5,000 contract price and the $7,000 paid to Printco, *plus* any consequential damages resulting from the late mailing of the brochures. Choice **A** is wrong only because it doesn't recognize that Piper may be entitled to consequential damages. Choice **B** is wrong because $7,000 overstates its damages. It has to subtract the original contract price. Choice **D** is wrong because Litho will not prevail. It breached the agreement and then tried to impose a penalty on Piper.

56. **A** The facts deal with an installment contract between Builder and Seller providing for nine separate deliveries. Builder has a right to reject one installment only if the defect substantially impairs the value of that installment. UCC §2-612(2). The right to cancel future installments arises only if the defect in one installment "substantially impairs the value of the whole contract." UCC §2-612(3). Here, the first installment was late, but that minor defect did not substantially impair its value. The second installment involved the wrong goods, a more serious breach, permitting rejection of that delivery. But nothing in that delivery impaired the value of future installments. Builder's fears of future defects gave it a right to demand adequate assurances of performance, but no right to cancel the entire contract at this time. UCC §2-612, cmt. 6. The correct answer is therefore **A**. Choice **B** is incorrect because Builder did reject the second installment, which Seller cured the next day. The UCC will reinstate the contract if the aggrieved party accepts a nonconforming installment without seasonable notice of cancellation. Since Builder accepted Seller's cure before giving notice of cancellation, this provision probably would not apply. Choice **C** misstates the rule. Material breach is the standard under the Restatement 2d, but not under the UCC. The question involves whether the breaches so far substantially impair the value of the future installments. No facts suggest that future installments have lost their value. In fact, Builder almost certainly still requires future windows to finish the building. Choice **D** is wrong because under the UCC, the "perfect tender rule" does not apply to installment contracts. UCC §§2-601, 2-612.

57. **B** A party to a contract may by his conduct indicate that he does not intend to perform the terms of the contract. In these circumstances,

the party will be deemed to have committed an anticipatory repudiation of the contract. The other party to the agreement may then cancel his own performance and may generally institute a suit for damages even before his performance is due. Here, Seller's conduct in conveying title to a third party before July 1 was a clear and voluntary repudiation of his contract with Buyer. Rest. 2d §250(b). The correct answer is **B**. Choice **A** is not the correct answer because Buyer has no obligation to do anything following the Seller's repudiation. Choice **C** is not a correct statement of the law. Buyer does not have to wait until the date for his own performance, but may accept the Seller's act as a repudiation and sue immediately. Choice **D** is incorrect. Buyer does not have to analyze or construe Seller's intent or mental state. His conduct speaks for itself. His act of conveying to a third party is a repudiation of the contract with Buyer.

58. **B** An ***anticipatory repudiation*** can occur either as a result of a party's conduct or by his unequivocal statement that he will not perform. In either case, the other party may commence an action for ***breach of contract*** immediately. And he does not have to ask for assurances of performance if the repudiating party's statement is unambiguous, as it is here. When Seller advised Buyer that the home would not be conveyed, Seller's conduct constituted a clear and voluntary anticipatory repudiation. Choice **A** is incorrect because an anticipatory repudiation can be marked by a clear and unequivocal statement that the party is unwilling to perform, without any further action. Choice **C** is incorrect because when an anticipatory repudiation has occurred, the aggrieved party can commence an action even though the date for performance has not yet arrived. Finally, Choice **D** is incorrect because the aggrieved party may commence an action immediately; she does not have to wait to see if the other party really means what he says.

59. **A** If the promised performances of both parties to a contract ***can*** occur at the same time, the courts will normally require that they be performed ***simultaneously***. The performances are then said to be conditions of each other, or ***concurrent conditions***. Each party is expected to be ready to perform at the time designated. Normally, he manifests this by ***tendering*** his performance. The concept is used especially in contracts relating to the sale of goods and of land. Rest. 2d §234(1). Buyer's tender of payment is sufficient to establish readiness to perform on his part. The correct answer is **A**. Choice

B is incorrect because Buyer need only show an ability or readiness to perform by tendering payment (it would obviously be incongruous to require actual payment). Choice **C** is incorrect. Buyer is required to *tender* performance (i.e. payment) to show that he has the ability to perform. Seller need not deliver a deed if Buyer is unprepared or unwilling to perform. Choice **D** is wrong. Land contracts and title closings are the primary example of transactions involving the requirement of simultaneous performance, not alternating and dependent performances.

60. D Under the written addendum to their contract, the parties created an express condition to payment of the balance by Erik. Provisions of this kind (i.e., those requiring the approval of a specified architect) are very common in construction contracts. Rest. 2d §227, cmt. c; §228, cmt. b. Under the majority view, the condition will be enforced even if the designated architect is unreasonable (so long as he acts in good faith). Some states require that the architect act reasonably (New York is among this minority). Under these facts, Mitch's refusal to issue a certificate will prevent recovery on the contract by Myron. Under the majority view, Myron cannot rely on the certification by Paul Right. Only in those states following the minority view will he be able to argue that Paul Right's judgment raises questions about Mitch's reasonableness. Choice **A** is therefore incorrect. Choice **C** is wrong because most courts will allow Myron to recover something, either damages under the contract (if the breach was not material) or the fair market value of the services (if the breach was material). In either event, Myron is in default as measured by Mitch's refusal to issue a certificate of completion, so his recovery will be limited by the damages Erik may recover for Myron's breach. The best answer is therefore **D**. Choice **B** is wrong because the agreement did not empower Mitch to fix Erik's damages in the event of breach. He is entitled to deduct his actual damages.

61. D Sally honestly believed that she had a legal claim against Bob. She was wrong. Nonetheless, her agreement not to press the claim would be valid consideration for Bob's promise to pay her medical bills. Choice **C** is incorrect. Choice **A** is incorrect because the agreement did not have to be in writing. Choice **B** is plausible. The existence of consideration will not negate a defense of mutual mistake. The mistake involved here is a mistake not of fact but of law (both parties believed that the applicable law made the property owner responsible to clear snow and ice from the sidewalk). Originally, courts would not afford relief to a party claiming a mistake of law. The modern view, however, is to treat a mistake in law in the same way as any other mistake, on the theory that a mistake of law is "part of the total state of facts at that time." Rest. 2d §151, cmt. b. This defense, however, cannot apply to settlement contracts. Uncertainty over who might prevail (either on the law or the facts) is one risk the settlement resolves. No settlement would be secure if a party could avoid the contract by pleading a mistake of fact or law pertaining to the merits of the claim or defense justified rescission. Rather, mistake applies when a mistake of law (say, a zoning ordinance) materially affects the underlying consideration (say, a land sale). It is not pertinent to mistakes concerning who is right in litigation.

62. C Parties to a commercial agreement often argue over the quality or scope of performance by one of the parties. To encourage settlement of these disputes, the courts will generally enforce a general release of claims given by one party to the other. This practice is recognized by the UCC. UCC §1-107 (UCC §1-306 under the 2001 revisions to article 1). Choice **A** is therefore incorrect: no consideration was necessary for the execution of Owner's release. However, these facts confront us with a more difficult issue, i.e., can the party executing the release reassert his claim if the release was given under a mistake or misunderstanding? When the relationship is a commercial one, the answer is no. *Sears, Roebuck & Co. v. Jardel Co.* The result may be different when the relationship is noncommercial, as in the case of a release from a personal injury plaintiff to an insurance company. The correct answer is **C**. Because this was a commercial transaction, Owner cannot avoid his release because he gave it to Builder on the mistaken impression that Builder was a lodge fellow. In any event, this is probably not the kind of mistake that would justify redress to Owner. The mistake did not relate to the underlying contract or transaction but to an extraneous and collateral fact. Choice **B** is therefore incorrect. Choice **D** is wrong because it states a conclusion that is contrary to the facts.

63. D The best answer is **D**. However, under an alternative interpretation of the facts, the best answer would be **C**. The solution depends on whether we are dealing with an accord and satisfaction or with a substituted agreement. In an accord and satisfaction, one party offers and the other accepts a substitute performance in the future in discharge of an existing obligation. The promise is called an *executory accord*. Here, the executory accord was Orville's promise to convey title to his station wagon. If an executory accord is made, no discharge occurs until the new terms are performed. In the meantime, the old debt or obligation *is not discharged*. If neither the old debt nor the promised accord is performed or satisfied, the other party has an option: he may sue on either the original obligation or on the promised accord. Rest. 2d §281. In a substituted agreement, the parties agree that the old obligation will be discharged and a new one substituted. If the substituted agreement is not performed, the aggrieved party can sue only on the new promise, not the old one. Rest. 2d §279(2). Whether a particular transaction is an accord and satisfaction or a substituted agreement depends on the intent of the parties. Here, the agreement looks, feels, and smells more like an accord and satisfaction than a substituted agreement, so we prefer choice **D** to choice **C**, which would be the correct answer if we had a substituted agreement. Choice **A** is wrong under either theory: a substitute would wipe out the debt, not the car; an accord would not wipe out either one. Choice **B** is wrong because Bradford cannot recover both, but must choose one or the other, even under an accord.

64. **C** If a promise is conditioned on the occurrence of an event that is within the exclusive or partial control of one party, most modern courts will imply an obligation on the part of the promisor to use his best efforts to make the event happen. Barney must make at least a good faith effort to locate a purchaser for his business. If he fails to do so, Sampson can successfully assert a breach of contract claim. Choice **C** is the right answer. Choice **D** is not the best answer, although it correctly states that a promise contingent on the occurrence of some event will satisfy the requirement of consideration. Choice **C** is a better answer than **D** because even though we find consideration, we must subsequently analyze what effect Barney's unwillingness to find a buyer would have on Sampson's promise. Choice **A** is incorrect because the court will read into the condition (because it is within Barney's control) the obligation to use his best efforts to find a buyer. Choice **B** is not correct. The fact that a promise is executory does not mean that it fails to supply consideration.

65. **D** The parties to a written agreement usually engage in extensive oral discussions and negotiations before they sign the agreement. Once

the agreement is signed, the parol evidence rule operates to exclude any evidence of these oral discussions that differ from the writing. The assumption is that the written agreement represents the final expression of the parties' intent. If it does, the agreement is deemed a **total integration.** If, on the other hand, the agreement is not intended to include all the details of their agreement, the agreement is deemed a **partial integration.** In the latter case, evidence of a prior oral understanding may be admitted if it does not contradict a term of the agreement. The judge, not the jury, will usually determine whether the agreement is a partial or total integration. The best answer on these facts is **D.** If the judge decides the agreement was a partial integration — a logical conclusion when we consider that the writing specified only a total price without dealing with the distribution of the price between cash and mortgage — then Barney will be able to introduce the oral understanding and win. Choice **C** is wrong because a decision that the agreement was a partial integration is not helpful to Sampson's case. Choice **A** is wrong because it offers only an objective test of whether we are dealing with a total integration or a partial integration. The issue to be resolved is the intent of the parties, and that can be determined only by the judge after hearing the evidence. Choice **B** is wrong for the same reason. (**Note:** Two other theories, not offered in any of the answers, might be tried. One argues that the agreement should be reformed to include the condition that Barney's business be sold entirely for cash. The other argues that the agreement, though totally integrated, was conditioned on an event that did not occur. The theory is weak because the condition was included in the writing. Thus, arguing that the entire writing became effective only if the condition occurred is less persuasive.)

66. C Under these facts, Barney's best argument is probably that the agreement as written is unconscionable. The courts will not enforce an agreement that is so one-sided as to be essentially unfair. Both the Restatement and the UCC make provision for rejection of an unconscionable agreement. Rest. 2d §208; UCC §2-302(1). Several facts make performance of this agreement by Barney unfair: (1) he is being forced to sell an existing business; (2) he has to move to a new city; (3) he has to pay more for Sampson's business than his own business is worth; (4) Sampson is the one who has failed to negotiate a new lease; and (5) he has no assurance that his new business will be allowed to remain in its present location, or, indeed, be able to find a new location. Under these circumstances, the court can easily help

Barney to be relieved of his bad bargain by reforming the agreement to conform to the oral modification. *Gianni Sport Ltd. v. Gantos.* Choice **B** is arguably as good an answer. Most oral modifications of written agreements will be enforced without consideration, but there is always the risk that the court will insist on some showing of consideration, especially where the contract as written contains no reference to Sampson's lease. Choice **A** is wrong because there is no ambiguity in the writing as described. Choice **D** is not the best answer. Under some circumstances, the court will impose a condition as a matter of law to ensure fairness. However, constructive conditions are not normally used to impose new terms on the parties.

67. **B** The best answer is **B**. The facts we are given show only that the parties had a dispute and that they resolved their dispute in a modification that involved two basic ingredients: a promise by Jack to perform additional services in caring for the trees, and his agreement to wait for payment until the end of the year. These facts create neither an accord and satisfaction (i.e., an agreement to give a new performance in exchange for an old one) nor a substituted agreement (i.e., an agreement to perform a different duty in satisfaction of an existing one), but simply the modification of an existing contract by a change in terms. A modification of an existing contract is enforceable without consideration even if it benefits only one party. UCC §2-209(1). Under these facts, Jill could reasonably ask for the modification to which Jack agreed. Because one of the modifications was a delay in payment for a period of one year, Jack's suit is premature. If, however, Jill repudiated the contract, choice **B** would not be correct. Choice **A** is wrong because the original agreement was not supplanted. We do not have a substituted agreement, but the modification of an existing one. In addition, the modification did not eliminate Jack's right to compensation, but merely delayed it for a year. Choice **C** is wrong because we cannot measure Jack's remedy at this time. If the trees do not survive, Jack may recover nothing. If they all survive, Jack's failure to water them may cause no damage to Jill. If only some of them survive, his recovery will have to be calculated. Choice **D** is an arguable choice, but it is not as good as **B**. While Jack has not performed the modifications, his failure may not be material. If all the trees survive after one year despite Jack's failure to perform the modifications, he will probably be entitled to the agreed price of $10,000.

68. D An "assignment of rights and obligations" operates both as an assignment and a delegation. An assignment is a transfer of rights; a delegation is a transfer of duties. UCC §2-210(5) (UCC §2-210(3) under the 2003 revisions to article 2). Here, Scents transferred both to Parfumco. All contract rights are assignable unless the assignment materially increases the risks to the obligor, in this case, Aroma. Rest. 2d §317(2). The facts here involve a requirements contract: Aroma contracted with Scents for all its oils for a period of one year. Before the UCC, requirements contracts were not assignable. The UCC now recognizes such assignments under the proper circumstances. UCC §§2-306(1), 2-210(2) (UCC §2-210(1)(a) under the 2003 revisions to article 2). The assignment from Scents to Parfumco was therefore valid without the consent or acknowledgment of Aroma. Choice **A** is not the best answer because there is no inherent right in the obligor to prevent an assignment. Choice **B** is wrong for essentially the same reason. Scents had a right to assign and did not breach the agreement with Aroma by assigning; the agreement did not contain a no-assignment clause, and prohibitions against assignment are frowned on anyway. If Aroma suspects that Parfumco cannot or will not perform as well as Scents and that the risks to it will be increased unacceptably, it can ask for assurances because the assignment is coupled with a delegation. UCC §§2-210(5), 2-609 (UCC §2-210(2)(c) under the 2003 revisions to article 2). Failure of Parfumco to give adequate assurances will entitle Aroma to cancel the agreement. Choice **D** is therefore the best answer. Choice **C** is not the correct answer because, on the facts, Parfumco had already confirmed the assignment in writing.

69. D The facts illustrate the difference between two different circumstances, each of which can operate to relieve a party from performing the terms of a contract. The first arises when the contract calls for delivery of particular goods and the goods are destroyed. When this happens, the contract is discharged if the goods are essential to the contract. On these facts, we have to ask two questions: Were the live flowers essential to the contract? And were flowers from Iris the subject matter of the contract? The answer to the first question is yes, but the answer to the second question has to be no. The flowers from Iris were not the subject matter of the contract. The contract did not specify a particular source for the flowers. Many suppliers have live flowers, and OSI's duty was not to deliver the Iris flowers, but to deliver live flowers from any reasonable source. UCC §2-615. Choice **B** is therefore wrong. The other circumstance that will relieve a party of its duty to perform is impracticability.

Impracticability is akin to impossibility, but different enough to suggest a different result in this case. It was not impossible for OSI to perform, but it was impracticable (i.e., performance would be too costly and might jeopardize OSI's very existence). The modern view is to permit discharge under these circumstances. The cost increase must be extreme, must not be foreseeable, and must not be implicit in the contract. Rest. 2d §261, cmt. d; UCC §2-615. The increase in price may not be enough by itself to justify discharge, but the threat to OSI's very existence probably is. Choice **D** is the best answer. Choice **A** is wrong under our analysis of the facts because OSI is excused from performing. Choice **C** is not the best answer; although it is one way of restating the nature of the event confronting OSI, it doesn't help us to analyze the subtleties involved.

70. **B** These facts involve a dispute between the two parties over the completion of a building contract. The issue is the measure of damages following a dispute over performance. Because we are told that an architect has certified a defect in performance, we have to conclude that the defect did occur and that Contractor was in breach. Unless the breach is material, Contractor can recover on the contract, but the balance due will be offset by any damages the breach caused Homeowner. (If the breach was material, Homeowner might elect to cancel the contract, in which case Contractor could not sue on the contract, but must instead recover in *quasi-contract* for the fair market value of the services performed, less any damages to Homeowner.) Because the breach does not seem to be material, the measure of damage is the contract price, less the damages for defendant's breach. If the architect's estimate is correct, Contractor's recovery will be $7,000, the difference between the contract price and the cost to Homeowner of replacing the wrong material. Choice **A** is wrong because it does not compensate Homeowner for the cost of correcting Contractor's breach. Choice **C** is wrong because the result would be to confer a windfall on Homeowner. Choice **D** is wrong. The defect here is a breach of Contractor's duty, not the failure of a condition. Unless the breach is material, which it does not appear to be, Homeowner must perform and seek damages rather than withhold performance.

71. **B** An *assignee* ordinarily *stands in the shoes* of his assignor with respect to the original contract. Since Ed was Carl's assignee under a continuing contract, he was entitled to have Dan render

performance to him. Choice **C** is incorrect because Ed, having assumed Carl's obligations, would be obliged to purchase his requirement of doughnuts from Dan. Choice **D** is incorrect because a
vendee under a requirements contract may not require an amount
that is unreasonably disproportionate to comparable prior requirements. Finally, Choice **A** is incorrect because Ed has only those
rights that Carl had against Dan under the original contract.

72. **A** As Harpo's attorney, your responsibility is not only to guide him to
the maximum possible recovery but also to prevent him from actions that may ultimately work to his disadvantage or detriment.
Choice **D** is the only choice that contemplates the completion of the
yacht in an effort to improve Harpo's position. It is a course of
action that is covered under the UCC. UCC §§2-703, 2-704(2).
The UCC recognizes the right of a reasonable seller to complete
the manufacture of an article and resell it in the event of a breach
by the buyer. However, under these facts, which tell us that construction has not begun and that the resale price is purely speculative, it would not be advisable for Harpo to proceed with
construction. Choice **D** is not the best answer. The other three
choices all anticipate that Harpo will sell the materials for
$30,000 and sue Roland for damages. What is the best measure
of his damages? Choice **C** is not the best answer. Restitution is
available only when the plaintiff has performed a part of the contract and conferred some benefit on the defendant. In other words,
the plaintiff's restitution interest is the value to the defendant of the
plaintiff's performance. Rest. 2d §370. Here, Roland has received
no benefit, and restitution is not the best theory to proceed on.
Choice **B** is incorrect because the UCC does not provide a separate
remedy based on reliance. Both UCC §§2-706 and 2-708 (the basic
remedies for repudiation) start by allowing buyer to recover the
contract price, then subtract resale price (here, salvage value) and
costs saved (here, the expense of finishing construction of the
yacht). This at least will include recovery for expenses, but allows
(almost requires) Harpo to try to prove that a profit would have
remained after accounting for savings. Rather than give up now,
Harpo should try to prove expenses. Choice **A** is the best answer. It
may be difficult to prove how much Harpo saved by not completing
the yacht (since construction has not begun, it is almost impossible
to calculate all of Harpo's costs at this time). Still, Harpo has the cost
projections he used to compute the price, which serve as some basis
for proving savings. Harpo's profit is somewhat speculative. Still,

choice A comports best with the damage formulations allowable under the UCC and with Harpo's best interests.

73. **A** Because the associate's assignment is to construe the facts in a way that will be most beneficial to Builder, the best answer is **A**. We know that Subdivider threw Builder off the job. Unless excused by a Builder's breach or nonoccurrence of a condition, Subdivider's conduct breaches the contract. It would be hard to argue the breach was not material since it completely severed all remaining duties. Material breach may allow Builder to recover more than $375,000. Damages would be the contract price ($750,000) minus any costs saved (by not building the remaining five houses). Unless costs of construction on the last five houses will exceed $375,000, this remedy exceeds recovery on a severability theory. Choice **B** is tenable. Construction contracts are often divisible (i.e., they can be divided logically into a series of separate contracts in which services are performed in stages in exchange for payments of money). Rest. 2d §240. Not all construction contracts are divisible, but this contract would seem to qualify. The houses are all the same, the price for each is the same and is separately identifiable, and the event that triggers payment — the satisfactory completion of each house — is clearly stated. If we rely on the theory of divisibility, Builder will be likely to recover the $175,000 he asked for. Choice **B** would be the best answer if facts suggested either that Subdivider was justified in throwing Builder off the job or that finishing the work would cost Builder more than $375,000. Choice **C**, promissory estoppel, is not the best theory to rely on. It is applied generally in situations in which one party relies to her detriment on another's promise and is usually used as a substitute for consideration. Rest. 2d §90(1). It is not applied in bilateral contracts in which the rights and obligations of each party are clearly stated. Choice **D** is not the best answer. Quantum meruit is used in those cases in which the plaintiff has failed to give all the performance that was required by the contract, but has given a measure of performance that has conferred some value or benefit on the defendant. The plaintiff is allowed to recover the reasonable value of the benefit. The fair market value of the homes might be less than the contract price and certainly won't include the profit on the remaining five houses. The doctrine is not appropriate here because, at this point, Builder has given a measure of performance that can easily and reasonably be translated into Subdivider's obligation to pay a measurable sum.

74. D The parties to a contract sometimes intend that a third party shall receive the benefit arising from their contract. For example, A may agree to perform services for B with the understanding that B will pay A's earnings to C, to whom A owes a debt. C is the third party beneficiary of the contract between A and B. The Restatement distinguishes between "intended" beneficiaries and "incidental" beneficiaries. An intended beneficiary is one to whom the parties mean to give an interest that can be protected in the courts. Rest. 2d §302, cmt. b. A beneficiary who is not the intended beneficiary is an incidental beneficiary. Rest. 2d §302(2). Under these facts, the Harriot was clearly not the intended beneficiary of either Kiwanis or Delwood. The parties were concerned merely about supplying lodging to Delwood. They did not intend to confer on the Harriot the right to benefit from their promise. The Harriot is the incidental beneficiary of their agreement, not the intended one. The correct answer is **D**. Since the Harriot is not the intended beneficiary, choices **A**, **B**, and **C** are all wrong. Kiwanis intended no greater benefit to Harriot than to any other hotel that might lodge Delwood. And Delwood owed no duty to the Harriot whatever. He was free to use any hotel he wished.

75. C Arthur is the third party beneficiary of the contract between Joe and Bob. The ***original parties to a third party beneficiary contract*** may, by mutual agreement, alter or extinguish the third party beneficiary's rights ***prior to the time*** the third party beneficiary (1) manifests his assent to the promisor's promise, (2) materially changes his position in justifiable reliance on the third party beneficiary contract, ***or*** (3) brings a lawsuit to enforce the promisor's promise. Rest. 2d §311(2)-(3). Joe and Bob could, by mutual agreement only, divest Arthur of his rights under the agreement since none of the three circumstances that would cause Arthur's rights to vest had occurred. Choice **D** is incorrect because the original parties to the third party beneficiary contract do not require the consent of the third party beneficiary to modify their agreement, unless the beneficiary's rights have already vested as required by Rest. 2d §311. Choice **A** is incorrect because Joe could not unilaterally commit an anticipatory repudiation of his contract with Bob simply because Jack had not yet examined the car (an act that was not scheduled to occur until January 30). Finally, choice **B** is incorrect because Bob's promise was not made illusory by requiring Jack's certification.

76. C A third party beneficiary under a valid contract may sue the promisor directly if the promisor fails to perform as required. Arthur is the intended beneficiary of the contract between Bob and Joe. An **intended beneficiary** is created when "the performance of the promise will satisfy an obligation of the promisee to pay money to the beneficiary." Rest. 2d §302(1)(a). That is certainly the case here. Once Jack certified that the car was worth $5,000, Bob had an obligation to pay Arthur directly. Arthur did not, however, lose his right to sue Joe as well. Most courts agree that the third party beneficiary may also sue the promisee on the contract. Rest. 2d §310(1). Of course, the beneficiary is limited to one satisfaction. That is particularly true because Joe owed Arthur the money, and nothing in this contract precludes Arthur from suing Joe on that original debt. Choice **C** is the right answer. All the other choices are wrong because they prevent recovery against either one or both of the parties to the contract.

77. C The original parties to a third party beneficiary contract may, by mutual agreement, modify, alter, or extinguish the third party beneficiary's rights until such time as **the third party beneficiary** (1) manifests his assent to the promisor's promise, (2) materially changes his position in justifiable reliance on the third party beneficiary contract, **or** (3) brings a lawsuit to enforce the promisor's promise. Rest. 2d §311(2)-(3). Under these facts, Joe and Bob were free to modify their agreement in any way required to protect their own interests. If Joe and Bob recognized that they had made a mutual mistake by inserting the number $5,000 instead of $4,000, they were entitled to amend the agreement. If Jack came in with an appraisal of $4,000 instead of $5,000, they were entitled to agree on the new figure. Since both I and II are available to Bob as partial defenses, **C** is the correct answer. B would have a partial defense with respect to the difference between $4,000 and $5,000. Choices **A, B,** and **D** are incorrect because I and II are **both** correct.

78. D The **promisor** under a **third party beneficiary contract** may assert any defenses against the third party beneficiary that she could have asserted against the promisee under the underlying contract. Rest. 2d §309(2). In a contract for the sale of an identified article, the destruction of the article operates to discharge the seller if the risk of loss has not passed to the buyer. When the car was destroyed on January 14, it became impossible for Joe to perform his obligations to Bob on January 30, and on January 14, the risk of loss had not passed to Bob. UCC §2-613(a). Choice **D** is the right answer. Choice **A** is the wrong answer because in the absence of the car's destruction, Bob's repudiation on January 15 would be an anticipatory breach entitling Arthur to sue for damages. Choice **B** is incorrect because Joe's statement was not relevant to the rights of the parties as they existed on January 15. Choice **C** is wrong because Arthur's statement was wrong. Once the car was destroyed, Bob could avoid the agreement.

79. D The best answer is **D**. The contract between Fabrico and Zippro is a fairly typical output and requirements contract. These contracts are covered under UCC §2-306. Because no specific quantities are set forth, the UCC imposes the requirement that the parties act in good faith to ensure a reasonably foreseeable and constant quantity. The facts tell us that Fabrico treats Zippro as its exclusive source. This commitment by Fabrico acts as the consideration for Zippro's promise to meet Fabrico's needs and imposes on Zippro the obligation to deal with Fabrico in good faith. *See Eastern Airlines Inc. v. Gulf Oil Corp.* Because Fabrico was a good, loyal, and constant customer for three years, Zippro did not act in good faith when it cut Fabrico off completely and prevented it from getting any zippers. The decline in Fabrico's needs was caused not by any action on its part but by the intrusion of a stronger competitor. Zippro's actions were especially egregious when you consider that it preferred Skisuit to Fabrico. Zippro could easily have served all the needs of Fabrico and some of the needs of Skisuit. Choice **A** is wrong because the facts tell us that Zippro did not expand its facilities, but merely geared up to full capacity. Choice **B** is wrong because Zippro could have sold to Skisuit without cutting Fabrico off entirely. Choice **C** is plausible if 200,000 zippers is disproportionate to the prior year's orders and that difference constitutes a material breach. (The perfect tender rule applies to buyers, not sellers. UCC §2-601.) On the facts, the orders may be disproportionately small, permitting Zippro to recover damages for the breach, if any. But no factors supporting termination for material breach appear in the facts. The courts will supply the level of requirements based on the parties' needs and business history, so long as the parties are acting in good faith.

80. B Brown and White entered into a bilateral contract under which Brown agreed to pay for White's performance. However, there was a condition to White's performance that was in the control solely of Brown (i.e., the bringing in of the sheep). Before the Restatement 2d, this would constitute a *condition precedent* to distinguish it from a *condition subsequent*. The Restatement has abandoned the distinction completely. What was formerly known as a condition precedent is now merely a condition. Rest. 2d §224. What was known as a condition subsequent is now treated as an event of discharge. Rest. 2d §230. An event can be made a condition by the agreement of the parties. Rest. 2d §226. Under these facts, the condition was understood by both parties. Also, Brown was under a duty to bring the sheep in because he knew that White would rely on his performance. Brown breached this duty by failing to bring the sheep in. White is discharged from any duty to dig the well. Choice **B** is the correct answer. Rest. 2d §225(3). Choice **A** is wrong because a specific date for performance was not necessary. Implicit in the agreement was White's duty to dig the well within a few days after Labor Day and, in any event, before "winter." Choice **C** is wrong because the perfect tender rule is applicable only in connection with contracts involving the sale of goods. UCC §2-601. Choice **D** is wrong because construction contracts are not within the Statute of Frauds; only contracts involving the transfer of an interest in land come within the statute. Rest. 2d §125.

81. **A** These facts illustrate the importance of requiring a formal written agreement in those circumstances in which the parties have had extensive discussions and negotiations of some, but not all, of the essential terms. Sue and Mark have exchanged a series of invitations, offers, and counteroffers. When Sue offered to perform for $20,000 and Mark "accepted her terms," they reached agreement on price, dates, and roles, but Sue's insistence on a written contract "for my approval" obviously confirmed her need to be sure that other possible terms — e.g., the identity of the conductor, the names of other members of the cast, her hotel accommodations — would be acceptable to her. Mark's agreement — "a contract follows" — established that he also felt a written memorialization was required. For these reasons, there was no "meeting of the minds" and no contract, and **A** is the best answer. Choice **C** comes close to being the best answer. But the parties had agreed on many material terms. Without the express reservations about the writing, a court easily might find oral assent and fill in the remaining terms. Thus, choice **C** is not as good an answer as **A**. Choice **B** is wrong because, although Mark's offer was a counteroffer, the parties continued to negotiate and reached agreement on a figure of $20,000. Choice **D**

is wrong precisely because not all sopranos are equal. If the parties had reached agreement, Mark might well be damaged because Sue might have been the best of the candidates.

82. B The parties to a contract will often neglect to specify the order of performance. To provide a workable formula wherever possible, the courts have developed a number of general rules. The applicable rule on these facts specifies that, in the absence of language to the contrary, When only one party's performance requires a period of time to complete, that party will be required to substantially complete performance before the obligation of the other party to pay for the services arises. Performance is said to be a *constructive condition* to payment. Rest. 2d §234(2). Felix was obligated to prune the trees before requiring payment. Choice **B** is the correct answer. Choice **A** is not the best answer. It correctly states one rationale behind the rule but not the applicable rule itself. In addition, it implies a broader right than Oscar has. He might not have the right to see Felix's performance first if his own performance also required time to complete. Choice **C** is wrong because it is essentially illogical. If each party had a right to insist that the other go first, no contract that failed to specify the order of performance would ever be enforced. Finally, choice **D** is incorrect because the hiring of men and the procurement of equipment are essential and foreseeable elements in a contract for tree pruning.

83. C The critical issue on these facts is whether in pruning only one of two trees, Felix committed a material breach of the contract or whether he had substantially performed the contract. Under some circumstances, it is not easy to determine whether the performance is substantial. If the performance is substantial, the party giving the performance is entitled to recover on the contract, i.e., sue for his expectation damages, in this case, the contract price less a setoff for defendants damages. The defendant's damages will be measured by the cost of remedying plaintiff's default. Under those circumstances, choice **D** might be correct. But pruning one tree may not be substantial performance of the contract. The question is a close one because the work was easily divisible into two equal parts. Arguably, Felix could recover $250 for the half of the contract he completed, though this choice was not offered as an answer. For two reasons, it seems Felix did not substantially perform: (1) Felix walked off the job and should be charged with the default; and (2) the value of his work can be assessed by the cost imposed on Oscar to remedy his default ($150), given that the two trees were identical and, thus, pruning one would be no different from pruning the other. The most equitable result is to limit Felix to recover under quasi-contract in **quantum meruit**. This is the appropriate remedy when the plaintiff has materially breached the contract, but has given the defendant part performance that is of value to the defendant. In that case, the plaintiff will be limited to the reasonable value of his work. This is especially true in construction cases. Since the reasonable value of Felix's work can be readily measured by the cost of Murray's work, the correct answer is **C**. Choice **D** is not the right answer because, as we have seen, Felix is not entitled to his expectation damages because he materially breached the contract. Choice **A** is probably not the right answer, but it is a close call. Many courts will not allow any recovery to a plaintiff who has committed a "willful" default, which may be the case on these facts. Rest. 2d §374. Choice **B** is wrong for the same reason that **A** is wrong. Having performed some valuable services, it would be unjust to allow Oscar to keep the services without any compensation to Felix.

84. **C** When Otto agreed to pay $4,000 to Albert in exchange for Bart's painting of Otto's house, Albert became the third party beneficiary of Otto's promise. Under the common law, a third party beneficiary could not sue because he was considered not to be "in privity" with the promisor—in this case, Otto. Even the first Restatement allowed a third party beneficiary to sue only if she was either a creditor beneficiary or a donee beneficiary. As now revised, the Restatement has eliminated these two classes of beneficiary and has created two new ones—*intended beneficiaries* (who can sue) and *incidental beneficiaries* (who cannot). Here, Albert is clearly the intended beneficiary of the agreement between Bart and Otto. (*See* Rest. 2d, Chapter 14 Introductory Note for a history of the beneficiary concept.) Rest. 2d §302(1). An intended beneficiary has the right to sue to enforce the promisee's promise. The choices here raise the issue: which one of the parties may he sue? May he sue both? The third party beneficiary may certainly sue the promisor, who, in this case, has received value for his promise. May he also sue the promisee? The majority view is that he may. Rest. 2d §310(1). Of course, he is entitled to one satisfaction of his claim. Rest. 2d §310(2). The best answer is therefore **C**. Albert may recover against both Bart and Otto, so long as he collects only $4,000 from either or both. Choice **A** is wrong because Albert is not limited to a suit against Bart.

Choice **B** is wrong because he is not limited to a suit against Otto. Choice **D** is wrong because the intended beneficiary may initiate a suit in his own name and does not have to wait for the promisee (Bart) to recover against the promisor (Otto).

85. B The modern view is that all contracts are assignable, except under circumstances that would make the assignment inherently unfair to the obligor, such as by increasing the burden or risk to the promisor. UCC §2-210(2) (§2-210(1)(a) under the 2003 revisions of article 2). Here, Viburnum expressed two concerns: (1) that Poplar may have greater demands than Maples and (2) that Poplar may not pay as quickly as Maples. The UCC protects Viburnum from excessive demands by limiting the quantity Poplar can require to an amount reasonably proportionate to the amounts Maples demanded in the past. UCC §2-306(1). Viburnum may refuse to fill excessive demands, but may not refuse to fill demands within the range demanded by Maples. The UCC protects Viburnum from the second concern by allowing it to demand adequate assurances that Poplar will perform the contract. UCC §2-210(5) (§2-210(2)(c) under the 2003 revisions to article 2). If Poplar fails to provide adequate assurance, Viburnum then may have a right to terminate the contract based on an implied repudiation by Poplar. UCC §2-609. Neither potential problem seems to justify an immediate termination of the contract. No breach by Maples or Poplar justifies that preemptive move. If specific performance prevents all of Poplar's damages, it may not receive both remedies. However, choice **B** remains the best choice because some damages might occur before the court orders specific performance. Choice **A** is incorrect. Even if Viburnum's performance is not unique, other appropriate circumstances may justify specific performance, including a shortage of the goods. Poplar's inability to find another supplier suggests that a shortage exists. Choice **C** is plausible if the court refuses to enforce the assignment because facts essential to the original agreement are no longer applicable. *Crane Ice Cream Co. v. Terminal Freezing & Heating Co.* Choice **D** is wrong because Poplar need not establish the similarities to prevail. Rather, the assignment will be presumed effective. Viburnum may resist excessive requirements or poor credit under the UCC, but may not reject the assignment based on unsubstantiated fears that these might arise.

86. B The best answer is **B**. The letter sent by Sunset Hotel was not an offer but an invitation to reserve its accommodations for a specific

weekend. Offers by hotels, airlines, cruise ships, theatrical performances, sports events, and other similar attractions are understood
by everyone to include the condition of limited availability. In this
sense, they fall into the category of offers controlled by "trade
usage." Trade usage is defined in the UCC as "any practice . . .
having such regularity in a . . . trade as to justify an expectation
that it will be observed with respect to the transaction in question."
UCC §1-205(2). Since the hotel notified Maxwell that it was sold
out (i.e., rejected his offer) and did not confirm his reservation (i.e.,
accept his offer), there was no contract. Choice **A** is wrong because it
assumes the hotel made an offer. If the hotel had made an offer,
Maxwell's method of acceptance probably would be deemed
reasonable, certainly more reasonable than just showing up and
attempting to register and use the room! Choice **C** is wrong because
Sunset did not make an offer that Maxwell was empowered to
accept. Choice **D** is not the best answer because, although it states
the facts correctly, Maxwell's knowledge would make no difference
if, in fact, the hotel's letter had been an offer. The hotel can limit the
offer to first come, first served, but its failure to do so would come at
its own risk, not Maxwell's.

87. **C** The call was not a repudiation for two reasons. First, it did not
unequivocally state that Farnsworth would not perform starting
February 1, but simply expressed the possibility that he would be
unprepared to begin until February. 10. Repudiation requires an
unequivocal statement that the party will commit a breach. Rest. 2d
§250(a). Second, the breach threatened was not material. Rather,
Farnsworth's statement at most suggested he would miss 10 days on
a 24-month (730-day) contract. While Jones would be entitled to
damages for the breach, the breach is not sufficiently material to
justify termination of the entire contract. Thus, no cause of action
for total breach would arise, as required under Rest. 2d §250(a).
Choice **A** is wrong for these two reasons: the statement was equi-
vocal, and the breach was not material. Choice **B** is wrong because
the only unequivocal statements count as repudiation. No matter
how reasonable Jones's interpretation may have seemed, uncertainty must be resolved by recourse to a request for adequate assurances of performance, not by assuming the words in fact signal a
breach when they did not clearly so state. Rest. 2d §251. (If this case
arose under the 2003 revisions to article 2 of the UCC, choice
B might be correct. That rule defines repudiation to include
"language that a reasonable person would interpret to mean that

the other party will not or cannot make a performance still due under the contract," and does not expressly require that the threatened breach be material. UCC §2-610(2).) Choice **D** is wrong because nothing requires that a repudiation be in writing. It may be accomplished orally or by deed.

88. C The issue presented by these facts is: did Farnsworth's failure to appear on February 1 constitute a material breach entitling Jones to cancel the contract and sue for damages? It's not always easy to decide if a breach is material. The courts resort to several tests: How much has the aggrieved party been damaged? What is the essence of the contract? Can the aggrieved party be compensated adequately? What is the relationship in value between the defaulted performance and the balance of the contract? How extensive is the delay? Was the breach willful? Can the aggrieved party make other arrangements? On these facts, it's hard to see how Farnsworth's breach can be deemed material. He had a two-year contract. His failure to appear was not willful (though evidence that he could have returned earlier but willfully remained in China might negate this). He suggested a temporary placement. He kept his promise to appear on the 10th. The best answer is therefore **C**. Jones, however, would have the right to set off against Farnsworth's salary any damages resulting from his delay in appearing. Choice **A** is incorrect as a matter of law; only a material breach, not just any breach, will justify terminating the contract. Choice **B** is wrong because Farnsworth's breach was not material, and Jones can be adequately compensated for his damage. Choice **D** is wrong. Although it can be argued that Farnsworth should have given earlier notice, Jones was not entitled to cancel the contract because the notice included a promise of material performance by Farnsworth.

89. D If the death or illness of a party makes performance impracticable, that party is excused, at least for the duration of the disability. Farnsworth's injuries were severe enough to relieve him of his responsibility to appear and entitle Jones to seek a replacement. However, because the contract was for two years and the period of injury was only two months, the contract was discharged only partially and could be enforced anew by either party once Farnsworth was able to sing again. Since Farnsworth's performance was excused, he is not responsible to reimburse Jones for the additional fees paid to Young. The correct answer is **D**. Choice **A** is not correct. It's immaterial to the outcome whether Jones was responsible in any way. Choice **B** is incorrect on the facts. There is no indication that Farnsworth was the drunk driver or in any other way contributed to the injury. Choice **C** is wrong because permanent injury is not required; temporary incapacity is sufficient.

90. **B** When one party to a contract has breached, the other party is entitled to compensatory damages. The usual measure of damages is to put the aggrieved party in the same position as if the contract had not been breached by the other party. These are called ***expectation damages.*** In this case, Jones has been forced to incur additional costs of $300 per month by Farnsworth's breach. To award him these costs is to put him back in the same position as if Farnsworth had not breached. Rest. 2d §347. The correct answer is **B**. Jones is entitled to damages for all of February because that month has passed, and to the present value of the excess costs in future months. (If, at the time of judgment, additional months have passed, they will be recovered in full plus prejudgment interest. Only months that still have not occurred will be reduced to present value.) If Jones can prove that Farnsworth would have captured bigger turnouts than Stone, he may also be entitled to his lost profits. Rest. 2d §347(b). Choice **C** is incorrect because Jones's damages are the difference between the Farnsworth contract and Stone contract. Choice **A** is incorrect because, since Farnsworth repudiated the contract, Jones is entitled to recover for the entire period of the contract. Finally, Choice **D** is incorrect because Jones was not required to give notice to Farnsworth. He was entitled to rely on the fact that Farnsworth had not appeared and was performing elsewhere.

91. **A** The parties to a written contract will often agree on a no-assignment clause. These clauses are not regarded favorably by most courts. In the same spirit, both the Restatement and the UCC place restrictions on these clauses, although they do permit them. Rest. 2d §322; UCC §2-210. In this case, Multiplex consented to a one-time modification of the written contract to permit an assignment by Construct to its bank. This could be a valid waiver of a right or a limited modification of the contract. In either event, assent by both parties seems adequate to make it enforceable, absent a defense. Choice **A** is the best answer because the modification would not have been effective without the consent of Multiplex. Choice **B** would appear to be a good answer, but it is not the best answer because it is only the statement of a general legal principle. Just because the parties can enter an oral modification does not mean

that they did, as specified by choice **A**. Choice **C** is an accurate statement of a general legal principle, but it is not relevant under these facts. Neither the original contract nor the contract *as modified* comes under the statute. Neither involves the transfer of an interest in land, but only services relating to land. Choice **D** is wrong because, as we have seen, it is not an accurate statement of the law.

92. A Lord Northchild's offer to pay $25,000 created a unilateral contract that Casso could enforce by performing the services requested (i.e., paint the Lady's portrait). The distinction between unilateral and bilateral contracts has been eliminated by the Restatement, which distinguishes instead between an acceptance "by rendering a performance" (Rest. 2d §45(1)) and promissory acceptance. Once Casso began the performance, he accepted the offer. However, he had to complete the portrait before he could recover. The measure of his recovery when the work was finished and rejected by Lord Northchild was his expectation damages, in this case, the agreed price of $25,000. UCC §2-709(1)(b). Because very few others seem likely to want a portrait of Lady Northchild, attempts to resell at a reasonable price probably will be unavailing. This is the most appropriate remedy under these facts. Choice **A** is therefore the best answer. Choice **B** states the remedy for quantum meruit, but Casso has an enforceable contract and need not resort to this (less lucrative) cause of action. Choice **C** is not the right answer. Although the UCC requires a writing when the price is $500 or more ($5,000 or more under the 2003 revisions of article 2), UCC §2-201(1), the UCC includes an exception for specially manufactured goods once performance has begun. UCC §2-201(3)(a). Here, the goods were produced specifically for Lord Northchild and were not suitable for sale to another. The goods are not only begun, but completed. The writing requirement will not preclude enforcement on these facts. Choice **D** is wrong because the Lord did not include a condition that the painting be satisfactory, but expressed a preference to be surprised by the result.

93. D* The analysis will differ depending on whether the 2003 revisions to article 2 have been enacted. In either case, however, each of Shelly's defenses should fail, leaving Terry with an enforceable contract. Choice **A** would be correct if no acceptance occurred before Shelly sent the email informing Terry that the goods were back-ordered. The electronic confirmation, however, seems to be an acceptance. Even if it will not serve as a writing, it can satisfy the requirement of assent. Choice **A** could be correct if choice **C** were correct — in which case, choice **C** would be a better answer since it negates acceptance by itself, without regard to any other answer. Choice **C** is incorrect because Shelly can authorize any agent she wishes to respond for her. The computer confirmed the order under program instructions she supplied (or hired another to supply). Her failure to consider each offer consciously is no defense. (Shelly would not want it to be a defense if Terry, rather than Shelly, tried to cancel the order after confirmation. Shelly probably sends emails only when problems arise. If so, none of her customers get a human acceptance in the normal course, which could leave Shelly without any enforceable rights.) The revisions to article 2 codify the ability of electronic agents to bind a party. UCC §2-204(4) (2003 revisions). Choice **B** is incorrect under the 2003 revisions for two reasons. First, the Statute of Frauds applies to sales of $5,000 or more, but the sale here is only $2,000. Second, the statute requires a signed "record," not a signed "writing." UCC §2-201(1) (2003 revisions). A record includes "information that is inscribed on a tangible medium or that is stored in an electronic or other medium and is retrievable in perceivable form." UCC §2-103(1)(m) (2003 revisions). Thus, the email confirmation would satisfy the Statute of Frauds if signed. The signature requirement under the UCC is quite minimal — any symbol, such as initials or a logo, may suffice. UCC §§2-103(1)(p) (2003 revisions), 1-201(39) (original), 1-201(37) (2001 revisions). As long as the email confirmation includes the company name, it seems likely to satisfy the Statute of Frauds. * Choice **B** presents a much closer case under the unrevised UCC, and may in fact be a better answer. The statute required a writing, which was defined as reducing the information to tangible form. An email is not a tangible form and thus not a writing. A court may refuse to get caught up in these niceties, recognizing that the purposes of the statute are fully satisfied by an email that can be printed out. Indeed, if Shelly printed out a copy of the email, that would be a writing, even if the printout was never sent to Terry. (A writing must exist, but need not be sent to the other party.)

94. D* The analysis of this problem is no different from the preceding problem. The order by Terry was always treated as the offer. The terms and conditions, therefore, do not change anything. The confirmation accepted the offer before any counteroffer or rejection was received by Terry. Choice **A**, therefore, is factually correct, but legally irrelevant. Choice **C** is wrong because Terry probably is bound by the terms and conditions. While some websites force users to scroll through all the terms to reach a button labeled "I agree" before they will consummate the transaction, nothing in the law requires this practice. The claim that the terms and conditions should not apply to Terry is no more persuasive than a claim that someone who signed a written agreement without reading it should be excused from the terms of the writing because of his own neglect. * Choice **B** remains a plausible choice under the UCC as it exists today, but will be incorrect if states adopt the 2003 revisions to article 2.

95. **C** The mailbox rule applies to email. A revocation is effective on receipt at a place the other party designated for its delivery. Thus, Terry's revocation was effective the moment Shelly received the email — which the question says is the same moment she sent the email. But an acceptance is effective from the time it is dispatched. Because Shelly's website dispatched the acceptance before Terry's revocation was received, the contract was formed at that moment. Choice **A** is incorrect as a statement of law because the important time for revocation is the time of receipt, not the time of dispatch. Because dispatch and receipt were simultaneous, it describes the facts well enough, but is not as good as choice **C**, which accurately states the rule. Choice **B** would be correct if the mailbox rule did not apply. Even though no one read the message until morning, it was received when it arrived in Shelly's inbox — the place designated for such communications. Rest. 2d §68. Without the mailbox rule, all communications are effective on receipt. The rule, however, is not limited to snail mail, but makes any acceptance effective once it leaves the offeree's possession. Rest. 2d §63. Choice **D** is factually accurate, but irrelevant under the legal rule.

96. **A*** The Statute of Frauds is Terry's best hope (until and unless the 2003 revisions to the UCC become law). Terry's order and email are both electronic, not in tangible form. They do not satisfy the requirement of writing under the existing law. While a court may decide to treat them as writings anyway because they serve most of the same functions, a court that scrupulously follows the language of the UCC will not enforce the contract against Terry.* Choice **B** is a plausible answer and would be a better answer if the 2003 revisions to article 2 become law. Once courts recognize an electronic record as sufficient to satisfy the Statute of Frauds, Terry's reliance on the Statute of Frauds will fail. Unilateral mistake is hard to apply to these facts,

but might work. The quantity was a basic assumption; it has a material effect on the exchange (Terry would need to pay 10 times the price expected, though Terry would also receive 10 times as much in return). The risk of mistake is not allocated to Terry by the agreement — though a review of the unread terms and conditions would be required to confirm this. Conscious ignorance might allocate the risk to Terry: Terry knew she had not reviewed the final confirmation carefully but submitted the order anyway. But perhaps this was mere negligence on Terry's part, not conscious ignorance. Finally, the deal may have been too good to be true, putting Shelly on notice that Terry was mistaken. This may depend on how often Shelly gets other orders of this size. Choice **C** is incorrect because reformation corrects a writing to reflect the agreement the parties actually made, not the agreement one of them wished she had made. This is not a case where the parties agreed on 100, but the writing erroneously said 1,000. Shelly agreed to sell 1,000 candles, the only number in the record at the time Shelly accepted. Unilateral mistake justifies reformation when the other party commits fraud or nondisclosure. No such misconduct applies to Shelly here. While canceling the order might be plausible, reforming it to 100 would be unusual. Choice **D** is incorrect. Nothing in the facts suggests that the deal is unfair; the candles seem to be worth the price, and free shipping on an order this large makes the deal even better. The terms were not concealed from Terry. In fact, the terms to which Terry objects were terms typed in by Terry, not terms Shelly imposed on Terry. No basis for unconscionability exists.

97. B Under the perfect tender rule, any defect in delivery permits the buyer to reject the whole, accept the whole, or reject any commercial unit and reject the rest. UCC §2-601. The failure to deliver 1,000 candles within 10 business days fails to conform to the contract, permitting Terry to resort to this section. Choice **A** is incorrect in that it implies Terry can reject only the portion that was late. Even though Terry accepted the first two boxes, that happened before the breach occurred (i.e., before any right to reject arose). The breach creates a right that Terry can exercise as to the whole shipment (or only the 9 boxes Terry didn't intend to order) at Terry's option. Choice **C** is a correct statement of the law, but does not apply to this case. Terry did not order candles to be shipped in installments (say, 100 per month). Terry placed a single order for 1,000 candles, all due at the same time. Shelly's decision, for her own convenience, to ship the 10 boxes at different times does not convert a single order into an installment contract. If shipment in a single lot (not a single box, but one lot with all 10 boxes) was constrained by external factors, not just Shelly's own convenience, Shelly might argue that these circumstances authorized shipment in lots. UCC §2-307. If so, this would be an installment contract as defined in UCC §2-612(1) and choice **C** would be correct. Choice **D** is incorrect because the perfect tender rule applies to any failure to conform to the contract, not just defects in the goods themselves. (**Note:** If Shelly could argue that the contract did not require delivery within 7-10 business days, she might prevail on the ground that no breach occurred. The estimate of delivery might not be deemed a promise. The default UCC term would fix delivery when Shelly put the boxes in the hands of the carrier. UCC §2-308(a). In this case, choice **D**, though not phrased with this position in mind, would be the best answer. Because the parties' negotiations mentioned the delivery time, it seems likely this became an express term, overriding the UCC's default term.)

98. **D*** The contract formed on the phone — computer for price — was complete in itself. Both parties performed it: Sean paid, and Compco shipped the goods. Subsequent negotiations could modify it, but neither party can be compelled to accept different terms if they prefer to retain the terms of the original contract. Compco's record included with the computer was not part of the terms mentioned on the phone, but proposed additional or different terms. (Compco could have demanded these terms if the salesperson had noted, before the agreement was final, that all sales were subject to terms and conditions contained in the box. Sean could not accept an offer without those terms if Compco's offer included those terms, at least by reference.) Because Sean is not a merchant of computers, proposals to modify the contract will not be accepted by silence, but require express assent. UCC §2-207(2) (deleted in the 2003 revisions of article 2). The same result would be reached under revised §2-207. The new terms were not part of the records of both parties nor part of the default provisions under the code. Unless assent by Sean was found, they would not become part of the transaction. Choice **A** is incorrect because modification under the UCC does not require consideration if made in good faith. UCC §2-209. Sean might question good faith here: nothing changed after the phone call to make the new terms more important than before. Sean should have more success challenging the acceptance of the modified terms. * Choice **B** is incorrect because the phone

conversation between the parties stated a complete agreement. There would be no basis for either party to challenge the enforceability of the terms reached at that time. Nonetheless, at least one prominent court has concluded that sales of this type are not final during the phone conversation, even though payment occurs at that time. Rather, the offer consists of shipping the goods, which the consumer has an option to accept after reviewing the terms in the box. Keeping the goods then signals acceptance. *See Hill v. Gateway 2000.* So far, other courts have not adopted this reasoning. Choice **C** is wrong because Sean's conduct is ambiguous. Keeping the computer could express assent, if Sean so intended. Rest. 2d §69(1)(b). But silence also could express rejection of the modification and a decision to keep the computer under the terms of the original contract. Compco cannot force Sean to relinquish the original contract right (to keep the computer) as the only way to reject the modification.

99. B The UCC permits recovery of "any loss resulting from the general or particular requirements and needs of which the seller at the time of contracting had reason to know and which could not reasonably be prevented by cover or otherwise." UCC §2-715(2)(a). If Sean made known his requirements for the computer, including the need for wireless access, then losses resulting from seller's failure to meet these needs seem to fall within the definition. Choice **A** is incorrect. Not all (nor perhaps most) laptop buyers use them for business, especially in a way that would produce losses if wireless access were interrupted for a few days. Just because some do does not mean that Compco should foresee these losses without notice. Such a general foreseeability requirement would virtually eliminate this restriction on consequential damages. Choice **C** is incorrect, or at best depends on facts not in the question. Dial-up may not fully substitute for wireless access. It requires a phone line, which might not always be available while traveling. It also is significantly slower than wireless, which may make it less effective. While dial-up might have avoided these losses, that is not certain on these facts. Choice **D** is incorrect. Notice to the seller would lay the groundwork for consequential damages, as long as the notice was sufficiently detailed. The precise nature of what Sean would need to reveal may be subject to some debate: is it enough that Compco know Sean conducts transactions via computer, or would Sean need to reveal specific deals and the amount of potential losses in each to give sufficient notice? But, at some point, full disclosure would satisfy the requirements of the UCC.

Table of References to the Uniform Commercial Code

Codes in brackets refer to the 2001 revisions to Article 1 and the 2003 revisions to Article 2.

Table of References to the
Restatement (Second) of Contracts

Index